the Bible culminating in the final victory of the triune God over all that opposes him (the eschaton). As we press the claims of Christ we must in no way compromise 'the self-attesting Christ of Scripture as mapped out in biblical revelation and summarized in the ecumenical creeds of the early church and the Reformed confessions.' His method represented a radical departure from the evidentialist apologetic method he was taught at Princeton Seminary. Dennison very helpfully takes us through the criticisms Van Til encountered in his own Reformed camp, both from those who opposed his method and from those who sympathetically aligned themselves with his initiative. Van Til would say to his students that if we stand on the shoulders of our fathers in the faith we ought to be able to see a little further. Van Til's own work illustrates that point, and so also does Dennison's. 'Taking Van Til's own acknowledgement that [Geerhardus] Vos was his most influential teacher [at Princeton], I have attempted to push Van Til's biblical apologetic deeper into the fabric of God's revelation.' Tying Van Til's apologetic method into a biblical philosophy of history is the most valuable contribution of this book. Dennison helps us by strengthening the apologetic backbone of believers as we face up to new challenges posed by rapid changes in the intellectual and cultural landscape where we are called to serve today."

—**Norman Shepherd**
Pastor, Holland, Michigan

"For those not familiar with Dr. Dennison's work, his distinctive contributions in this series of articles outline the implications for Christian apologetics of the evident intrinsic integration that exists in Van Til's thought with the philosophy of history inherent in the Biblical Reformed theology of Geerhardus Vos. In this volume, Dennison provides the Reformed church and the Christian academy with a key that helps to unlock a Biblically faithful defense and declaration of the Christian faith. From this starting point, Dennison provides a cogent critique of structural and substantial shortcomings in the arguments of the most prominent proponents of classical apologetics and education. He also effectively critiques the most recent previous, popular, and prevailing interpreters of Van Til in a way that calls for a fuller response from them. Taken together, this book presents a challenge to any and all existing models for human thought that do not hold as necessary and sufficient the aeonic, historical character of divine redemptive revelation fulfilled in the self-attesting Christ of the Scriptures. As such, this volume offers, at once, an elenctic indictment against unbelieving and biblically inconsistent thought and a faithfully Reformed and ecumenical invitation to defend this faith by all who hold to and love the Bible as the infallible Word of God. To be sure, this seminal contribution requires and deserves greater elaboration even beyond this collection. What Dennison himself admits concerning one article may also be affirmed with regard to this brief book: 'My study is only meant to be an introduction. I have not provided a comprehensive presentation of Van Til's philosophy of history, epistemology, or his connection with Vos. Van Tilians must have a renewed commitment to disclose, understand, and carefully reexamine the basic presuppositions that underlie the structure of his thought.' The book, however, does afford, as a starting point, manifold opportunities for continuing dialogue, discussion, and debate on how we evangelize our communities, educate in our schools, and counsel in our churches. This prospect all by itself makes a careful and critical reading of this book well worthwhile. My prayer is that Dennison's arguments herein will be considered carefully, engaged faithfully, and applied persuasively to 'destroy arguments and every lofty opinion raised against the knowledge of God, and [to] take every thought captive to obey Christ' (II Corinthians 10:5, ESV)."

—**Christopher H. Wisdom**
Vice President and Professor of Practical Theology, Erskine Theological Seminary

"It would be impossible for me to overestimate the influence of Van Til's apologetic on my thought and indeed my life. Navigating the halls of three secular postgraduate academic institutions, I have carried with me the toolkit of transcendental critique and, more specifically, an awareness of the myth of objectivity, which I weave through my teaching and my conversations with unbelievers. In making Van Til's work accessible, Bill Dennison offers in this collection an invaluable means of putting on the full armour of God so that we may resist captivity by the philosophies of the world. Reading his essays has refreshed me, and I highly recommend them to every Christian."

—**Valerie Hobbs**
Lecturer in Applied Linguistics, University of Sheffield; Fellow in Christianity and Language and Associate Director of the Lydia Center for Women and Families, Greystone Theological Institute

"The influence of Geerhardus Vos and Cornelius Van Til stands like a colossus in the story of the development of reformed theology in the 20th century. For me their contribution was defining. They figured hugely in my own education at seminary and beyond into a lifetime of ministry. Dr. Dennison understands their significance and his encyclopedic knowledge of his subject makes him a sure guide to their thought and its importance for the world and the church."

—**Liam Goligher**
Senior Minister, Tenth Presbyterian Church, Philadelphia, Pennsylvania

"*In Defense of the Eschaton* is an invaluable compilation of Dr. Dennison's biblically faithful and insightful efforts in defense of the faith. With every expectation of our Lord's blessing, I commend to the reader the work of Dr. Dennison, which is produced with scholarly excellence and theological integrity. Dr. Dennison highlights topics that will undoubtedly advance biblical theology united with presuppositional apologetics."

—**Harry L. Reeder**
Senior Pastor, Briarwood Presbyterian Church, Birmingham, Alabama

"Cornelius Van Til has suffered the misfortune of either being dismissed or slavishly idolized. It is the merit of Dennison's work that although Van Til is definitely his teacher, he is guilty of neither but in a clear and accessible manner illumines the profound issues of revelation, common grace, antithesis and Christian thinking that dominated discussions in the Christian Reformed and Presbyterian world of the 20th century. One need not agree with him (or Van Til) on every point to appreciate the significant historical/systematic service Dennison has provided in clarifying the Vos/Van Til nexus for a generation inclined to forget its own roots. This volume is a valuable contribution to making a fair and honest conversation possible which would be a refreshing development."

—**John Bolt**
Professor of Systematic Theology, Calvin Theological Seminary

"Geerhardus Vos and Cornelius Van Til were among the most significant Reformed thinkers of the last century, their legacy an enduring one. William Dennison is an eminent scholar, a leading exponent of their thought but with distinctive contributions of his own. This collection of his writings, building on both Vos and Van Til, will be of great interest to all who recognize that only when our thinking and living is shaped and directed by the trinitarian God can we be true to his revelation in the Bible."

—Robert Letham
Senior Lecturer in Systematic and Historical Theology and Director of Research, Wales Evangelical School of Theology

"Cornelius Van Til regularly expressed his indebtedness to the biblical theology of Geerhardus Vos throughout his professorial career. Those privileged to hear Van Til preach or pray surely understood why. But because Vos's influence on apologetics was subtle and indirect, Van Til's claim has generally eluded many readers of his works. Among interpreters, Bill Dennison stands virtually alone for consistently underscoring this connection. As displayed first in his *Paul's Two Age Construction and Apologetics* (1986), Dennison's essays and articles, gathered helpfully in this anthology, demonstrate the necessity of reckoning with the eschatological dimension of Van Til's work in order fully to assess his contribution to Reformed apologetics."

—John R. Muether
Dean of Libraries and Professor of Church History, Reformed Theological Seminary, Orlando

"Do not be misled by the word "eschaton" in the tile of this collection of the shorter writings of William Dennison. His book has nothing to do with differences between premillennialists and postmillennialists or related issues, but has everything to do with how we go about presenting our Christian faith in a world that is bitterly opposed to this faith. No one has spoken more pointedly to this question in recent times than Cornelius Van Til of Westminster Theological Seminary in Philadelphia, PA. Dennison undertakes to unfold, explain, and illustrate Van Til's apologetic method in a compelling way. Van Til's strength as an apologist lay in consistently maintaining his starting point and method in the redemptive history of

"Whether one agrees or not with the apologetic methods of Cornelius Van Til, his unique contributions to the discipline must be considered. William Dennison has spent a lifetime engaged in this work and his students and readers have been the beneficiaries. In the collected pages of this volume, the reader is helpfully led by the hand into the mind and thoughts of one of the most unique theologians of the modern age."

—Jason Helopoulos
Associate Pastor, University Reformed Church, East Lansing, Michigan

"I am very pleased that James Baird has collated and edited these fine selections from the prolific pen of William Dennison in *In Defense of the Eschaton*. Dennison has reminded us anew of the influence of Geerhardus Vos on his pupil Cornelius Van Til. Dennison demonstrates the *essential nexus* between covenantal (presuppositional) apologetics and the eschatalogically infused redemptive history. It is impossible to go away from reading *In Defense of the Eschaton* and not now see how the truth that "eschatology precedes soteriology" suffuses the apologetic task. The antithesis between belief and unbelief reflects the reality of the overlap of this present evil age and the age to come. If I say that Dennison is brilliant and solidly biblical and Reformed, it is true but an understatement. This volume leaves the reader wanting more."

—Jeffrey C. Waddington
Stated Supply, Knox Orthodox Presbyterian Church, Lansdowne, Pennsylvania

"In these essays, Dr. Dennison builds faithfully upon the apologetic method of Cornelius Van Til rooted in the biblical theology of Geerhardus Vos. He effectively demonstrates its wide-ranging relevance for a consistently Christian approach to not only 'practical' apologetics, but also inter-disciplinary issues involving philosophy, rhetoric, Christian education, and the perennial debate over 'Christ and culture.' The appearance of these essays in a more permanent form is a welcome addition in the library of any minister or student of Christian theology who seeks in all things to exalt the preeminence of Jesus Christ."

—Benjamin W. Swinburnson
Minister, Lynnwood Orthodox Presbyterian Church, Lynnwood, Washington

"This book is exactly the kind we should all read more of today. It is not about this or that hot topic, or this or that current debate. Instead, it is persistently about what is ultimate: how we can know anything at all and live consistently with that. Bill Dennison shows us how by filling our vision with the self-authenticating Lord Jesus Christ, to know whom is life eternal. How can we confess this One in the face of the world's denial and Christian scholarship's open betrayal? Is to live really Christ, as Paul says? Take and read!"

—**Marcus A. Mininger**
Assistant Professor of New Testament, Mid-America Reformed Seminary

"As a young teen Dr. Dennison introduced me to the fundamentals of Christian theology. Now as a colleague, he has refreshed my exposure to the apologetics of Van Til. Anyone wanting to think further about the applications of Van Til's thought will be helped by this collection."

—**Thomas K. Groelsema**
Senior Pastor, First Christian Reformed Church, Byron Center, Michigan

"This marvelous collection of apologetic essays will encourage faith in Christ even as it sharpens the mind. It represents an eschatological approach to the life of the mind, rooting traditional Augustinian-Reformed apologetics in the rich soil of Scripture and its unapologetically firm faith in the Lord of nature, history, and rationality. Many thanks to Bill Dennison for staying true to his tribe (Presbyterian confessionalists and students of Van Til) while developing its insights in important, new ways to meet the needs of our own day."

—**Douglas A. Sweeney**
Professor of Church History and the History of Christian Thought and Director of the Jonathan Edwards Center, Trinity Evangelical Divinity School

"It is good to see these important essays gathered in one place, forming as a whole what they couldn't individually—a comprehensive and sustained witness to the effectiveness of a presuppositional apologetic and to the cohesiveness of Van Til's theological and philosophical thought. Dennison's treatment is by turn powerful, convicting, and cumulatively overwhelming in its analysis."

—**Derek W. H. Thomas**
Robert Strong Professor of Systematic and Pastoral Theology, Reformed Theological Seminary, Atlanta; Senior Minister, First Presbyterian Church, Columbia, South Carolina

"This collection of essays is a must read for those interested in the apologetic work of Cornelius Van Til. Dr. Dennison not only helpfully describes and illumines some key aspects of Van Til's thought (e.g., common grace, the relationship between natural and special revelation, and critique of non-Christian thought), he also develops Van Til's apologetic in ways not often discussed. By showing Van Til's dependence upon the pioneering work of Geerhardus Vos, Dennison offers a more robust understanding of Van Til's work by grounding it in a sound biblical theology and then illustrating how this biblical grounding wonderfully applies to the doing of apologetics. For anyone interested in faithfully and consistently bringing the intellectual challenge of the Gospel to our day, this book is for you. Take, read, enjoy, and put it to work!"

—**Stephen J. Wellum**
Professor of Christian Theology, The Southern Baptist Theological Seminary

"Professor Dennison and I have not seen eye-to-eye with regard to Van Til, and after twenty years I am still bewildered by his critique of my approach (chapter 2 of this book). But Dennison and I both seek to honor Jesus Christ and to recognize his claims on human thought, and I honor him for that. Further, Dennison does us a service by drawing attention to Van Til, one of the most significant Christian thinkers of recent years. However one evaluates it, Dennison's analysis of Van Til is distinctive and has influenced many students. Indeed, nobody can fully appreciate the discussion of presuppositional apologetics over the last century without taking Dennison's approach into account. For that reason I am glad to see the book available, and I recommend it to serious students of the debates over apologetic method."

—**John M. Frame**
J. D. Trimble Professor of Systematic Theology and Philosophy, Reformed Theological Seminary, Orlando

"The voice of Bill Dennison is loud (for those who've heard him in person) and strong (for those who've read him). But Bill is not loud because he's proud, but because he profoundly believes the Word of the Lord. For many today, epistemic skepticism is a virtue and is thought to be 'humble apologetics.' It is no true humility, however, to fail to take God at His Word and to refuse to acknowledge the systemic lack of intelligibility that pertains apart from the ontological Trinity and the self-attesting Christ of Scripture. There is no neutrality, Bill reminds us—we all come from the perspective of those who have been united with Christ and seated with him in heavenly places or from the vantage of those who remain only 'in Adam' and who are indeed the living dead. Truly, this is an apologetics rooted in redemptive history and biblical eschatology. Bill's eschatological apologetics is a great contribution to the enterprise of defending the faith but has not sprung full-grown as Athena from the head of Zeus. Bill builds all that he does on the Word of God as understood by Augustine, Calvin, Vos, Van Til, and others of that tradition. As noted herein, however, Bill no more simply repristinates Vos and Van Til than they did Augustine and Calvin. Bill, as these first-rate integrative contributions to Van Til studies and redemptive history will show, as well as the book reviews, advances the discussion on all fronts, deftly synthesizing apologetics and eschatology more ably than any other practitioner I know. I heartily commend these essays to all readers concerned about these matters in a day in which autonomy is thought sophisticated and in which God and His Word is regarded as passé. Here we hear Bill, with all his learning and devotion to Christ, athwart history yelling 'Stop' to all the naysayers of Christ and His Word, seeking truly to bring every thought captive to the obedience of Christ, walking according to the coming age while challenging those yet living in this age, appreciating both common grace and antithesis, seeking to address all in this world from the heavenly perspective of the believer, and to engage truly in a transcendental analysis of all life and thought. Take, read, apply, and enjoy! SDG!"

—**Alan D. Strange**
Professor of Church History, Mid-America Reformed Seminary

"This stimulating collection of essays presents a robust explanation and defense of Van Til's apologetic for the twenty-first century. It will both make Van Til more accessible to the beginning reader and greatly assist the more discerning reader probe even more deeply into the profound truths he propagated."

—**Joel R. Beeke**
President and Professor of Systematic Theology and Homiletics, Puritan Reformed Theological Seminary

In Defense of the Eschaton

In Defense of the Eschaton

Essays in Reformed Apologetics

WILLIAM D. DENNISON

Edited by
James Douglas Baird

Foreword by
Lane G. Tipton

Preface by
Mark A. Garcia

WIPF & STOCK · Eugene, Oregon

IN DEFENSE OF THE ESCHATON
Essays in Reformed Apologetics

Copyright © 2015 William D. Dennison. All rights reserved. Except for brief quotations in critical publications or reviews, no part of this book may be reproduced in any manner without prior written permission from the publisher. Write: Permissions, Wipf and Stock Publishers, 199 W. 8th Ave., Suite 3, Eugene, OR 97401.

Wipf & Stock
An Imprint of Wipf and Stock Publishers
199 W. 8th Ave., Suite 3
Eugene, OR 97401

www.wipfandstock.com

ISBN 13: 978-1-4982-2633-2

Manufactured in the U.S.A.   10/15/2015

To
Richard B. Gaffin Jr.
Teacher and Friend

Do you fear the foe? To be sure Satan's power and ingenuity are great. But one little Word shall fell him. This Word tells the story of the Christ who came into the world conquering and to conquer. The powers of hell cannot prevail against him as he establishes his kingdom.

—Cornelius Van Til, "Why Westminster Today?"

Contents

Permissions | ix
Foreword by Lane G. Tipton | xi
Preface by Mark A. Garcia | xiii
Acknowledgments | xix
Introduction | xxi
Abbreviations | xxviii

Part 1: Van Til Studies
1 Van Til's Critique of Human Thought | 3
2 Van Til's Epistemology and Analytic Philosophy | 9
3 Van Til and Common Grace | 36
4 Antithesis, Common Grace, and Plato's View of the Soul | 55
5 Van Til and Classical Christian Education | 81

Part 2: Redemptive History and Apologetics
6 The Christian Apologist in the Present State of Redemptive History | 105
7 The Eschatological Implications of Genesis 2:15 for Apologetics | 118
8 A Reassessment of Natural and Special Revelation | 132

Part 3: Book Reviews
9 A Review of Greg Bahnsen's *Van Til's Apologetic* | 155
10 A Review of John Muether's *Cornelius Van Til* | 159
11 A Review of Timothy Keller's *The Reason for God* | 162

Bibliography | 171
Other Works by William D. Dennison | 179
Subject Index | 183
Names Index | 189
Scripture Index | 193

Permissions

Chapter 1 originally appeared as "Van Til's Critique of Human Thought," *New Horizons*, October 2004, 9–10. Used by permission.

Chapter 2 originally appeared as "Analytic Philosophy and Van Til's Epistemology," *Westminster Theological Journal* 57, no. 1 (Spring 1995) 33–56. Used by permission.

Chapter 3 originally appeared as "Van Til and Common Grace," *Mid-America Journal of Theology* 9 (Fall 1993) 225–47. Used by permission.

Chapter 4 originally appeared as "The Christian Academy: Antithesis, Common Grace, and Plato's View of the Soul," *Journal of the Evangelical Theological Society* 54, no. 1 (March 2011) 109–31. Used by permission.

Chapter 5 originally appeared as "Is Classical Christian Education Truly Christian?: Cornelius Van Til and Classical Christian Education," in *Confident of Better Things: Essays Commemorating Seventy-Five Years of the Orthodox Presbyterian Church*, edited by John R. Muether and Danny E. Olinger (Willow Grove, PA: The Committee for the Historian of the OPC, 2011) 101–25. Used by permission.

Chapter 6 originally appeared as "The Christian Apologist in the Present State of Redemptive-History," *Kerux: The Journal of Northwest Theological Seminary* 25, no. 3 (December 2010) 11–24. Used by permission.

Chapter 7 originally appeared as "The Eschatological Implications of Genesis 2:15 for Apologetics," in Chapter 10 of *Revelation and Reason: New Essays in Reformed Apologetics*, edited by K. Scott Oliphint and Lane G. Tipton (Phillipsburg, NJ: P&R, 2007) 190–204. ISBN 978-1-59638-596-9 This material is used by permission of P&R Publishing Co. P O Box 817 Phillipsburg N.J. 08865 www.prpbooks.com

Chapter 8 originally appeared as "Natural and Special Revelation: A Reassessment,"

Permissions

Kerux: The Journal of Northwest Theological Seminary 21, no. 2 (September 2006) 13–34. Used by permission.

Chapter 9 originally appeared as a review of *Van Til's Apologetic: Readings and Analysis*, by Greg L. Bahnsen, *Calvin Theological Journal* 39, no. 1 (April 2004) 188–91. Used by permission.

Chapter 10 originally appeared as a review of *Cornelius Van Til: Reformed Apologist and Churchman*, by John R. Muether, *Ordained Servant* 17 (2008) 123–5. Used by permission.

Chapter 11 originally appeared as a review of *The Reason for God: Belief in an Age of Skepticism*, by Timothy Keller, *Ordained Servant* 17 (2008) 147–51. Used by permission.

Scripture quotations marked (ESV) are from The Holy Bible, English Standard Version® (ESV®), copyright © 2001 by Crossway. Used by permission. All rights reserved.

Scripture quotations marked (KJV) are from the King James Version.

Scripture quotations marked (NASB) are taken from the New American Standard Bible®, Copyright © 1960, 1962, 1963, 1968, 1971, 1972, 1973, 1975, 1977, 1995 by The Lockman Foundation. Used by permission. www.Lockman.org

Scripture quotations marked (NIV) are taken from the Holy Bible, New International Version®, NIV®. Copyright © 1973, 1978, 1984, 2011 by Biblica, Inc.™ Used by permission of Zondervan. All rights reserved worldwide. www.zondervan.com The "NIV" and "New International Version" are trademarks registered in the United States Patent and Trademark Office by Biblica, Inc.™

Scripture quotations marked (NKJV) are taken from the New King James Version®. Copyright © 1982 by Thomas Nelson. Used by permission. All rights reserved.

Scripture quotations marked (ASV) are from the 1901 American Standard Version.

Foreword

The theology of Geerhardus Vos and the apologetics of Cornelius Van Til stand out in the twentieth century as the purest antidotes for the destructive methodologies of modern philosophy and theology.

Given the developments in the wake of Kant's critical philosophy, modern theology and philosophy have united in asserting that the self-contained ontological Trinity, sovereign author of a history of special revelation that has the eschatological kingdom of God in Christ at its center, cannot be allowed to form the presuppositional context for all theological and philosophical reflection. Nor can appeal be made to an inerrant, revelational record of that history of special revelation, which the confessional Reformed tradition understands as the Scriptures of the Old and New Testaments. Modern theology and philosophy sacrifice this remnant of an "older" Augustinian and Calvinistic theology on the altar of autonomous scholarship. However, both Vos and Van Til self-consciously seek to defend the genius of Reformed theology in this post-Enlightenment context.

Vos's formulation of a supernatural, progressive, and organic conception of a history of special revelation positions his notion of biblical theology over against all forms of "modern" biblical theology indebted to Gabler and the so-called critical tradition. In turn, Van Til's robust apologetic, which begins with the ontological Trinity and his comprehensive covenantal revelation, both general and special, places the concrete claims of the Christian worldview over against all forms of the non-Christian philosophy of life.

Nevertheless, neither Vos nor Van Til seeks merely to repristinate Augustine or Calvin. Both extend the genius of Augustinian Calvinism

Foreword

beyond its pre-Enlightenment expressions in order to deal with the unique problems that arise on the other side of the Enlightenment.

Vos seeks to set a self-consciously Reformed understanding of the history of special revelation over against various permutations of a critical notion of biblical theology. He engages the critical tradition and advances an orthodox understanding of biblical theology by dealing head on with the special problems that arise within that critical tradition.

Van Til's apologetic is self-consciously set within the context of both modern theology and modern philosophy. Van Til never tires of setting Calvinism over against modern philosophy—whether it be absolute idealism or pragmatism—or modern theology—whether liberal or neo-orthodox. Even a cursory reading of his *A Survey of Christian Epistemology* or *The Defense of the Faith* will make this point emphatically.

Vos and Van Til unite in reasserting the theological convictions central to Augustinian Calvinism, *but they enrich and apply those convictions to the new developments that arise from the pressing issues of their day*. Not a shred of the older theology is abandoned. Yet that older theology begins to develop in a richer way as a result of critical engagement with those whose presuppositions and methods would seek to destroy that older theology.

It is squarely within this context that William D. Dennison has labored as a theologian and apologist. The essays in this volume are not mere restatements of Vos or Van Til. Rather, you will find here creative and constructive *applications* of their basic insights to topics that advance Reformed theology and apologetics.

Dr. Dennison's work as a whole represents a high-level synthesis of the methodologies of Vos and Van Til. He seeks to apply a radically non-speculative, revelationally regulated methodology to a host of issues that neither Vos nor Van Til had opportunity to address. I enthusiastically commend to the reader the work of Dr. Dennison. His insights are penetrating, and his interests are wide-ranging. He has taken up the mantle of Vos and Van Til in both the polemical defense and constructive extension of the Reformed faith. I pray this volume finds a wide and appreciative readership.

Lane G. Tipton
Westminster Theological Seminary
April 16, 2015

Preface

Of all the seemingly ineradicable myths concerning the Christian Scriptures, none enjoyed greater traction in the heyday of modern criticism than the wildly naïve conviction that the meaning of biblical text is decipherable through acts of what we may call literary archaeology. *Getting behind* the text—penetrating to its allegedly more primitive and thus "authentic" redactional layers, interpreting newly discovered artifacts to accumulate authoritative near Eastern parallels, framing the relationship of the New Testament to the Old in evolutionary terms of sophisticated development—was long the presumed key to truly *getting* the text. We only understand the text, it was thought, if we dig behind it and look around.

Thankfully, the story of biblical studies and theology in the twentieth century included episodic arousals from the long slumber of this kind of historical criticism. To be sure, the more sober voices in this chorus of objectors have never suggested dispensing with redaction criticism, archaeology, or the hard questions of relating the apostolic witness to the Scriptures of Israel. But we find ourselves blessed to live in a time in which that most primitive and most conspicuously Christian conviction regarding Scripture is being reaffirmed for its hermeneutical and theological importance: these are, the whole and not only a part of them, the *Christian* Scriptures, the Scriptures of the church—and as they are *given*, coming down authoritatively from above and not merely arising from below, they are given *as a whole*, not in a panoply of disparate parts. In response to the cul-de-sac of the text-*behind-and-backwards* approach, we are hearing more and more of the text-*forward* reading and thinking.

Preface

We can imagine the difference this makes. Nahum, for instance, is a text with its own integrity to be sure. It should be read as Nahum. But, for the Christian reading, there is no such thing as a Nahum which is not part of the organic and divinely-given wholeness of the canon of Holy Scripture. There is no Nahum in the abstract; there is only the Nahum contextualized by the canon to which it invariably and providentially belongs. And this makes a difference in how we read Nahum, in what we think Nahum "means." To answer this question of meaning, we must permit ourselves to be instructed by the meaning given Nahum by the canon as a whole, by the "message" of the canonical Scriptures in their unity. Thus the *Christian* reading refuses to read Nahum as though it could be read faithfully in any other way. Reading the text *as given*, then, believing it to be given, means reading in light of the canonical whole given to the church by the Triune God in divine inspiration and providence. Finally, this requires our admitting from the start that the Author's locus of meaning, according to this very canonical whole, is a Person, Lord Jesus Christ, crucified, risen, and ascended. The quest for the edifying, spiritually nurturing meaning of Nahum must begin with (hermeneutical) confession of that Lord.

In regard to this last claim, it bears more than passing mention that this salutary development goes hand in hand with the explosion of interest in the history of Scripture's *reception*, namely, pre-modern, and particularly patristic, hermeneutics. Their subtlety, richness, and living density has come home to us again, as numerous recent projects and publication series demonstrate. The earliest of these post-biblical adumbrations of Christian reading is the so-called "Rule of Faith" (*regula fidei*), a creed-like Rule that in fact is more canonical in origins than patristic, having its roots in the critically important phenomenon of the Scriptures reading themselves. The Rule is in Irenaeus, Hyppolytus, and Clement of Alexandria, yes, but only after it was (in ways fitting their covenantal-historical location) in the Shema of Deuteronomy 6:4, the "yet for us" of 1 Corinthians 8:6, and the "elementary doctrine of Christ" of Hebrews 6:1–2. In short, the "Rule," which is a brief Christologically-focused sketch of the most central and non-negotiable of Christian convictions, "ruled" or determined right readings of particular Scriptures in light of the meaning of the whole.

The Rule is again entrancing modern scholars of text and theology, for, in a time of disenchantment with historical criticism, it challenges the assumptions that drove biblical studies into the wilderness for generations. Recovery of the Rule reminds us that, in the Scriptures, we behold Christ

Preface

and we hear Christ as a matter of faith, not as a matter of historical sight or archaeological skill. It is a simple, practical confidence that Christ's voice in his Word is heard most faithfully by his sheep who hear and who follow. In other words, the church is not an obstacle to rigorous biblical study and theology. The Rule provides, if you like, the precondition of a faithful reading of the Scriptures, the things which—at once arising from the Word and also illumining that same Word—must be presupposed to hear this Word well, to hear it *as a Christian*.

To be sure, these voices have been rather lonely and have not (yet?) won the day. Biblical scholars and theologians continue regularly to assume Gabler's infamous division of biblical studies from theology, treating Scripture as (in fact, as less than) any other human text. Theologians continue to labor to bridge Lessing's ditch between revelation and history.

But not all. Enter Cornelius Van Til.

Yes, Van Til may be the last person to come to mind in light of the foregoing. Known for his pointed criticisms of both foes and allies of the Christian faith, his often impenetrable and painful prose, and his sometimes maddening revisionist use of vocabulary, he seems an unlikely ally for advancing anything like the hermeneutical and theological catholicity just described. But behind those undeniable features of the man's work stands what many regard as one of the finest theological minds of the last century. And by all accounts, this mind was animated not by mere intellectual curiosity or by an unsavory predilection for conflict, but by love and fear of the Lord. Van Til knew the Lion which appeared as a Lamb, and he was fiercely committed to a simple fact which the best of Reformed theology had always insisted to be true: when the One who is the Truth speaks, the humble creature must listen, believe, and rejoice. Anything less is anarchic rebellion. Indeed, Van Til knew that in the Scriptures, this Lion-Lamb has truly spoken, as in history he has truly acted. Our place is to follow with awe and thanksgiving.

What, though, does Van Til have to do with the Rule and the Christian reading of Scripture in the life and fellowship of the church? On review, we notice in the Rule the distinctive Christian seedbed of Van Til's insistence that we come to our experiences, to facts or information, or to the Scriptures themselves, not as impartial and neutral observers. Rather, we come in one or another relation to the Author of history and of Holy Writ. We come in submission or in rebellion.

Preface

This is the conviction Van Til labored tirelessly to carry out himself and to summon from his best-intentioned but as-yet-unpersuaded colleagues in the Kingdom. And, if we relate this conviction to the Rule, I suggest we meet with a refreshing and stimulating harmony. It is a harmony worth energetic exploration and requiring patient development, to be sure, but I suggest it is necessary for the ongoing development of Reformed theology.

In brief, the harmony, and the promise of it, is this: for Van Til, the Christian Faith must be assumed as true in order to make sense of anything. No doubt, some will continue the tired cry that this is an example of one's dogmatic system imposing itself improperly upon the allegedly neutral task of reading Scripture. But we labor in a time when that vacuous objection, too, has been exposed for what it is, namely, the authoritative primacy of the individual over the text's Author. Returning to Van Til in our context means hearing his pulsating commitment to the hermeneutical priority of God's Triune existence as a commitment potentially enriched by, and enriching, the contemporary rediscovery of the Rule, in nub or in kernel, and within the framework of the confessional Reformed tradition. Contemporary rediscovery of the hermeneutical significance of the patristic (biblical) Rule needs the work of Van Til to apply that rediscovery more faithfully, more profitably and usefully. On the other hand, Van Til's students need to rediscover the hermeneutical significance of the Rule (in relation to Scripture) as a way to do fuller justice to Van Til's insight that, in theology and biblical exegesis as in all of life, we must conscientiously presuppose not merely some amorphous body of Christian affirmation but the Christian faith most faithfully summarized in the plotted points (what the early Reformed called the "most necessary doctrines") of the catholic confessions of the Reformed tradition. We need both. The Rule without the catholic confessional Reformed tradition is mere primitivism, lacking specificity in a day of specific questions and challenges; the Reformed confessions without a sophisticated grasp of the significance of the biblical-patristic Rule is sheer traditionalism, ironically lacking catholicity. One yields a weak ecumenism and denies providence, the other turns theology into church history and denies the authority of Scripture. Van Til can help us confront both of these dangers.

In a preface I am expected not to write my own book but to say something of the book to follow, and I hope by now it is clear I have been doing just that. What is Dr. William Dennison doing in these pages? As a longtime churchman and college professor, Dr. Dennison has written for many years on the relationship between Van Til's theology and the nature of biblical text as redemptive revelation. It is a relationship he has explored richly, patiently, and effectively, pulling into view a wide range of concerns in apologetics, pedagogy, and ecclesiastical life. In the pages to follow, we benefit from his labors and have the special opportunity to think with him about what it might mean to share Van Til's commitment to the consequences for life and thought of the church's guiding conviction that the Lion-Lamb has spoken. For he has spoken, and, however we may wish to put this or that differently from Dr. Dennison—in a collection with this range of subject matter, we should consider that inevitable—let us rejoice at the opportunity. Moreover, I would also encourage the reader to participate in an edifying pleasure it commends, namely, the joy many have found in critical interpretation and appropriation of Van Til's thought. We are greatly in need of a second and fresh look at Van Til in the light of the questions being asked in biblical studies and theology, questions for which Van Til puts us in a uniquely advantageous and promising position. To be sure, the definitive interpretive account of Van Til's theology has yet to be written. But I trust you, too, will discover that this collection nudges in the direction of what useful biblical, theological, and ethical terrain such work might traverse.

If you please, though, I would offer one more comment on locating Dr. Dennison's essays. Luke tells us that in the earliest days of the church, a gifted preacher and apologist arrived in Ephesus. Eloquent, educated at avant-garde Alexandria, and skilled in the Scriptures, he combined zeal with knowledge, and with notable success. He had been instructed in the way of the Lord, and Luke tells us confidently that what he taught concerning Jesus he taught accurately. But he lacked something. He knew only the baptism of John, not that of Jesus and the Spirit. Priscilla and Aquila heard this man, Apollos, and, out of loving concern for him and their own zeal for the good of the church, they took him under their wings and "explained to him the way of God more accurately" (Acts 18:26 ESV). It was an invaluable service rendered in charitable patience on their part, and evidently received with humble grace on his part.

Dr. Dennison here renders a Priscilla-and-Aquila-like service. There are many fine teachers, preachers, apologists, and theologians advancing the cause of the Gospel in our day. Some seem even to have the gifts of an Apollos. Dr. Dennison does not suggest otherwise; nor should we. "Getting" Van Til is not a prerequisite to usefulness. But, in this collection of

Preface

essays, Dr. Dennison comes alongside us all to explain the way of God "more accurately." This is the contribution, among others, that Van Til made to his own students and colleagues. You may not identify with every conclusion or step in the arguments made, but do not let this deter you from the gold here. After all, if we come away from this exercise of heart and intellect better attuned to the voice of our Shepherd, that is everything to his sheep. This was Van Til's animating desire, and it is Dr. Dennison's as well. Confident you will enjoy that very blessing, I warmly commend Dr. Dennison's essays to you.

Mark A. Garcia
Pastor, Immanuel Presbyterian Church (OPC), Coraopolis, PA
President and Fellow in Scripture and Theology, Greystone Theological Institute
April 8, 2015

Acknowledgments

When James Baird came to me and spoke of this project, I did not show much excitement about the venture. However, as a result of his own unique persistent manner and our continual interaction concerning the work of Cornelius Van Til and Christian apologetics, I finally capitulated and told him to go ahead with the project. In giving permission to proceed, I told him that it would be his endeavor and that I would have little to do with it. He definitely took this directive to heart; he owns the selection, the organization, and all the work in bringing this volume to fruition. I want to thank him, and the wonderful patience of his dear wife, Georgia, for all the hours and the work he has done to make this a reality. James has been an extraordinary student who has sought to embrace faithfully Van Til's apologetic starting point, that is, no compromise with the self-attesting Christ of Scripture. One of the best blessings teachers can receive is that their students surpass them; James Baird is such a student. I am humbled and honored that he has benefited from my work on Van Til and that he thinks it would be well for others to have this collection of essays in one volume. Moreover, the reader should examine closely his introductory essay, which captures my specific interest in and understanding of Van Til.

For editorial reasons, James Baird decided to remove the initial footnote in the chapters in which I acknowledge the specific occasion of the essay and/or convey thanks to those who helped in the production of the essay. He asked if I would place those comments here.

The third chapter, "Van Til and Common Grace," is an essay based upon two Reformation Day lectures, which I presented to the Ohio Presbytery of the Orthodox Presbyterian Church in Morgantown, West Virginia,

Acknowledgments

on October 28, 1995. The lectures were given to commemorate the centennial celebration of Cornelius Van Til's birth. They were based solely upon Van Til's volume, *Common Grace and the Gospel,* which contains a collection of his articles on common grace from 1947–1968. Reverend Larry Semel coordinated the event for the Ohio Presbytery. For chapter four, "Antithesis, Common Grace, and Plato's View of the Soul," special thanks to the library staff of Covenant College, who provided much assistance for this project, especially Barbara Beckman, Thomas Horner, and John Holberg. It should be noted that chapter six, "The Christian Apologist in the Present State of Redemptive History," is an abridged edition of the opening section of my course "Christian Apologetics" at Northwest Theological Seminary in Lynnwood, Washington. Moreover, chapter eight, "A Reassessment of Natural and Special Revelation," with some revisions, is an essay based on a public lecture on August 13, 2005, at Northwest Theological Seminary in Lynnwood, Washington, under the title, "Apologetics and Creation." Although delivered in August 2005, the lecture was part of the program for the Kerux Conference in May 2005. I wish to thank the Lilly Endowment through the Kaleo Center at Covenant College for a grant to research this subject. Specifically, I thank Dr. Kevin Eames, Director of the Center for Theological Exploration of the Kaleo Center, who graciously approved the grant.

Special mention and appreciation must be given to Miriam Mindeman for her excellent editorial work, comments, and suggestions on the essays appearing in chapters 4, 5, 6, and 8.

Again, thank you James Baird!

William D. Dennison
Covenant College
March 29, 2015

Introduction

In the aftermath of orthodox Christianity's twentieth-century conflict with theological liberalism, too few Christians now write with scholarly conviction; even fewer write with robust commitment to the Holy Scriptures and the Reformed confessions. The popular Christian response to the advances of liberal scholarship is either to retreat into the half-built fortress of fundamentalistic dogmatism, or to capitulate to modernism's demands, even if an inch at a time. A limited number of Christian scholars have a clear vision of the truth: the best response to liberalism—and the best response to its cognates, produced as they are by the same anti-Christian spirit—is to plant oneself squarely on the foundation of the inerrant Scriptures and the Reformed confessions, and then, on that presuppositional basis, to address the hard questions of scholarship with meticulous research and serious reflection. This procedure was implemented by the greats of the Reformed tradition, and it is the superior route toward which Dr. William D. Dennison has worked hard to encourage Christians.

In Defense of the Eschaton is an anthology of Dr. Dennison's most valuable essays on the Reformed apologetics of Cornelius Van Til, all of which carry the mark of being written with Dr. Dennison's erudite Reformed confessionalism. The essays in this book do not comprise all of Dr. Dennison's writings on apologetics—much less do they comprise all of his writings! He has published on a variety of topics, including biblical theology, practical theology, interdisciplinary studies, and intellectual history. A strong argument could be made that, since Van Til's thought has influenced the full scope of Dr. Dennison's scholarship, all of Dr. Dennison's other essays should be added to this anthology. Such additions would turn this book into a hefty tome, indeed. My aim for this anthology, however, is for readers to glean a deeper

Introduction

understanding of Van Til's Reformed apologetic method from Dr. Dennison's exegesis and research. I have attempted to make up for the absence of Dr. Dennison's other writings by including after the general bibliography, a bibliography of his published materials, excluding the essays herein republished.

I have edited the component essays of this volume (some more heavily than others), but I have made no attempt to interweave the chapters. Each essay stands alone with its own particular goals and motives. Nonetheless, common themes join the chapters together, as they are vital participants in Dr. Dennison's overarching project to elucidate, apply, and extend Van Til's thought. My hope is that, as Dr. Dennison's project comes to expression in this volume, readers will gain a greater appreciation of the redemptive-historical structure of a truly biblical defense of the Christian faith.

I would like to thank the respective editors of *New Horizons*, the *Westminster Theological Journal*, the *Mid-America Journal of Theology*, the *Journal of the Evangelical Theological Society*, *Kerux*, the *Calvin Theological Journal*, and the *Ordained Servant*, as well as the Committee for the Historian of the OPC and P&R Publishing for kindly granting us permission to use the articles herein republished. I am especially grateful to Dr. Lane G. Tipton for his foreword and to Dr. Mark A. Garcia for his preface. I am obliged to Wipf and Stock Publishers and to Matthew Wimer for his wonderful assistance in the publication process. Thanks are in order to Anna Baird, Nate Groelsema, Vierow Lynn Weber, my great friend Thomas Buiter, and my patient wife, Georgia, for their assistance in preparing the manuscript for publication. I am indebted to John Holberg and Tom Horner for their help in compiling the bibliography, and to Miriam Mindeman for her extensive and exceptional editing.

My last word of thanks goes to Dr. Dennison for his abounding trust, encouragement, and generosity. Dr. Dennison, I regard you as my esteemed teacher. To work alongside you on such a substantial project has been a true privilege—an honor I will never forget.

The remainder of this introduction is a synopsis of Dr. Dennison's published reflections on Reformed apologetic methodology and related topics. Rather than seeking to capture Dr. Dennison's thought comprehensively, the following is intended only to highlight the primary contours of his apologetic endeavors in order to orient readers and provide them with perspective on the subsequent chapters.

Introduction

* * * * *

William D. Dennison initiated his academic career as a Reformed apologist with his ThM thesis, *Paul's Two-Age Construction: Its Significance for Apologetics*.[1] His basic argument in that work has set the trajectory for his scholarship up to the present: Paul teaches that a unique mindset is implanted into believers upon their union with Christ, and Paul persistently harkens back to that implanted mindset when issuing imperatives for believer's thought-lives (see Col 3:1–4). In union with Jesus Christ, believers are remade to think in a certain way, and believers are called to think in this way for the sake of Christ. Although this biblical way of thinking may be given various labels, Dennison has appropriately titled it *eschatological*. By using the term *eschatology*, Dennison emphasizes that, if Christians are to think biblically, they must think in a way that is principally shaped not by abstract systematic categories, but rather by the epochal structure of redemptive history as set forth in Scripture. Paul was mentally drawn up into the progressive unfolding of the triune God's plan; as Dennison argues, so should we be drawn up, especially when confronting the challenges of unbelief.

According to the Apostle Paul's eschatology, there are two historic aeons that comprise two radically distinct world-and-life views for their respective participants.[2] The believer has been united by faith to the resurrected and ascended Christ. As a result, the believer has been lifted into the heavenly world to come; he has been placed in the *eschaton*. The unbeliever, however, is united by nature to the fallen first man, Adam. The unbeliever is consequently bound to the carnal pattern of life inherent in this present evil age. Apologetics, in Dennison's view, is not about a casual exchange of ideas over coffee or the presentation of the rational ground of Christian belief—or, for that matter, an explanation of why belief in God does not require propositional evidence to be rational.[3] The apologist may use these tactics while in dialogue with his unbelieving friend, as long as he keeps in mind the antithesis between their two respective ways of thinking. The believer is insolubly united to the heavenly Christ. His thinking is not defined by a so-called "neutral" use of reason and experience, but instead by a heart filled to the brim with glorified life. The unbeliever, on the other

---

1. This thesis is now published with Wipf and Stock as *Paul's Two-Age Construction and Apologetics*.
2. Ibid., 27–53.
3. See Plantinga, "Reason and Belief in God."

Introduction

hand, is a slave to sin in active rebellion against his Creator. The believer must, then, confront the unbeliever as one offering intellectual, moral, and religious life to the willfully and helplessly dead. Apologetics is above all else a testimony and defense of the hope and life in Christ. Because this testimony and defense is given by the believer who is in heaven to the unbeliever who is of the earth, the nature of the apologetic dialogue will be one of radical conflict grounded in two definitively diverging starting points. For the believer to begin interacting with the unbeliever from a neutral starting point is tantamount to giving up his heavenly position in Christ; so Dennison states, "My hope is that the church will establish itself with Paul in the *eschaton*."[4]

Dennison's eschatological approach to apologetics has strong affinity (if not identity) with the presuppositional approach of Cornelius Van Til. Dennison has frequently claimed that he never intended to be original; his goal has been to be more consistently Calvinistic than Van Til—or, if you will, to be more Van Tilian than Van Til himself. Hence, Dennison has devoted a major portion of his apologetic corpus to elaborating the redemptive-historical structure of Van Til's Reformed apologetic.[5] Recently, K. Scott Oliphint has proposed a renaming of Van Til's apologetic approach from *presuppositional* to *covenantal*.[6] This name change corroborates Dennison's contention that the primary thrust of Van Til's apologetic is not speculatively philosophical, but rather biblically *eschatological*. In Dennison's estimation, the genius of Van Til was his programmatic attack on unbelieving thought-systems, a confrontation that issued out of his starting point in the self-attesting Christ of redemptive revelation. According to Dennison, Van Til essentially taught that the heavenly world-and-life view secured and required by the believer's union with Christ supplies the believer with everything needed to engage the world of unbelief properly. Dennison's writings on apologetics have thus sought to establish the connection between Van Til's apologetic and the biblical theology of Van Til's most beloved professor, Geerhardus Vos.

Dennison has also aptly shown how Vos's insight into the nature of revelation deeply shaped Van Til's view of human understanding.[7] The

---

4. W. Dennison, *Paul's Construction*, 106. Emphasis in original.
5. See, for example, chapter 2, chapter 6, and chapter 7 below.
6. See Oliphint, *Covenantal Apologetics*.
7. See chapter 8 below.

Introduction

influence of Vos on Van Til can be seen in *An Introduction to Systematic Theology*, where Van Til states the following:

> In paradise . . . God revealed his will with respect to the Tree of Good and Evil. Man could not know from nature itself nor from himself in relation to nature that the result of eating from the Tree of Good and Evil would spell his death. . . . It had to be a direct communication of thought content on the part of God to man. . . . We may speak of this revelation as *supernatural* in opposition to natural. . . .
>
> It is this revelation that Dr. Vos speaks of as pre-redemptive, special revelation. . . . It is of prime importance to observe that even in paradise man was never meant to study nature by means of observation and experiment without connection with positive *supernatural* thought communication given to him by God. Nature could not be observed for what it actually is except in relation to history, and history cannot be seen for what it is at any stage except it be viewed in relation to its final end. And only by direct supernatural revelation could man have an adequate notion of this end.[8]

Van Til's point in this passage is that even when we engage in simple observations of the physical universe, we are designed by God to understand his creation in light of himself and his one great plan of redemption, as fulfilled in the eschatological person and work of Jesus Christ, and as inerrantly revealed in Holy Scripture. Van Til, in *Common Grace and the Gospel*, puts the issue this way: "Natural revelation must not be separated from this supernatural revelation. To separate the two is to deal with two abstractions instead of with one concrete situation."[9]

Dennison has supplied additional exegetical support from Paul's letter to the Romans for the Vos-Van Til idea that natural revelation and special revelation are organically intertwined.[10] According to Dennison's investigations, Paul teaches that the invisible things of God—invisible things we ordinarily categorize as belonging to special revelation—are made known in the natural world by God's triune activity (Rom 1:19–20). For example, the entire creation proclaims the redemptive work of Christ by following in his footsteps—by being humiliated in expectation of the glorification of God's elect (Rom 8:19–23; 10:18; cf. Col 1:23). Dennison's conclusion is

---

8. Van Til, *Systematic Theology*, 125–26. For Vos's position on the nature of preredemptive revelation, see Vos, *Biblical Theology*, 19–40.

9. Van Til, *Common Grace*, 69.

10. See chapter 8 below.

Introduction

that the apologist must not begin to convince the unbeliever of the truth of Christianity by appealing to the natural world or natural reason, as if natural revelation can be correctly understood without being brought together with special revelation; for, to begin abstractly in this way is to deny the Christian truth for which the apologist means to contend.

Another focus of Dennison's writings on apologetics is Christian education, a favored topic shared with Van Til.[11] In education, believers are required to learn and teach the ideas of unbelievers. How can this be done consistently with the believer's life in Christ? The answer to this question is much the same answer Dennison gave to the problem of engaging unbelievers in apologetic discussion: the subject matter of the academic disciplines must be addressed by the believer from his heavenly perspective. This means that the believer must give proper attention to the common grace insights of unbelievers while at the same time realizing that these insights must be recontextualized into a Christian world-and-life view before they can be fully accepted.[12] The unbeliever's hatred toward God and blindness to Spiritual things so taints his academic procedures that he suppresses the truth about God with which he is always in noetic contact as he investigates God's world. As long as unbelievers disconnect truths about God's creation from truths about God and his redemptive plan revealed in Scripture, their theories about reality will be wrongheaded in the strongest sense. The Christian academic must, therefore, discard those ideas that are inconsistent with the teaching of Scripture and must biblically reorient those ideas that are true but bent by the principle of death clinging to the darkened mind of the unbeliever (see 2 Cor 4:4–6). In order to burn through these ideological impurities and rework the metal of the unbeliever's thought-system, the Christian academic must perform a *transcendental analysis*.[13]

A transcendental analysis is the first step of Van Til's transcendental argument for Christianity. Van Til taught that the Christian apologist must argue for the truth of Christianity by showing the unbeliever that only Christianity can make cogent sense of reality. This argument requires the apologist to demonstrate to the unbeliever that his unbelieving thought-system is inadequate, inevitably harmed by internal inconsistencies. Dennison contends

---

11. See Van Til, *Essays on Christian Education*. See also chapter 4 and chapter 5 below.

12. See chapter 3 below for more on Dennison's interpretation of Van Til's unique conception of common grace.

13. Dennison also calls Van Til's transcendental analysis a *transcendental critique*. See chapter 1 and chapter 5 below.

Introduction

that the apologist must therefore dig deep into the structure of the unbeliever's thought-system in search of its controlling ideological commitment in order to show the unbeliever that the foundation of his thought as well as its superstructure is flawed beyond repair. Transcendental analysis is this mining into the unbeliever's system of thought. Put in Pauline terminology, a transcendental argument is simply the Christian academic's effort to "destroy arguments and every lofty opinion raised against the knowledge of God," and a transcendental analysis is his effort to "take every thought captive to obey Christ" (2 Cor 10:5 ESV). Without transcendental analysis, believers would consistently be taken "captive by philosophy and empty deceit, according to human tradition, according to the elemental spirits of the world, and not according to Christ" (Col 2:8 ESV).

Finally, the controlling incentive driving Dennison's work in Reformed apologetics is deeply ecclesiastical: Dennison is concerned for the fidelity of Christ's church. In the marketplace of ideas, the lies of Satan tempt believers to compromise their commitment to the Word of God. To aid the laity in their battle against the Devil, Dennison has worked hard to convey Van Til's biblical defense of the faith at a more understandable level.[14] On the other hand, Dennison's profound interest in the health of the church has also motivated him to interrogate Reformed scholarship, critically examining its biblical, confessional, and academic astuteness.[15] Most central to Dennison's writings, then, is his call for believers (laity, pastors, and academics alike) to be *epistemologically self-conscious*—that is, to live faithful thought-lives in Christ. In its essence, Dennison's work in Reformed apologetics is an exhortation for believers as they sojourn through this foolish and evil world—to cling to their Savior by faith and to rely on the might of his heavenly wisdom.

James Douglas Baird
Lookout Mountain, GA
May 2015

---

14. See, for example, chapter 1 and chapter 3 below.
15. See, for example, chapter 9, chapter 10, and chapter 11 below.

Abbreviations

CTJ	Calvin Theological Journal
CRC	Christian Reformed Church
JHMTH	Journal for the History of Modern Theology
JETS	Journal of the Evangelical Theological Society
JIS	Journal of Interdisciplinary Studies
NH	New Horizons
NICNT	New International Commentary on the New Testament
OPC	Orthodox Presbyterian Church
SPCK	Society for Promoting Christian Knowledge
TZ	Theologische Zeitschrift
WCF	Westminster Confession of Faith
WTJ	Westminster Theological Journal

Yet among the mature we do impart wisdom, although it is not a wisdom of this age or of the rulers of this age, who are doomed to pass away. But we impart a secret and hidden wisdom of God, which God decreed before the ages for our glory. None of the rulers of this age understood this, for if they had, they would not have crucified the Lord of glory. But, as it is written,

> "What no eye has seen, nor ear heard,
> nor the heart of man imagined,
> what God has prepared for those who love him"—

these things God has revealed to us through the Spirit. For the Spirit searches everything, even the depths of God. For who knows a person's thoughts except the spirit of that person, which is in him? So also no one comprehends the thoughts of God except the Spirit of God. Now we have received not the spirit of the world, but the Spirit who is from God, that we might understand the things freely given us by God. And we impart this in words not taught by human wisdom but taught by the Spirit, interpreting spiritual truths to those who are spiritual.

The natural person does not accept the things of the Spirit of God, for they are folly to him, and he is not able to understand them because they are spiritually discerned. The spiritual person judges all things, but is himself to be judged by no one. "For who has understood the mind of the Lord so as to instruct him?" But we have the mind of Christ.

—1 Corinthians 2:6–16 ESV

PART 1

Van Til Studies

1

Van Til's Critique of Human Thought

> Thus the transcendental argument seeks to discover what sort of foundations the house of human knowledge must have, in order to be what it is.
>
> —Cornelius Van Til, *A Survey of Christian Epistemology*

Educators have always been concerned with how information transfers from the teacher to the pupil. Specifically, does the student acquire a sufficient understanding of a subject in order to apply it to life? Over the years, students have voiced this concern with regard to Cornelius Van Til (1895–1987)—they find his language difficult to understand and difficult to apply to apologetic situations.

One reason for this is that they are not trained in philosophy. Even so, their failure to comprehend and apply Van Til's philosophical language has not diminished their enthusiasm for his apologetic starting point, which is the self-attesting Christ of Scripture. For them, the authority of God's Word and the preeminence of Jesus Christ transcend their ignorance of philosophy. They know that the apologist is not to compromise the Christ of Scripture with any principle or system of secularization! Even if Van Til's philosophical language is unclear, his students support his initial commitment to the gospel found in the infallible Word of God.

These students, while applauding Van Til's starting point, struggle to apply the truth of the self-attesting Christ of Scripture to secular thought, Christian thought, and their own thought. Perhaps their efforts are impeded once again by Van Til's philosophical language, for he asks them to employ the "transcendental critique." For Van Til, this critique is the method of examining a principle or system of thought in order to uncover the central presupposition (idea, belief, *Archimedean point*) that shapes it. In this case, the term *transcendental* refers to the one principle that is foundational to the whole system of belief. For Christians committed to Van Til's apologetic, that basic principle is the self-attesting Christ of Scripture. Non-Christians offer such principles as reason, experience, imagination, power, and dialectic. Contrary to what many think, the basis for Van Til's transcendental critique is not obscure or theoretical. His critique of human thought merely employs Christ's teaching that out of the heart flow the issues of life (cf. Matt 12:34–35; 15:18–19; Mark 7:21; Luke 12:34; 16:15). By participating in Christ's words, the apologist is to uncover and expose the heart of humanity. For Van Til, no one is exempt from this critical analysis. The transcendental critique reveals the deep roots of sin in the heart of man, and it demands the purity of biblical truth in the church as well as in the individual Christian.

HOW IT WORKS

How does the transcendental critique work? Let us say, for example, that I believe that discussion (negotiation) and experience can resolve all disputes between nations. The transcendental critique attempts to figure out *why* I hold that position. As you begin your analysis of my thought, as a Christian apologist, you must have a self-conscious understanding of God's revelation from Genesis to Revelation. Specifically, you must *participate self-consciously* in Christ's message to the church (the Bible) as you attempt to disclose the foundation (root) of my system. By your participation in the biblical text, theory and practice are brought together. With a biblical consciousness of God's revelatory truth in place, you are ready to begin your analysis and critique of my thought.

Your transcendental critique functions like a drill penetrating the earth in order to find coal. You begin at the surface—with the statement that I have placed before you. The drilling process begins by asking questions graciously in order to uncover the various layers of my thought (1 Pet 3:15–16). A drill removes layers of dirt and rock as it makes its way to the coal; likewise, you will ask me questions that reveal the layers or "structures" of my thought as you make your way toward my most fundamental belief. In Van Til's apologetic, this part of the transcendental critique is known as "structural analysis." For example, your questioning should reveal that one of the structures of my thought is the belief that people are basically good. Moreover, you should discover my belief that people desire to live at peace with one another.

PRESUPPOSITIONS

With these structures before us, the question remains: why do I hold these beliefs? At this point, the drill seems to be approaching the coal—my core belief. You begin to realize that my fundamental concept of human rationality dictates my convictions that people are basically good and that people wish to live in peace. You have exposed the central *presupposition* of my thought—the assumption that most minds embrace inherent goodness and peaceful coexistence. Diplomatic negotiations will solve conflicts between nations, in my view, because all humanity shares a common desire for goodness and peace. This concept of human rationality is my core belief.

One might react to my illustration by recalling Augustine's (354–430 AD) conception of man as the image of God. In his *City of God*, Augustine writes that man's goodness and desire for peace are central elements of that image. So, is my view of human rationality secular or Christian? At this point, the Christian apologist has to be very perceptive as he applies the transcendental critique to the structures of my thought. He has to connect the dots of each response that I give to his questions. Moreover, he is responsible to construct my worldview honestly as I disclose any various beliefs. That is, the apologist must endeavor to understand his opponent's position better than his opponent understands it.

In our example, let us say that as your investigation advances toward my core belief, it becomes apparent that the tenets of modernity shape my view of rationality—for example, I do not believe in God, and I do not accept the biblical view that man is God's image. Neither the Bible nor Augustine is determining my understanding of the role of goodness and peace in the arena of diplomacy. Rather, enlightened humanism, as it came to expression in John Stuart Mill (1806–1873), has conditioned my conceptions of goodness and peace.

In his essay *On Liberty* (1859), Mill sounded the alarm that the majority could become tyrannical in a democratic state. In order to prevent this abuse of power, Mill maintained that people must put all differences aside and appeal to the collective constitution of human reason. By doing this, all parties (majority and minority) are capable of resolving their problems through "discussion and experience." They can be confident that rational discourse will easily resolve all conflicts, as each party invokes the experience of history and human collectivity. Mill's position is dependent on what he calls the "quality" and "respectability" of the human mind to construct an intellectual and moral society—that is, a society that is dependent on the goodness of man, and man's ability to create an environment of peace and harmony. If Mill's political philosophy is embraced and executed, then the biblical doctrine of man's fall into sin must be rejected, and the realization of a human utopia seems to be placed within man's grasp. For those committed to classic democratic liberalism, Mill's principle of utility—"discussion and experience"—became the solution to all human conflict.

COUNTERARGUMENTS

After the Christian apologist has uncovered the central presupposition of his opponent, he is in a position to move on to the next step: to demonstrate that his opponent cannot live consistently from his presupposition(s). Keep in mind that, according to Van Til, apologetics is not a battle between competing presuppositions. The object of apologetics is not to show that my presupposition is better than your presupposition. Rather, for the Christian apologist, the presupposition of the absolute authority and truth of the self-attesting Christ of Scripture calls all men to repentance and faith in Christ as their presuppositions and systems of thought are brought into the open. For Van Til, there is an *antithesis* between the Christian presupposition and all other presuppositions.

To see this, let us return to our illustration. Two examples are sufficient to show the folly of the secular view of rationality that I espoused (Mill's view). First, we know that dictators and tyrants have invoked Machiavelli's (1469–1527) *The Prince* in order to justify their evil behavior. History is full of instances in which "discussion and experience" had no impact as these ruthless "princes" terminated the lives of millions. Second, since my

(Mill's) perspective of utopian idealism is grounded in the Enlightenment's view that rationality would lead to the cessation of war, its folly is exposed by the two world wars of the twentieth century—and the continuing strife of our day. Although many continue to give blind allegiance to this ideal, there is no evidence, as we enter the twenty-first century, that "discussion and experience" will pacify man's evil quest for power over others.

By using these counterarguments, the Christian apologist has shown the absurdity of my core belief and my inability to apply my view of rationality to the affairs of humanity consistently. The counterarguments affirm the antithetical instruction of the Psalmist to put no confidence in princes. Instead, we are to put our confidence in the sovereign providence of God, who has reserved the inheritance of the nations for his Son (Pss 2:1–12; 118:9; 146:3). The apologist will place before his rival this statement of the Psalmist in the hope of seeing repentance and faith in Christ.

I want you to learn from my illustration that it is not necessary to know someone's thought thoroughly in order to critique it. I tried to demonstrate this point by not revealing Mill's name until the transcendental critique had uncovered his basic presupposition. In other words, my aim was to show that a competent understanding of Van Til's critique is sufficient for pastors and laymen to expose the starting point and structures of a rival's thought. A competent use of the critique does not require knowledge of the history of philosophy. I attempted to show that knowledge of the history of philosophy will add context and substance to the critique, but such knowledge is not imperative for the pastor or layman. Indeed, competency in the method enables one to combat effectively the secular presuppositions of the world, as well as to withstand the invasion of secularism into Christ's church and the believer's life.

CHRISTIAN SELF-ANALYSIS

Although my example is from the arena of secular thought, I do not want to overlook the responsibility of the church and the believer to employ the method in self-analysis. For a church that proclaims the truth of the gospel, and for the believer who loves Christ, apologetics is not only the defending of the Christ of Scripture from the world, but also the constant cleansing of our union with Christ from the pollution of sinful thought. Through the power of Christ's Spirit, we are to live out our self-conscious identity in Christ (Gal 2:20). As pastors prepare to preach, the transcendental method will need to be employed. As the church makes decisions about her philosophy of ministry, the method will need to be employed. As believers watch TV, view a film, read a book, counsel a friend, listen in the classroom, and hear a political candidate, the method will need to be employed. Simply put, the church, the pastor, and the believer must critically analyze everything that passes through the brain. As the Holy Spirit maintains our participation in the self-attesting Christ of Scripture, such analysis thwarts the evil one!

2

Van Til's Epistemology and Analytic Philosophy

> Man was created as a historical being.... Moreover, [man's] consciousness of objects and of self in time meant consciousness of history in relationship to the plan of God back of history.
>
> —CORNELIUS VAN TIL, *CHRISTIAN APOLOGETICS*

Imagine, Van Til's apologetic leads to Hegelian pantheism! In 1953, philosophy professors Cecil De Boer (Calvin College) and Jesse De Boer (University of Kentucky) made such an accusation concerning Van Til's apologetic. Cecil De Boer stated their thesis clearly: "The new apologetic [Van Til's] seems to have taken over uncritically the idealist theory of knowledge and truth, a theory leading logically to a kind of [Hegelian] pantheism."[1] Moreover, the De Boers fused their thesis with an attack on Van Til's claim that he was presenting a pure Christian epistemology, free from the corruption of non-Christian thought. In their estimation, Van Til's formulation was tainted by the language of modern idealism,

---

1. C. De Boer, "Editorial," 3.

especially terminology found in Immanuel Kant (1724–1804) and G. W. F. Hegel (1770–1831). Hence, they believed that Van Til's purism turned into a "boomerang" against his own system; Van Til was not a purist since "modern idealism is no friend of Christianity."[2]

In contrast to the De Boers, many of the disciples of Van Til, led by Professor John Frame (now at Reformed Theological Seminary in Orlando), have maintained that Van Til presented a biblically consistent epistemology despite his reliance upon the language of idealistic philosophy. These disciples acknowledge that Van Til received his philosophical education in the idealistic tradition. They hold, however, that Van Til adequately criticized idealism and redefined its terminology within the framework of his presuppositions and method. Even so, it should be noted that these comrades of Van Til, like the De Boers, focus on his use of language. There is, however, an obvious difference between the two approaches. For the De Boers, Van Til's use of idealistic language creates a confusing, ambiguous, and at times nonsensical epistemology. In contrast, the Van Tilians maintain that his use of idealistic language creates a somewhat complex epistemology, but that his terminology is understandable if interpreted in the context of his presuppositions.

From my perspective, both critic and disciple have assessed Van Til's epistemology by analyzing his particular dependency upon the terminology of idealism. Although the results of their analyses are different, I believe that both sides have failed to perceive the foundation of Van Til's epistemology because of a similar methodological procedure. Instead of dissecting the terminology of Van Til, both sides should have analyzed the underlying structures of Van Til's thought. In my judgment, if both sides had followed such a procedure, they may have discovered that a philosophy of history and the rubrics of systematic theology ground Van Til's epistemology. Specifically, his epistemology is rooted in the Christian God of revelational history and the content of the Reformed confessions.[3]

---

2. J. De Boer, "Bramble Patch," 11.

3. In light of this thesis, the reader must keep two points in mind. First, this study is primarily interested in presenting the place of Van Til's philosophy of history in his epistemology. Presently, I am not concerned with a comprehensive study of Van Til's philosophy of history or his epistemology. Second, this study will avoid any elaborate discussion of the rubrics of systematic theology since my immediate concern is the position of history in Van Til's epistemology.

Van Til's Epistemology and Analytic Philosophy

THE DE BOERS

During the second quarter of the twentieth century, there existed a sincere respect among Westminster Theological Seminary, Calvin College, and Calvin Theological Seminary, and the two Reformed denominations that mainly supported those institutions: the Orthodox Presbyterian Church (hereafter OPC), which has strong ties with Westminster Theological Seminary, and the Christian Reformed Church (hereafter CRC), to which Calvin College and Calvin Theological Seminary are affiliated. In the early 1950s, however, their mutual respect began to be tested. The so-called "progressives" (a new breed of intellectual leaders at Calvin College and within the CRC) began a serious assault on the most prominent Reformed leader at Westminster Theological Seminary, who was himself bred in the CRC—Cornelius Van Til. Although now a member of the OPC, Van Til remained a spokesman for the so-called "traditionalists" in the CRC who fought to maintain a rigid interpretation of the Reformed confessions and a clear antithesis between Christian and non-Christian thought. Unlike the "traditionalists," the "progressives" opposed a rigid interpretation of the confessions, and they raised questions concerning the clarity of antithetical Christian thinking. In view of Van Til's popularity, the "progressives" believed that the success of their future agenda was tied partially to raising speculations concerning his thought.[4] Possibly, they could convince the membership of the CRC that Van Til was not a friend of the historic decisions made in the CRC, and that his Reformed theology was not pure. Hence, they instigated a public assault upon Van Til which followed a twofold strategy: (1) demonstrate that Van Til's and Herman Hoeksema's (1886–1965) views on common grace were essentially the same, thereby showing that Van Til opposed the decision of the 1924 CRC Synod against Hoeksema; and (2) demonstrate that Van Til's Christian philosophy was not pure or competent. James Daane spearheaded the attack upon Van Til's view of common grace with articles in the new magazine, *The Reformed Journal*, whereas Cecil De Boer spearheaded the attack upon Van Til's work as a Christian philosopher with articles in *The Calvin Forum*.[5] If their strategy successfully discredited Van Til, then

---

4. Bratt, *Dutch Calvinism*, 187–203.

5. Quickly, in the second issue of the *Reformed Journal*, Daane began his attack on Van Til's view of common grace. However, the clarity of his thesis appeared later: "Thus although Hoeksema denies common grace and Schilder and Van Til affirm it, there is no difference in their conceptions of grace" (Daane, "A Theology of Grace—II," 9). Daane also published a book on Van Til's view of common grace entitled *A Theology of Grace*.

the "progressives" would take an important step in establishing a foothold within the CRC. Although the discussion on common grace is relevant to the current state of affairs, presently I am concerned only with the attack upon Van Til's philosophy.

In order to discredit the popularity of Van Til in the CRC, Cecil and Jesse De Boer engaged in an analytical-critical investigation of Van Til's epistemological language. Such an investigation focused on linguistic and conceptual units within Van Til's epistemology. This critical method is limited since it is usually directed toward isolated propositions and not toward the full-orbed spectrum of a person's thought. After all, can a philosopher who subscribes to analyzing linguistic and conceptual units critique a holistic philosophy of life pictured in the context of speculative idealism? I maintain that he can, provided that he has a firm grasp of the holistic picture being criticized. In many cases, however, an analytic philosopher does not seem to apprehend the holistic picture because he is content merely to focus on linguistic and conceptual units. In my judgment, the De Boers fell into this trap. Hence, they never observed or comprehended the holistic picture of Van Til's epistemology, built as it is upon the foundation of a philosophy of history.

As the De Boers worked within the framework of analytic philosophy, they accused Van Til's epistemology of being idealistic, intolerant, and without common sense. Beginning with idealism, C. De Boer maintained that Van Til borrowed his entire epistemological scheme from idealism, and, thus, it led uncritically to a species of pantheism, not theism.[6] In order to verify his point, C. De Boer took issue with Van Til's understanding of "God-interpreted facts." He reasoned that if the "givens with which we

---

Although William Masselink (1897–1973) was not a "progressive," the "progressives" solicited his support when they discovered that he also attacked Van Til's view of common grace in a published book (see Masselink, *General Revelation and Common Grace*) as well as in articles that appeared in *The Calvin Forum*. Masselink's criticism of Van Til was helpful to the "progressives" because he had divided the issue of common grace into two camps: the traditional Reformed view (Abraham Kuyper [1837–1920], Herman Bavinck [1854–1921], B. B. Warfield [1851–1921], Charles Hodge [1797–1878], J. Gresham Machen [1881–1937], Louis Berkhof [1873–1957], and Valentine Hepp [1879–1950]) and the "Reconstructionist" view (Klaas Schilder [1890–1952], D. H. Th. Vollenhoven [1892–1978], Herman Dooyeweerd [1889–1977], and Van Til). For the "progressives," the genius of Masselink's work was demonstrating Van Til to be an enemy of Kuyper, Old Princeton, Berkhof, and even Van Til's hero, Machen. Hence, from their perspective, Van Til could not be revered as a spokesman for the historic Reformed faith, or, in this case, the historic CRC.

6. C. De Boer, "Editorial," 3.

must begin are not facts but 'God-interpreted facts,'" then one cannot really distinguish between the facts and the identity of God's knowledge, that is, "if God's knowledge constitutes the facts, the facts must constitute God's knowledge."[7] Hence, Van Til's epistemological scheme leads to pantheism.

C. De Boer's criticism was serious; he had cast doubt on a fundamental distinction in Van Til's epistemology, that is, the Creator-creature distinction and his pure conception of Christian theism. After all, Van Til was dogmatic about the Creator-creature distinction: "As God has self-contained being and all other being has created or derivative being, so also God has self-contained and man has derivative knowledge."[8] Simply, Van Til affirmed that God's being and knowledge are self-contained; God does not derive his being and knowledge from any other substance or essence. Moreover, Van Til held that man's true knowledge of the creation was dependent upon, and derived from, God's knowledge of the creation. Thereby, at all points in the epistemological scheme, the Creator remains the Creator, the creature remains the creature, and the creation remains the creation. Hence, in contrast to C. De Boer's accusation, the creature's knowledge is not comprehensively identical with the knowledge of God, and the creation does not constitute God's knowledge of the creation.[9] In fact, Van Til delivered a strident indictment of ancient and modern idealism:

> In reality, no form of idealism, even if it uses the term creation, will admit that which is to us most important of all, namely, that God is absolutely self-existent and absolutely self-conscious. Idealism will not admit that the one and the many are equally eternal and are harmonized in the church's conception of the Trinity. No idealist can admit the biblical doctrine of creation *ex nihilo*. Idealism includes the God and the universe of Christianity in what it calls the Universe of the Whole. God is then the a priori aspect of Reality, and no more.[10]

---

7. Ibid.

8. Van Til, *Apologetics* syllabus, 9. In this section, we must keep in mind that the De Boers based their criticism upon four documents by Van Til: *The Intellectual Challenge of the Gospel*, *Apologetics* syllabus, *Introduction to Systematic Theology* syllabus, and *Christian-Theistic Evidences* syllabus. Also, one should keep in mind that his writings on common grace were available to them as well. For this reason, my response to the De Boers will be dependent mainly upon these documents.

9. See C. De Boer, "Editorial," 3.

10. Van Til, *Systematic Theology* syllabus, 23.

In light of these words, it is difficult to comprehend C. De Boer's claim that Van Til's epistemology leads logically to an uncritical pantheism. Van Til was adamant; indeed, idealism was pantheistic, and therefore it had no place within the confines of Christian theism. For this reason, Van Til's own critical assessment of idealism was consistent with his view that true theism is inseparable from Christianity. For him, no other form of theism exists except Christian theism. Alternatively, to put it another way, all forms of theism are idols to an unknown god, including the god of Plato, Kant, and Hegel.

Although it should be apparent that Van Til was critical of non-Christian idealism, it is still conceivable that he did not adequately distance himself from that system. Often in the history of thought, a person criticizes a philosophical system, declares that he has overcome it, only later to discover that the underlying structures of his thought place him back within that system. Herein lies a further contention by the De Boers against Van Til; they held that Van Til failed to oppose idealism although he believed that he had successfully distanced himself from such a false philosophy. In contrast to their judgment, could it be that the underlying structures of Van Til's thought were in line with orthodox Christian theism as his claims were set forth with idealistic language? For example, when Van Til discussed the incomprehensibility of God, he wrote:

> It does not mean that God is incomprehensible to himself. On the contrary, man's inability to comprehend God is founded on the very fact that God is *completely self-comprehensive*. God is absolute rationality. He was and is the only self-contained whole, the system of absolute truth. God's knowledge is, therefore, exclusively *analytic*, that is self-dependent. There never were any facts existing independent of God which he had to investigate. God is the one and only ultimate Fact. In him, i.e., with respect to his own Being, apart from the world, fact and interpretation of fact are coterminous.[11]

In view of this quote, it would be foolish to deny that Van Til used idealistic language. Statements such as "God is absolute rationality," God is "the only self-contained *whole*" and God is "the *system* of absolute truth" tend to verify the De Boers' criticism that ambiguous idealistic language surrounds Van Til's view of God. Is God really "rationality," a "self-contained whole," and a "system"? On the surface, C. De Boer's criticism may seem correct,

---

11. Ibid., 10.

that is, Van Til, like any idealist, used language that sets up his ultimate presupposition or major premise to be the foundation of an entire deductive system.[12] In this case, God is the presupposition and the major premise.

In contrast to C. De Boer's assessment, could it be that Van Til attempted to say something profoundly biblical, not idealist? Simply, that the logical attribute of God is constitutive of his being; there is no concept of logic or reason outside of himself by which he defines himself or to which he appeals. Moreover, his being is a self-contained whole. Nothing can be added to or subtracted from God's being, that is, God cannot add love to his being and he cannot subtract justice from his being. Also, God's knowledge of himself does not increase and it does not decrease. His being is always complete. Hence, all truth resides in him; his being contains the only legitimate system of truth. Although one may find it confusing that Van Til used idealistic language, it does not mean that he divorced himself from biblical orthodoxy. In fact, his understanding of God is profoundly orthodox despite the ambiguity surrounding his choice of language. The Bible clearly teaches that God is a self-contained, self-dependent being who is the foundation for knowing and understanding any object of truth.

Interestingly, J. De Boer befuddled the discussion when he criticized Van Til for not using Kant's term "analytic" in a correct Kantian manner.[13] In this case, Van Til found himself in a bizarre situation. On the one hand, the De Boers attacked him for using idealistic language while falling into its thought, whereas, on the other hand, he was attacked for not using Kant's terminology correctly. This puzzle leads one to wonder: even from the perspective of his critics, was Van Til's language and thought idealist or not? The fairest conclusion seems to be that Van Til's language was idealist, but the content and meaning of his terminology was not. For this reason, it would be difficult for Van Til to understand why anyone within the confines of biblical orthodoxy would object to saying that God's knowledge is self-dependent, that is, that God's knowledge is constituted and comprehended solely within his being. Hence, God's knowledge is not dependent upon laws of reason, cognition, intuition, experience, and other manifestations outside of himself. Simply, for Van Til, this language describes God's knowledge as analytical. Truly it is not Kantian; rather, it is grounded in biblical revelation.

---

12. See C. De Boer, "Editorial," 5.
13. See J. De Boer, "Bramble Patch," 8.

Following their analytical-critical method, the De Boers also attacked Van Til's intolerance toward any non-Reformed epistemology. In his initial article in *The Calvin Forum*, J. De Boer expressed his concern with Van Til's use of militant metaphors; he did not think that language that was reminiscent of war—"many types of weapons, comparable to bayonets, rifles, machine guns, heavy cannon, and atom bombs"—should be used to describe the apologetic task.[14] After all, it was J. De Boer's thesis that the goal of "apologetics is to clarify and defend the truth; it is not destruction."[15] Granted, against the background of World War II, J. De Boer's analysis of the apologetic task sounds positive and consoling. From Van Til's perspective, however, such a pious approach to the apologetic task would miss the biblical mandate. For the Apostle Paul writes: "We are destroying speculations and every lofty thing raised up against the knowledge of God, and we are taking every thought captive to the obedience of Christ" (2 Cor 10:5 NASB). In contrast to J. De Boer's viewpoint, Van Til held that the biblical language resembled his position: the Christian is to destroy (cast down) every aspect of thought raised up against the knowledge of God. Thereby, the Christian is enrolled in a militant battle between the kingdom of God and the kingdom of Satan; there is no middle ground to escape this war being fought.[16] One will either conquer or be destroyed; on the basis of Scripture, the believer knows that Jesus Christ is conquering the kingdom of Satan through the powerful and militant instrumentality of his Word in his church.

Even so, I believe that a deeper issue than merely the use of military metaphors drove J. De Boer's concern over Van Til's view of tolerance. His articles embodied the new "progressive" spirit of tolerance and accommodation within the CRC toward the secular world as well as Roman Catholic and evangelical thought. At first, one may think that my analysis is incorrect. After all, the De Boers scolded Van Til for not being purely Reformed while claiming their own faithfulness to the Reformed tradition.[17] Oddly,

---

14. Ibid., 7.

15. Ibid.

16. See Hughes, *Second Corinthians*, 352–3. Hughes pointed out that Paul's language in 2 Corinthians 10:5 is definitely militant imagery. He wrote: "Hence it is that the Christian warfare is aimed at the casting down of the reasonings which are the strongholds whereby the unbelieving mind seeks to fortify itself against the truths of human depravity and divine grace, and at the casting down also of every proud bulwark raised high against the knowledge of God" (ibid., 352).

17. J. De Boer concluded concerning Van Til's thought: "The Reformed scholar is

Van Til's Epistemology and Analytic Philosophy

as the De Boers scolded Van Til's presentation of a pure theology, they also scolded Van Til for trying to distance himself from so-called obvious tenets of common truth found in secular, Roman Catholic, and evangelical thought. From my perspective, the De Boers' admonishment seems contradictory. One could argue that the De Boers were upset merely with the fallacious, idealistic reasoning Van Til used to criticize and assess the various aspects of non-Reformed thinking. In my judgment, their criticism seems deeper than Van Til's association with idealism or his use of fallacious reasoning. Rather, the De Boers wished to accommodate a neutral realm of knowledge and truth for all men. Following their preferred philosophical method, they found Van Til's language too antithetical toward intellectuals outside Reformed orthodoxy. For this reason, I think it is best to comprehend their spirit of tolerance in the context of their commonsense theory of knowledge.

According to the De Boers, Van Til's antithetical epistemology is nonsense in the context of everyday thinking—whether it applies to the scientist or the common person. J. De Boer stated his position forcibly:

> I have contended that a non-Christian can make true statements about the ordinary properties of sensible or natural objects—after all, things *have* these properties and man *can* notice them without at the same time attending to creatureliness. One does not have to know God's relation to apples to learn how long it takes Winesaps to ripen. I contend that the non-Christian is not, in virtue of being non-Christian, disabled from doing science or acquiring ordinary empirical knowledge.[18]

Here J. De Boer, like the classical evidentialist, attacked what many have believed to be Van Til's most vulnerable point. According to J. De Boer, Van Til maintained that the non-Christian can make no accountable statement about himself and the world unless he presupposes the God of the Bible; for example, one has to know "God's relation to apples to learn how long

---

in peril of presumption if it is hinted and alleged that now for the first time a purely Reformed theology has been developed. And to cap it all, the purist version is impure, tainted not only with fallacious reasoning, but, what is still worse, with the logical and metaphysical legerdemain of absolute idealism. I suggest that Van Til's apologetics, because it does not grow out of painstaking and complete mastery of great Christian texts, ancient, medieval, and modern, is twisted and victimized by the categories and techniques of the idealists whose works he read in his student days" (J. De Boer, "God and Human Knowledge," 57).

18. Ibid., 55.

it takes Winesaps to ripen." This caricature of Van Til's position is absurd; indeed, the non-Christian can learn how long it takes Winesaps to ripen. Moreover, he can learn mathematical formulas without first asserting the God of Scripture.

Once again, however, the analytical-critical method prevented the De Boers from comprehending the holistic character of Van Til's epistemology. According to Van Til, a Christian theistic epistemology does not begin with isolated facts; rather, it begins with the Creator of the facts. Thereby, Van Til believed that one must view the facts of the universe in union with their Creator to view them rightly. In other words, our concepts and judgments of truth cannot be isolated from the ground of truthfulness—the ontological Trinity. Hence, Van Til's view of epistemology is quite simple: to understand, know, and interpret the facts correctly one must begin with the one who creates the facts. In contrast to this viewpoint, the De Boers wanted the legitimacy of understanding, knowing, and interpreting the facts in isolation from the Creator; they wanted the right to build an epistemology around particular facts, multiple facts, and abstract facts. According to Van Til, such a formulation removes the truthfulness of facts from the moral aspect of the fall and the eschatological judgment of God. To put it another way, the De Boers never permitted the noetic effects of the fall to enter their understanding of epistemology, and they did not demand an accountability on the part of the non-Christian for interpreting the facts apart from the God who created the facts. Thereby, they maintained a neutral view of truth; specifically, through an epistemology of common sense, they became tolerant of systems of thought outside Reformed orthodoxy.

In light of my threefold analysis (idealism, tolerance, and common sense), it is apparent to me that the De Boers failed to comprehend the entire structure of Van Til's project because of their alignment with the political nuances of the "progressive" movement, as well as their analytical-critical method. The De Boers had a political agenda; in order to capture the intellectual climate of the CRC, they had to create a skeptical atmosphere around Van Til's popularity. In my estimation, their agenda was threefold: (1) identify the opposition (Van Til) with a negative label (idealism and pantheism); (2) point out that the opponent is intolerant while creating a spirit of tolerance concerning one's own creed; and (3) caricature the nature of antithesis in the opponent's thought in order to claim the insights of all humanity under the rubric of common grace. The De Boers realized that if their agenda was successful in the church, then the "progressive" spirit would eventually overcome the laity. Their goal was achieved in the CRC; those who have followed the agenda of the De Boers (and other "progressives") have discarded Van Til's contribution to Reformed thought, and the average member of the church does not even know his name.

Moreover, concerning analytical criticism, historically this tradition of philosophy has been opposed to the tradition of idealistic philosophy. It is not surprising, therefore, to find the De Boers opposed to Van Til. After all, it cannot be denied that Van Til operated in the context of idealistic philosophy, which understood its task within the holistic medium of life—a *Weltanschauung* (worldview).[19] On the other hand, the De Boers understood philosophical criticism in the context of analyzing linguistic and conceptual units. For them, the critical task of philosophy was essentially the study of language; they sought to grasp meaning through employing an analysis of language. Immediately, a problem appears: Van Til was presenting a holistic philosophy of life in idealistic language, but the De Boers were analyzing linguistic and conceptual units in Van Til's thought. Since this analysis had a limited scope, the De Boers never grasped the total picture of Van Til's project; it remained obscure to them, even nonsensical. Perhaps it is more perplexing that a similar problem of method has appeared among Van Tilian analytic philosophers.

JOHN FRAME

Many of Van Til's disciples have also addressed his association with idealism. Specifically, these disciples have used Van Til's connection with German idealistic language as a positive as well as a negative element in their particular analysis of his thought. For example, John Frame has justified the introduction of modern analytic language philosophy into his theological system on the basis of Van Til's employment of idealistic language in his.[20]

---

19. Of course, it is legitimate to argue whether Van Til's use of idealistic language was the best procedure, but it is unfair to label Van Til's system of thought as idealist. From the beginning of Van Til's academic career, he asserted that idealism is the most repugnant philosophy of modern secular thought. In almost every discussion of the failures of modern philosophy and theology, Van Til begins with Kant. Kant and idealism are clearly of the enemy, manifesting the philosophy of the kingdom of Satan (see Van Til, "God and the Absolute").

20. See Frame, "Letter from John Frame," 10. From this, one should not think that Frame is unaware of Van Til's penetrating critique of non-Christian idealistic philosophy (see Frame, "Simplicity and Profundity," 4).

In making this connection, Frame argues positively that his procedure is consistent with Van Til's procedure. On the other hand, Frame's negative criticism of Van Til's idealistic language has been directed toward its inadequacy for the pastor and the laity in the church.[21] For Frame, Van Til's idealistic language is not practical for the local congregation.

In the context of this twofold analysis, it can be said that Frame's criticism of Van Til is different from the criticism offered by the De Boers. Unlike the De Boers, Frame holds that Van Til's terminology (when understood in the context of his thought) provides a Reformed epistemology adequately suited to overturn the system of idealism.[22] On the other hand, it can be said that both Frame and the De Boers evaluate Van Til by means of an analysis of language, that is, both sides focus on the meaning and interpretation of his terminology. Even so, both sides arrive at different conclusions. For the De Boers, Van Til's idealistic language is vague and confusing; it is detrimental to a distinctly Reformed epistemology. For Frame, Van Til's idealistic language is sufficient to counter idealism, but it needs clarification when applied to the contemporary academic and ecclesiastical scene. Here, we confront a dilemma: both the critic and the disciple working within the same philosophical school arrive at different assessments. Who is on the right track? As I have observed, the De Boers failed to penetrate and understand the presuppositional structure of Van Til's holistic thought; if they made a serious attempt in this direction, it is not evident in their writing. On the other hand, Frame points us in the right direction; he realizes that if one hopes to understand the meaning of Van Til's terminology, one must thoroughly penetrate the presuppositional structure of his thought. Frame's analysis demonstrates that one can work within the perimeter of analytic philosophy and at the same time comprehend the basic holistic character of a person's thought. Hence, Frame correctly writes:

> I find Van Til's major distinctiveness in the area of theological introduction or "meta-theology"—the theology of theology, the study of theological method and structure. This area is sometimes called "theological prolegomena," a term which designates those things that must be "said before" theology is done.[23]

21. Frame, "Letter," 9.

22. I believe that Frame attempts to give a careful interpretation of Van Til's language, including the terminology from idealism. See Frame, *Van Til: The Theologian*.

23. Frame, *Theologian*, 7. In fact, the first major section in this work by Frame is entitled, "Pro-System." Frame begins with an attempt to understand Van Til's thought as a whole.

Van Til's Epistemology and Analytic Philosophy

Unlike the De Boers, Frame directs his reader back to the first principles of Van Til's thought—the theological introduction that lies behind the theological system written on the page. Perhaps the De Boers would have understood Van Til better if they had followed such a procedure.

Although Frame has provided adequate direction in understanding Van Til's method, nevertheless, when one closely compares Frame and Van Til, it seems that the former also has overlooked the fundamental point underlying Van Til's Reformed epistemology. According to Van Til, his epistemology is built upon the foundation of a philosophy of history. It is within this context that Van Til developed his famous Creator-creature distinction and the other aspects of his epistemology. To my knowledge, Frame's writings have not noted this key point. Hence, the disciples of Van Til are faced with an interesting question: how can Frame provide such a thorough analysis of Van Til's thought (even to the point that he can be used to overturn the criticisms of the De Boers in the fifties) and yet also overlook the fundamental point of Van Til's epistemology? In my judgment, the answer lies in Frame's commitment to the method of analytic philosophy. This commitment has had, at least, a twofold effect upon his thought. First, he has made a conscious shift to move Van Tilian thought into the context of twentieth-century analytic philosophy. Although usually overlooked, this shift has begun to define a new Van Tilian epistemology, that is, a dualistic framework that consists of the ontological Trinity and human experience. Second, Frame has emerged as an eclectic and complex thinker. In the broad context of analytic philosophy, he rejects (or at least has a tendency to overlook) a sole Archimedean point that explains the whole picture of an individual's thought. Hence, his Van Tilian epistemology is formulated within the context of a perspectival conception of knowledge, whereas the main rubric of Van Til's epistemology—the philosophy of history—is not even investigated or presented. Let us look at these two points more closely.

In 1976, Frame announced that the analytic perspective is the future key to propagating, evaluating, and criticizing his mentor's thought.[24] Frame canonizes his analytic perspective to the degree that he opposes those Van Tilians who approach Van Til uncritically and non-analytically.[25] In my estimation, most Van Tilians have not examined the importance of Frame's announcement and his subsequent application of this principle. Frame's declaration presents a significant shift in propagating Van Til's thought—a

---

24. Ibid., 5–6. See also ibid., n10.
25. Ibid.

shift from constructing a Christian philosophical theology in the context of idealistic philosophy (Van Til) to constructing a Christian philosophical theology in the context of analytic philosophy (Frame). Such a shift may seem irrelevant to one who is ignorant of the history of philosophy. In truth, however, analytic philosophy arose in the late nineteenth century as a continuing critical response to idealistic philosophy. The analytic philosopher believed that idealism was living under the illusion of speculating about the grand metaphysical foundations of the universe, whereas the real focus of philosophy should be the understanding of the elements, structure, interrelationships, and meaning of language. Van Tilian scholars must not overlook these two opposing schools of thought. For example, although Van Til used idealistic terminology, such language was subsumed into the traditional content of Reformed systematics; his employment of idealist terms did not alter the traditional rubrics and substance of Reformed orthodoxy. Moreover, since most thinkers in the school of idealism focused upon the metaphysical and transcendental foundations of the universe, the terminology was somewhat easily transferable to Reformed Christian theism.

On the other hand, analytic philosophy arose as an attack upon any traditional metaphysical and transcendental scheme, whether in the fields of philosophy or orthodox Christian theology. It limits reality and truth to a logical and empirical investigation of language. In light of this method, a Christian theist who wishes to operate within the confines of analytic philosophy will comply with a dual epistemology: God and the logical-empirical meaning of language. In my estimation, methodologically this dualism is unavoidable. In fact, Frame's analytic perspective is evidence of this point; he presents and defends a Reformed Christian metaphysical system through the assistance of modern language philosophy. Unlike the result of Van Til's work in the context of idealism, Frame seems caught in a synthetic epistemology.

Indeed, Frame's epistemology begins with the transcendent God of the Bible; however, through the influence of analytic philosophy, a complementary or dualistic epistemology emerges.[26] As he grounds his epistemological construction in "God, the Covenant Lord," and the meaning of "divine lordship," he notes that "meanings of words are discovered through

26. In fairness to Frame, he claims that his view of epistemology does not "adopt a kind of Christianized variation on some secular theory or theories of knowledge. Rather, I began with Scripture and tried to determine what it says to us about matters epistemological" (Frame, *Word of God*, 5). As one shall see, I do not find his claim successful.

an investigation of their use, and such investigation does prove fruitful in the study of the lordship vocabulary in Scripture."[27] Frame's appeal to the empirical use of language is significant; it follows the logical positivists, who hold that "a sentence is cognitively meaningful if and only if it can be verified or falsified by experience."[28] Although Frame is not a logical positivist per se, certain factors are apparent. Is the ontological starting point of a Christian epistemology dependent upon the meaning of words in the realm of human experience? Specifically, is the epistemological understanding of "God, the Covenant Lord" or "divine lordship" dependent upon the meaning of those phrases in the realm of human experience? In terms of Frame's construction, the answer seems to be "yes"; he seems dangerously close to the evidentialist apologist who constructs his epistemology upon the foundation of human reason. In Frame's case, instead of reason, the human experience of language has a complementary position in a Van Tilian epistemological task.[29]

Moreover, there are two schools of analytic philosophy that have ramifications for epistemology: logical positivism and linguistic analysis. Both schools addressed philosophical problems through the analysis and meaning of language, and both schools agreed that language only had reference to empirical experience and not to a traditional metaphysical scheme that goes beyond experience. Even with these elements in common, there was a distinction. The logical positivists were known for addressing philosophical problems by using a rigorous scientific approach to philosophical language; in fact, they believed that "philosophy must develop its own vocabulary and set of concepts in order to resolve its problems."[30] Later, linguistic analysts held that "philosophical problems can best be approached by a careful analysis of the ordinary, natural language we all use to communicate with each other."[31] When closely investigated, Frame seems more sympathetic toward the school of linguistic analysis than the school of logical positivism

---

27. Frame, *Knowledge of God*, 12.

28. Stroud, "Logical Positivism," 262.

29. Upon close investigation, this task seems apparent in an earlier writing of Frame's, namely, "Biblical Language," 159–77. Consult also Notaro, *Evidence*, 65–77.

30. Ammerman, "Analytic Philosophy," 3.

31. Ibid. When viewing these two schools of thought, one point must be clear: Frame is extremely critical of their attack upon traditional metaphysics. On this point, Frame is a crusader against the destructive effects of language philosophy against Christian theism. Even so, Frame constructs his critical theology upon the backbone of language philosophy.

since he is concerned to communicate with ordinary language. Even so, if one attempts to analyze Frame exclusively within the categories of linguistic analysis, one will be misled.

The direction that Frame has taken is extremely complex; he is an eclectic thinker. For example, there has been a continual debate whether logical positivism was a new version of philosophical foundationalism. It has been said that the logical positivists were attempting to provide philosophical justification for scientific knowledge from an Archimedean point that was outside the historical sciences (the foundation of scientific sensory data in which mathematics and/or the use of language were fundamental). Some have argued that logical positivism is opposed to foundationalism, whereas others have argued that it built its conceptual superstructure upon the foundation of sensory data.[32]

In my estimation, the latter position is correct. Moreover, David Weissman has observed that in the philosophy of Rudolf Carnap (1891–1970)—a logical positivist—"epistemic foundationalism has its *ontological* correlate"; that is to say, "every thinkable reality is grounded in the mind that makes it."[33] If Weissman's assessment is correct, the mere observance of Carnap's correlation between epistemology and ontology is not out of line with a correlation between epistemology and ontology in Van Til's thought. However, the epistemic foundation of Carnap's ontology would be totally different from Van Til's.

Even so, at this point, certain suspicions are raised in regard to Frame's respect for logical positivism; he seems to be building a new foundation for a conceptual superstructure of Van Tilian epistemology. In my estimation, in Frame's epistemology the empirical sensory use of language is being tied together with the theistic ontological foundation of epistemology.[34] Perhaps this dual epistemological formulation explains his reassessment of the traditional theistic arguments for the existence of God. In the context of using meaningful language, Frame is willing to affirm, in contrast to Van Til's holistic scheme, that the traditional rational arguments for God's existence

---

32. In terms of this debate respectively, consult Friedman, "Logical Positivism"; and Weissman, "Logical Positivism."

33. Weissman, "Logical Positivism," 520–1.

34. See again Frame, *Knowledge of God*, 12. Also, it is worth noting that Frame has stated that "although we do not buy the whole logical positivist theory, many of us are quite impressed with the basic notion that *a fact ought to make a difference*" (Frame, "Biblical Language," 161).

Van Til's Epistemology and Analytic Philosophy

do not necessarily produce something less than the biblical God.[35] Thereby, through a rational and empirical examination and use of linguistic and conceptual units, one can reshape the traditional arguments in the context of the ontological God of the Bible. In my estimation, such a procedure is within the borders of Thomism.

Second, the logical positivists were known for artificially constructing language to confront philosophical questions. Although Frame identifies himself more with "ordinary language philosophy" (linguistic analysis), at times a new science of language—an element of logical positivism—appears periodically in his work (e.g., under the rubric of "speech acts," there are locutionary acts, illocutionary acts, and perlocutionary acts).[36] In fact, there is a new scientific structure to Van Tilian epistemology found in Frame's formulation: perspectivalism (the normative, situational, and existential perspectives). Although, to my knowledge, the perspectival construction cannot be identified with logical positivism, the principle that controlled logical positivism is alive: introduce and construct new scientific language to address philosophical issues and problems (in this case, theological issues and problems as well). One could argue that this is not new language; in fact, Frame points out that Dennis O'Brien, a Roman Catholic philosopher once teaching at Princeton University, introduced him to the perspectival viewpoint.[37] Moreover, Frame attempts to demonstrate that perspectivalism is in tune with historic Reformed theology.[38] On the other hand, one may argue that in the history of Reformed epistemology, the language is entirely new and foreign; indeed, a new system is being introduced into the Reformed community that is complex and scientifically unrecognizable—a principle that logical positivism would endorse. Ironically, this new perspectival theology seems distant from the common language of the laity.

More specifically, however, Frame declares an appreciation for the school of linguistic analysis (ordinary language philosophers).[39] In my view, there are a number of factors contributing to this appreciation. First, Frame found Van Til's formulations "not adequate to meet the needs of the pastor. [Van Til] wrote in the language of idealistic philosophy, which

---

35. See Frame, *Apologetics*, 71–77.

36. Frame, *Knowledge of God*, 203. Although Frame correctly associates this language with "ordinary language philosophers," this is an element from the logical positivists.

37. Ibid., xviii.

38. Ibid., 90.

39. See Frame, "Biblical Language," 166–75. See also Frame, *Knowledge of God*, 203.

not even philosophers understand anymore, let alone ordinary people. He also used technical theological jargon which was not understood except by seminary-trained reformed people."[40] In light of Frame's criticism, it seems plausible that Frame was looking for a philosophical school that advertised its desire to analyze and use ordinary language. The contemporary school that had been prominent in this respect was the school of linguistic analysis. This school provided Frame with what he thought was needed.

Second, John L. Austin (1911–1960), a member of the linguistic analysis school whom Frame seems to appreciate, held that the first step in philosophical problem-solving was to become knowledgeable about how our language operates. Of course, this presupposes the empirical investigation of the use of our language, which in turn is fundamental for the construction of a theory of knowledge. In my estimation, Frame does not distance himself from Austin's thesis; in fact, I find that Austin's thesis is a pervasive underlying necessity in constructing his Reformed epistemology.[41] If I am correct, then, a dual epistemology exists in Frame's construction for the sake of communicating to people in ordinary language.[42]

Third, there has been an ongoing passion and debate in Reformed thought to bring together doctrine and life, or the theoretical and the practical. In other words, it has been the contention that our theological constructions must be practical if they are going to be meaningful for the ordinary people in the church. In the context of this continual discussion, Frame has submitted the proposition that "theology is simply the application of Scripture to all areas of human life."[43] Again, it seems that Frame has come to this definition of theology in the context of linguistic analysis. Frame admits that he agrees with Ludwig Wittgenstein's (1889–1951) conception that "the meaning of an expression is its use"—that he is most helped by a "Wittgensteinian 'use view' that is grounded in distinct Christian norms."[44] According to Frame, the Wittgensteinian "use view" of

---

40. Frame, "Letter," 9. In Frame's handbook on apologetics, the same point is made: "Well, Van Til's work is still valuable, but it has always been in need of translation into more easily understood language" (Frame, *Apologetics*, xii).

41. For example, the thesis becomes more explicit in Frame, *Knowledge of God*, 93–98, 200–205, although it is implicit from the opening pages of the document.

42. Notaro summarizes Frame's thesis in "Biblical Language": "According to Frame, religious language is verifiable because it is ordinary language" (Notaro, *Evidence*, 75).

43. Frame, *Theologian*, 25.

44. Frame, *Knowledge of God*, 97.

language helps to explain his "earlier statement: 'Meaning is application.'"[45] Here we learn that Frame is interested in a dynamic, rather than a static, use of language. Language has meaning only in use and application. This view leads, however, to an interesting question: does the term "God" have meaning without application and use? Specifically, does Van Til's conception that God's knowledge of himself is analytical (the ground of Van Til's epistemology) have any meaning without human use and application? It seems that if Frame follows Wittgenstein's "use view" of language, he would answer no. If so, then Frame's construction presents a dangerous logical and empirical extract from the Archimedean point of Van Til's epistemology.[46]

In my judgment, Frame has been preoccupied with placing Van Tilian thought into the confines of twentieth-century analytic philosophy. In view of this agenda, a dual epistemology has emerged as foundational to a new Reformed perspectival theology, draped as it is in the ordinary and scientific language of analytic philosophy. Serious questions can be raised as to whether Frame has remained faithful to Van Til's epistemology, and whether Frame's language has resolved the alleged problem of complexity and impractical use in Van Til's language. Moreover, despite Frame's ability to view the holistic character of Van Til's thought, his preoccupation with linguistic and conceptual units, especially in the context of perspectivalism, has contributed to his failure to comprehend the full Archimedean point of Van Til's epistemology. In other words, for Frame, epistemology must be grounded in the normative, situational, and existential perspectives rather than the philosophy of history as defined by Van Til.

VAN TIL AND VOS

I have maintained that both the De Boers and Frame have failed to capture the key point of Van Til's epistemology because of their respective commitments to the method of analytic philosophy which proceeds by analyzing linguistic and conceptual units. In opening his discussion on the subject of Christian epistemology, Van Til remarked that "we shall have to approach the matter of a Christian world-and-life view from an historical

---

45. Ibid.

46. Perhaps this explains why Frame's section on Christian ethics in his lectures at Trinity Evangelical Divinity School began with the existential, then the situational, and finally the normative perspective (see Frame, *Word of God*, 39–56).

point of view."[47] Moreover, for Van Til, the problems of philosophy are not addressed in the context of an analysis of language, but rather in the general context of history.[48] Van Til's point seems to have escaped both the De Boers and Frame. Even so, his position is not trivial: epistemology, metaphysics, ethics, and the various problems of philosophy (e.g., the one and the many, facts, the interpretation of facts, point of contact, common grace, Christian-theistic evidences, human responsibility) have their meaning in the context of a philosophy of history.[49] Van Til clearly stated:

> For us history is the realization of the purposes and plans of the all-sufficient God revealed through Christ in Scripture. And if this is the case we are naturally persuaded that in history lies the best proof of our philosophy of human life. The core of our system of philosophy is our belief in the triune God of Scripture, and in what he has revealed concerning himself and his purposes for man and his world.[50]

Here, Van Til's definition of history appears in the context of his epistemology. For him, the initial domain of human epistemology is the realm of history; it is the spectrum of God's providence. Extreme caution must be followed here since there is a temptation to believe that Van Til also fell into a dual epistemology, for example, the ontological triune God and the realm of history. A careful exegesis of the quotation above should free him from such criticism since Van Til presented a unique construction of epistemology and history; a unique construction that both critics and many disciples of Van Til have overlooked.

Indeed, both critic and disciple have correctly observed that Van Til grounded his epistemology in the ontological Godhead of the Scripture. For Van Til, however, this ontological conception of knowledge is foundational

---

47. Van Til, *Christian Epistemology*, xiii.

48. Ibid.

49. Specifically, in introducing the subject of Christian-theistic evidences, Van Til wrote: "Nevertheless, in evidences it is primarily the factual question with which we deal. Christianity is an historical religion. It is based upon such facts as the death and resurrection of Christ. The question of miracle is at the heart of it. Kill miracle and you kill Christianity. But one cannot even define miracle except in relation to natural law.

"Thus, we face the question of God's providence. And providence, in turn, presupposes creation. We may say, then, that we seek to defend the fact of miracle, the fact of providence, the fact of creation, and, therefore, the fact of God, in relation to modern non-Christian science" (Van Til, *Evidences* syllabus, iii).

50. Van Til, *Christian Epistemology*, xiii.

Van Til's Epistemology and Analytic Philosophy

for a theory of knowledge in the realm of time and space (history); after all, in history, created human beings obtain a knowledge of God, the world, and man. In this construction, history is not a neutral point of contact between the believer and the unbeliever, and history is not an autonomous or complementary category of epistemology. Rather, Van Til held that an ontological knowledge of God is given to mankind in history by the revelation of the economic Trinity. Specifically, all epistemological issues within the creation have their initial solution in the economic, historical revelation of the God of Scripture, which God's ontology inherently grounds. Thereby, Van Til disclosed his obsession with consistency and Christian orthodoxy; a thorough Christian-theistic epistemology coheres in the context of God's ontological being as well as the economic disclosure of his being—the two cannot be separated.[51] For this reason, Van Til declared that a philosophy of history is the key to a Christian-theistic epistemology; our knowledge of anything is dependent upon the revelation of the economic Trinity in history. Alternatively, to put it another way, God's providential control of the creation is unfolded in the context of the ontological Trinity's revelation of himself in history (economic Trinity).[52] In my judgment, it is impossible to fall into a dual epistemology if one understands and applies Van Til's construction. Whether explicitly or implicitly, reason, experience, logic, cosmonomic law, language, and history do not have a complementary ontological status in Van Til's epistemology, since, even in time and space, all epistemological issues have their ground in the orthodox view of God—the ontological and economic Trinity.

In this construction of epistemology, Van Til believed that he was following John Calvin (1509–1564), that is, the true knowledge of self and the true knowledge of God are involved in one another, and this true God reveals himself in Scripture as the triune God.[53] For Van Til as well as for Calvin, we cannot overlook the phrase "the triune God of Scripture," since

---

51. Berkhof has summarized the orthodox position well; Van Til merely followed suit. Berkhof wrote: "This ontological Trinity is the metaphysical basis of the economical Trinity" (Berkhof, *Systematic Theology*, 89).

52. In the preface to his discussion on common grace, Van Til underlined this same starting point: "The 'system of truth' of Scripture presupposes the existence of the internally, eternally, self-coherent, triune God who reveals Himself to man with unqualified authority" (Van Til, *Common Grace*, v). In light of this presupposition, Van Til commented that "there is no way of discussing these problems [related to common grace] adequately except by way of setting forth the entire 'philosophy of history' as the Reformed confessions teach it" (ibid).

53. See Van Til, "Calvin," 5.

it presupposes that the "believer's whole philosophy of nature and history is but a conceptual expression of what Christ, in Scripture, has told him about the past, the present, and the future."[54] Specifically, the economic Trinity, who reveals himself in history, is in control of the course and facts of creation. For Van Til and Calvin, this truth is fundamental to the "story" of Scripture; in fact, only in the "story" of Scripture is this truth comprehended.[55]

On this basis, Van Til distinguished the thought of Calvin from that of Thomas Aquinas (1225–1274). Aquinas argued that "the Christian story needs the theism of the philosophers as its foundation" in order to show unbelievers that the story is reasonable.[56] Particularly, Van Til pointed out that "Aquinas sought to show the unbeliever that the Christian story is in accord with logic and in accord with fact. Calvin sought to show that 'logic' and 'fact' have meaning only in terms of the 'story.'"[57] Therefore, Van Til made a final appeal that "following Calvin rather than Aquinas, we may today point out that in all history of thought, except that which is based upon the Christian story, man cannot identify himself."[58] In other words, according to Van Til's version of Calvin, one must operate within the "story" of Scripture (the Christian story) in order to have a true epistemology. Directly, Van Til was referring to the providential revelation of the triune God in the biblical text.

Herein lies the crux of the problem: both the De Boers and Frame failed to perceive the importance and centrality of the "story" of Scripture (redemptive history) in Van Til's epistemology. Both sides failed to perceive the encompassing influence of Geerhardus Vos (1862–1949) upon his thought, including his epistemology. One may justify the De Boers' failure on this issue since they did not seem to be aware of the Vos-Van Til connection during Van Til's student days at Princeton.[59] On the other hand, Frame's failure is perplexing since he has recognized the status of Vos upon

---

54. Ibid., 6.

55. Ibid., 7. In another place, Van Til made his point in this manner: "Calvin and his followers hold to a primacy of Christ which begins from the fact of the clarity of his revelation in the space-time world" (Van Til, *Debate Today*, 5).

56. Van Til, "Calvin," 8.

57. Ibid.

58. Ibid., 9.

59. In my estimation, even if they were aware of the Vos-Van Til connection, that would not have changed their analysis of Van Til. Probably, it would have made them more critical of his competency in philosophy.

Van Til's Epistemology and Analytic Philosophy

Van Til's thought. Frame has noted: "Many critics are unaware of the fact that Van Til's favorite professor at Princeton was Vos, the brilliant biblical theologian. The influence of Vos upon Van Til is profound, though rarely seen on the surface of Van Til's writings."[60]

Perhaps Frame's observation is more accurate than he realizes since he has fallen prey to his own criticism. He has not seen on the surface of Van Til's epistemology the place of Vos's philosophy of history. I have been arguing that one of the main reasons for Frame's failure on this point is his association with analytic philosophy. There are further implications, however, in association with his commitment to perspectivalism. In this context, he provides subtle hints that he is distancing himself from Van Til. For example, he writes concerning his work on epistemology:

> Some parts merely gather together traditional ideas that have been stated by other authors (e.g., Van Tillian presuppositionalism, Van Til's rationalist-irrationalist dialectic). Other parts are rather new, at least in an orthodox context (theology as application, multiperspectivalism, appreciation for subjectivism, anti-anti-abstractionism, critiques of biblical and systematic theology, polemic against the ideal of total precision in theology, attack on word-level criticism, attack on "logical order," etc.). Thus I manage to offend both the traditionalists and the avant-garde.[61]

Frame's polemic is vague; there are, however, certain clues that one should not overlook. He informs his reader that he is introducing something new into the theological spectrum. Within the method of multiperspectivalism comes a serious criticism upon biblical theology. Although Frame holds that biblical theology is an exciting and thrilling discipline, he also desires his audience to be aware of its limitations.[62] It is limited by its perspec-

---

60. Frame, *Theologian*, 27.

61. Frame, *Knowledge of God*, xvi. Frame reveals the same subtle distance in his handbook on apologetics: "In good conscience I can describe this volume as 'Reformed' apologetics and as belonging to that special kind of Reformed apologetics developed by Van Til. I do not necessarily agree with every sentence Van Til wrote; indeed, some Van Tillians will describe this work as 'revisionist.' But I believe that Van Til's approach is still the best foundation for Christian apologetics at the present time. However, although I will refer to Van Til from time to time, it will not be my goal in this book to explain Van Til or to show the precise relationships between his ideas and mine. That will come later, God willing. . . . That book [future book on Van Til] will show more adequately than I can here why I continue to follow, and occasionally depart from, the Van Tillian method" (Frame, *Apologetics*, xi–xii).

62. Frame, *Knowledge of God*, 207, 209.

tive: "Scripture is a redemptive history but not *only* that. It does not belong exclusively to the historical *genre*."[63] According to Frame, it must be noted that the Bible also includes other literary *genres*: law, songs, proverbs, letters, and gospel. Specifically, the Bible is "intended not only to give us historical information but also to govern our lives here and now."[64] Hence, in light of these other perspectives, Frame "is willing to say that Scripture is a redemptive history, but . . . reluctant to say that this is the only way or the most important way of characterizing Scripture."[65] If one understands Vos and Van Til, then Frame's language elicits concern.

In light of Frame's affiliation with analytic philosophy and its kinship with literary criticism, he views redemptive history as one literary *genre* in Scripture (history); it is one perspective of the literary milieu found in the Bible. In Frame's construction, one must not overlook that he is not only criticizing Vos and biblical theology, but he is also implicitly criticizing Van Til's epistemology. He is attempting to reconstruct Van Til's epistemology in the context of verifying ordinary language statements that presuppose the experience and use of language, as well as the ontological Godhead. In contrast, Van Til's epistemology was not concerned primarily with the issue of literary-critical *genre*, rather he was concerned with a holistic philosophy of life embedded in a philosophy of history. Simply, Van Til was concerned with the full-orbed story of the Bible—from Genesis through Revelation—in which the economic Trinity grounds epistemology. Here Van Til follows Vos, who wrote,

> In redemption and revelation naturally not the human, subjective side, not the religious views and sentiments of men, stand in the foreground, but the great objective acts and interpositions of God, the history as it is in itself, not as it is reflected in the mind of man. Facts, rather than the spirit of times or consciousness of periods, should be here the primary object of investigation.[66]

As one can see, for Van Til and Vos, the primary issue in understanding biblical revelation and redemption is not an analysis of what literary genre is confronting us; rather, it is a confrontation with facts that presuppose a philosophy of history, which in turn presuppose the interpositions of the triune God of the Bible. Following Vos, Van Til places epistemology where

---

63. Ibid., 209.
64. Ibid.
65. Ibid.
66. Vos, "Bible History," 292.

Van Til's Epistemology and Analytic Philosophy

it truly belongs, within the eschatological status of history: either one is a member of the kingdom of God, with the knowledge of the truth (grounded in the triune God of the Bible), or one is a member of the kingdom of Satan, with the knowledge of a lie (grounded in the deception of Satan). In redemptive history, there is no other ground for human knowledge. One either stands with Christ as the source of all knowledge or against him.

When Van Til declared that the self-attesting Christ of Scripture had always been his starting-point for everything he had said,[67] he was telling Christ's church that the foundation of her knowledge must be the absolute authority of Christ as the "story" of the Bible (its redemptive-historical message) progressively reveals him. For this reason, both the critic and disciple of Van Til must comprehend that idealism never shaped his epistemology, and neither did his interactions with idealism; rather, the simple progressive story of the economic Trinity revealing himself in the facts of redemptive history shaped his epistemology. Van Til maintained that a philosophy of history—defined by Vos's conception of biblical theology—is the key to understanding a Christian-theistic view of epistemology. Thereby, Van Til was amazingly consistent and dedicated to Christian orthodoxy; his epistemology would not confuse any notion within the creature with the ontological and economic Trinity as revealed in Scripture and taught in the Reformed confessions.

On the basis of my study, it is apparent that both the critic and the disciple of Van Til have failed to come to grips with the holistic picture of Van Til's theory of knowledge, that is, the place of Van Til's philosophy of history in his epistemology. The same cause is behind their oversight: a commitment to analytical-critical philosophy and its method of investigating linguistic and conceptual units. Although contrasting motives exist in these parties, I do not find that any attempt to operate within the analytic school offers hope for criticizing, understanding, or reconstructing Van Til's epistemology. For example, building upon the work of the De Boers, subsequent "progressive" philosophers in the CRC in North America, Alvin Plantinga and Nicholas Wolterstorff, have attempted to operate within the context of analytic philosophy and construct a relevant Reformed epistemology. This Reformed epistemology has attempted to articulate a philosophical claim for the immediacy of our knowledge of God against modern positivism.[68]

---

67. Van Til, "My Credo," 3.
68. Hoitenga, *Faith and Reason*, ix.

One may view this project as an honorable task, but those committed to Reformed orthodoxy in the Westminster and Van Tilian tradition will note some serious problems. First, it does not maintain Christian theism as the starting point of epistemology.[69] Second, the noetic effects of the fall are not central to its epistemic issues.[70] Third, it has complementary epistemological alliances with Plato (428/427?–348/347 BC),[71] Scottish common-sense realism,[72] and Karl Barth (1886–1968).[73] Simply, when reviewing the entire project of the "progressive" Reformed epistemologists, the "story" of the Bible has no central place in their theory of knowledge.

Those disciples of Van Til working within the same parameters of analytic philosophy should be attentive to what has been found among the "progressives." In my estimation, these disciples have begun to compromise Van Til's epistemology. For Van Tilians, it is time to listen closely to the voice of our mentor when he compared Aquinas and Calvin: "Aquinas sought to show the unbeliever that the Christian story is in accord with logic and in accord with fact. Calvin sought to show that 'logic' and 'fact' have meaning only in terms of the 'story.'"[74] Specifically, in my judgment, Frame, akin to Aquinas, is viewing the Christian story in accord with the logical construction and the empirical experience of language. If he actually followed Van Til, he would perceive that language has meaning only in the context of the biblical story. In other words, language has meaning only in the context of a philosophy of history as defined by Van Til and Vos.

---

69. Nicholas Wolterstorff writes: "Central to Christianity, Judaism, and Islam alike is the conviction that we as human beings are called to believe in God—to trust in him, to rely on him, to place our confidence in him" (Wolterstorff, "Belief in God," 135). In his inaugural address as the John A. O'Brien Professor of Philosophy at the University of Notre Dame, Alvin Plantinga told his audience that "my aim, in this talk, is to give some advice to philosophers who are Christians. And although my advice is directed specifically to Christian philosophers, it is relevant to all philosophers who believe in God, whether Christian, Jewish or Moslem. I propose to give advice to the Christian or theistic philosophical community" (Plantinga, "Christian Philosophers," 254). In both cases, Wolterstorff and Plantinga demonstrate that they are interested in defending theism, not Christian theism.

70. See Plantinga, *Warrant and Proper Function*.

71. Ibid. See also Hoitenga, *Faith and Reason*, 1–33.

72. See Plantinga, *Proper Function*, x; Wolterstorff, "Thomas Reid," 43–69; and Clark, *Return to Reason*, 8, 143–51.

73. See Plantinga, "Natural Theology," 363–83.

74. Van Til, "Calvin," 8.

Van Til's Epistemology and Analytic Philosophy

If my analysis is correct, then Frame is a transitional figure. As most Van Tilians realize, Van Til fought diligently to purge the Reformed tradition from the remnants of scholasticism that remained in the thought of Old Princeton, Kuyper, and Bavinck. In light of that purging, presently it seems that those Van Tilians influenced by Frame are unsatisfied with Van Til's view that the sole Archimedean point of a Christian epistemology is the ontological and economic Trinity. Henceforth, these Van Tilians are beginning to supplement the ground of epistemology with something within the creation. As I see it, Frame has been the catalyst for this movement; he is the transitional figure. In this context, I predict that there will be a renewed appreciation for Aquinas and scholasticism, even among Van Tilians.[75]

My study is only meant to be an introduction. I have not provided a comprehensive presentation of Van Til's philosophy of history, epistemology, or his connection with Vos. Van Tilians must have a renewed commitment to disclose, understand, and carefully reexamine the basic presuppositions that underlie the structure of his thought. In my estimation, these presuppositions are so important that the heritage of biblical and Reformed orthodoxy is at stake within the Reformed institutions that are training the next generation of pastors. In respect to our present discussion, we must remain steadfast to the position that our knowledge has meaning only in the context of the biblical story (philosophy of history); that is to say, knowledge has meaning only in the context of the self-attesting Christ of Scripture.

---

75. Could we be witnessing the beginning of this phenomenon in Frame's reassessment of the traditional proofs for the existence of God? See Frame, *Apologetics*, 89–118.

3

Van Til and Common Grace

The common grace problem deals with this question: What do entities which will one day be wholly different from one another have in common before that final stage of separation is reached? . . . All common grace is earlier grace. Its commonness lies in its earliness.

—Cornelius Van Til, *Common Grace and the Gospel*

During my freshman year at Geneva College, I recall the occasion when my philosophy professor, Dr. Peter Steen (1935–1984), entered the classroom and began to tell his impressionable students about how he testified for the gospel to a number of young adults on the previous evening. He described how he had gone up to a gathering of non-Christians on the street corner and asked the question, "Does 2+2=4?" Needless to say, Steen remarked that he received some strange looks from those puzzled intellects. Finally, one remarked; "Yes, 2+2=4!" Steen told our class that this was exactly the response he hoped to receive. Immediately, he proceeded to ask his puzzled audience on the street corner the epistemological question: "But how do you *know* that 2+2=4?" "Because that is the way it is," responded one annoyed intellect. At this point, Steen told our class that he used this opportunity to confront his non-Christian audience with the point that unless one accepts the God of the Bible, one has no true basis on which to accept the mathematical proposition 2+2=4. Hence, the non-Christian can only substitute a world controlled by chance for a world controlled by the sovereign God of the Bible.

Steen's point was simple. He wanted the Christian students in his classroom to recognize that nothing can be said to be true unless the God of Scripture exists—the foundation of all true knowledge. Herein, Steen echoed the sentiments of his Reformed teachers, Herman Dooyeweerd and D. H. Th. Vollenhoven in the Netherlands, and Van Til at Westminster Theological Seminary in Philadelphia, PA. The sentiments of Steen and his teachers, however, have not found a consensus in Christian (Roman Catholic and Arminian traditions), or, for that matter, Reformed circles (Old Princeton tradition). Many Christian and Reformed individuals would view Steen's question about 2+2=4 as absurd. After all, does not God's common grace provide all men with the ability to rationally analyze and empirically perceive? For these Christian and Reformed thinkers, the mathematical proposition 2+2=4 is a neutral category, or at best a proposition that exists in the realm of natural or general revelation, that must be said to be true without qualification for the non-Christian and Christian alike.

For this reason, one may be compelled to say that the rightful place of common grace is in the doctrines of Roman Catholics and Arminian thinkers. Both traditions have accented what all men have in common: the correct use of the rational faculty, the empirical observation of human experience and natural phenomena, and the common comprehension on the part of all men of general and natural revelation. Indeed, it would seem that both traditions are the heralds of the benefits of common grace shared by the unbeliever and the believer. Van Til, Steen's beloved teacher, claimed, however, that only the Reformed tradition can provide the rightful context for the subject of common grace. After all, for Rome and the Arminian "it is a foregone conclusion that there are large areas of life on which the believer and the unbeliever agree without difference."[1]

According to Van Til, the Reformed tradition does not operate upon such a foundation. Rather, in the Reformed tradition common grace is a serious problem in view of her doctrine of total depravity. If one holds consistently to the doctrine of total depravity, then man's entire being is in rebellion against his Creator. Hence, how can one speak of anything

---

1. Van Til, *Common Grace*, 12.

that man knows as being in alignment with God's thoughts, or of anything that man does as being good? In light of the Reformed doctrine of total depravity, it is difficult for its comrades to articulate a position concerning the obvious commonness of certain truths espoused by non-Christians and Christians alike. For this reason, Van Til's writing on the subject of common grace was a quest to be consistently faithful to Scripture and the Reformed confessions.[2]

VAN TIL AND THE REFORMED POSITIONS

In order to achieve his goal on the subject of common grace, Van Til placed himself critically in the history of the Dutch Reformed discussion. In reviewing their discussion, he divided their heritage into three camps: 1) the traditional position; 2) the denial position; and 3) the reconstructionist position. In terms of the three camps, Van Til identified himself more closely with the reconstructionist camp, especially Dooyeweerd and Vollenhoven. One must be cautious here; Van Til viewed the reconstructionist movement as a *broad* movement in theology and philosophy which attempted "to build up the traditional Reformed position while yet to an extent rebuilding it."[3] In other words, Van Til saw himself as one who built upon the work of Abraham Kuyper, Herman Bavinck, and Valentine Hepp while assuring the Reformed community that certain reconstructions were necessary in order to enhance a consistent Reformed view of common grace. Hence, the only camp with which Van Til wished to have little, if any, identification was the group that denied common grace (Hoeksema and Henry Danhof). Such an observation is crucial since many critics of Van Til's view of common grace have attempted to label him as a denier of common grace, maintaining that he belongs in the Hoeksema camp.[4] Nothing could be more disingenuous to Van Til's position. In order to demonstrate this, however, permit me to

---

2. For Van Til, the problem with Old Princeton (the Hodges and Warfield) was that they were not consistent with the scriptural and confessional texts. They were more consistent with Roman and Arminian thought on the point of contact between believer and unbeliever in the apologetic enterprise.

3. Ibid., 23.

4. This accusation has been particularly popular among the "progressives" in the CRC and their legacy since the 1950s. One may wish to consult Bratt, *Dutch Calvinism*, 187–203; Masselink, *General Revelation and Common Grace*; Daane, *A Theology of Grace*; Vander Stelt, *Philosophy and Scripture*, 220–70; and the various articles in the *Reformed Journal* from 1951 to 1956.

highlight briefly Van Til's assessment of the three camps so that we can understand his project on the subject of common grace.[5]

The Traditional Position

Van Til proclaimed that he truly appreciated what he called the "traditional Reformed position on common grace." Its three main players were Dutch Calvinists: Kuyper, Bavinck, and Hepp. By the end of the nineteenth century, it had become evident that Kuyper had produced one of the main contributions to the Reformed tradition on the subject of common grace—he wrote a three-volume set on the topic. Van Til was basically pleased with Kuyper's contribution since Kuyper had placed common grace as well as special grace in relationship to total depravity. What particularly captured Van Til's attention in this relationship was the fact that Kuyper understood common grace as being grounded in God's work in history. Specifically, in the negative sense, common grace is viewed as God's work of restraining man's sinful and depraved state through history.[6] In the positive sense, although man is depraved, common grace is viewed as God's work of enabling man to express his gifts as an image-bearer of his Creator through history (e.g., art, music, and thought).[7] As Van Til praised Kuyper's negative and positive conceptions of common grace, he did not overlook another contribution from Kuyper's pen which related total depravity and common grace. Kuyper also had placed the interpretation of scientific knowledge in the context of regeneration. Specifically, a distinct epistemological difference exists between the way a person regenerated by the Holy Spirit interprets the world and the way a person who continues in the depravity of his sin interprets the world. Herein, Kuyper was maintaining that the status of the individual's *heart* determines his *holistic* understanding and interpretation of the facts. In this case, the knowledge and interpretation of the facts by the believer and the unbeliever are antithetical to each other.

Hence, an overview of Kuyper's position in respect to the unregenerate seems to convey that God restrains the unregenerate's depravity in history to the point that he makes a contribution to the world. At the same time, the depraved heart of the unregenerate cannot know or interpret the

---

5. Van Til's assessment of the three camps is very complex and technical. I will focus on only a few areas to serve our purpose.
6. See Van Til, *Common Grace*, 15.
7. Ibid.

facts *holistically* in a correct manner because his heart is at enmity with God (the exact opposite is true for the regenerate heart). Even so, as Van Til found these contributions vital to Reformed thought, he also found that Kuyper's view of common grace contained some serious flaws.

Van Til maintained that Kuyper's view of common grace was deficient in five areas.[8] I will focus on one area in order to give the reader an idea of the problem; specifically, Van Til believed that Kuyper promoted a Platonic/Kantian epistemology. For Van Til, one of the key aspects of this problem is revealed when Kuyper wrote that "our thinking is wholly and exclusively adapted to these (highest) relations [between universal objects], and these relations are the objectification of our thought."[9] Herein, Van Til maintained that Kuyper's view suffered from Kantian phenomenalism. Plato said that the distinction between the universals must be placed in the Form world, whereas Kant said that the distinction between universals belongs to the categories of the mind and its projections. Kuyper followed this Kantian line of thought, and, thus, Van Til claimed that "there is a vagueness inherent in Kuyper's treatment of common grace. He seems to be uncertain in his mind as to what is common to the believer and the non-believer."[10] What is this vagueness? According to Van Til, Kuyper began with a Platonic/Kantian understanding of the world; that is to say, the human mind shapes the world.

For Van Til, such a starting point was a serious mistake; rather, one should start with the ontological Trinity of Holy Scripture and say that the relations of the universe are dependent upon thinking God's thoughts after him. Van Til referred to his understanding of epistemology as analogical thinking or knowledge. Hence, from his perspective, Kuyper's epistemology was based upon the dualism of the human mind and the God of Scripture. It contained a kinship with medieval epistemology.

---

8. Permit me to summarize the five areas. First, it fell into abstraction; remnants of Rome's semi-Aristotelian epistemology remained. Second, Kuyper did not live up to the high ideal of his distinction between the regenerate and unregenerate. Van Til held that Dooyeweerd had adequately shown that Kuyper was too uncritically receptive of modern philosophical statements concerning the universal and the particular. Third, in terms of the classical, modern connection on epistemology, Van Til found a continual promotion of Platonic/Kantian epistemology. Fourth, Van Til believed that Kuyper followed Kant's *Ding-an-sich* in relation to the facts. Hence, in the fifth place, Van Til did not find in Kuyper a clear distinction between the Christian and the non-Christian ideal of knowledge. See Van Til, *Common Grace*, 35–44.

9. This quote appears in Van Til, *Common Grace*, 36.

10. Ibid., 40.

Van Til and Common Grace

Turning to Bavinck, Van Til noted that Bavinck wrote a booklet on the subject of *Common Grace* (1894) and that he also addressed the issue in his *Reformed Dogmatics*. Concerning Bavinck's contribution, Van Til appreciated the manner in which he stressed the mystery or incomprehensibility of God as being at the heart of dogmatic theology. Simply, "the revelation of the infinite God to the finite creature . . . cannot be exhaustive of the being of God."[11] The creature must submit to the mysterious sovereignty of God concerning the unfolding of God's saving grace to the elect as well as God's common grace to all mankind. Although Van Til praised Bavinck's concept of mystery, nevertheless, he was not specific about what he appreciated about Bavinck's view of mystery and common grace. Rather, he seemed more concerned with inconsistencies in Bavinck's position. Particularly, he focused on Bavinck's tendency to speak "as though the concept of the incomprehensibility of God entertained by Christian theology and that entertained by pagan philosophy were virtually the same."[12] According to Van Til, their similarity can be explained by principles of reason which led Bavinck to a metaphysical and epistemological position of "moderate realism." For Van Til, such a position lost the distinctiveness of a Reformed view of common grace.

In Van Til's eyes, like Kant before him, Bavinck wished to accept the good from empiricism and rationalism while he rejected the bad from both systems. Bavinck agreed with the rationalists that there are certain rational assumptions about reality that are made by the mind. Unlike the rationalists, however, Bavinck held that those assumptions correspond simultaneously with the perceptions of experience (moderate realism). Herein, Bavinck held that all men are naturally realists. In reaction, Van Til believed that Bavinck's moderate realism pushed him back to medieval scholasticism. Perhaps Van Til's accusation is best observed in his assessment of Bavinck's position on the theistic proofs for the existence of God. Bavinck held that the medieval arguments for God's existence were weak as proofs but strong as testimonies. One should take the theistic proofs, not as arguments that compel the unbeliever to believe in God; rather, the believer's faith may accept their testimony to defend himself against the attack of science and solidify the truth of God's revelation in creation.[13] According to Van Til, Bavinck's position on the proofs cannot solidify the testimony

---

11. Ibid., 46.
12. Ibid.
13. See ibid., 47, 48.

of the believer's faith because at the basis of the proofs is a non-Christian (Greek) conception of reason—a conception of reason that leads away from the God of the Bible, or at best, compromises him. Without this insight, Bavinck's moderate realism spoke "as though the only difference between the Christian and the non-Christian notions of the incomprehensibility of God were a matter of degree."[14] Both positions would begin with the same realistic view of God afforded to man through the means of human reason and experience (common grace). For example, by virtue of common grace, the unbeliever and the believer share by their conceptions of reason and their perceptions of experience a limited comprehension of the living God. However, by virtue of the Holy Spirit's revelation of Jesus Christ, the unbeliever does not share the additional comprehension of the living God disclosed to the believer. Thus, similar to Kuyper, Van Til thought that Bavinck's view of common grace has kinship to medieval scholasticism.[15]

If Kuyper and Bavinck did not adequately upstage the remnants of non-Christian epistemology and its effects upon common grace, perhaps Hepp could perform the task by placing Reformed epistemology upon the testimony of the Holy Spirit. According to Van Til, Hepp divided the testimony of the Holy Spirit into two domains: the special testimony of the Spirit and the general testimony of the Spirit. The special testimony of the Spirit testifies within us to the truth of Scripture (assures me of the truth of the revelation about me), whereas the general testimony of the Spirit testifies within us to truth in general (assures me of central truths only). The general testimony of the Holy Spirit is of particular interest to the discussion on common grace. According to Hepp, there are three groups of general truths: God, man, and the world. Concerning God, Hepp held that the general testimony of the Holy Spirit presses upon the conscience of all men the theistic proofs. Here, the Spirit does not give absolute certainty, but he does provide a general testimony that enables man to have a general understanding of God. Likewise, man is certain of his own existence by means of the general testimony of the Holy Spirit, and furthermore, man can only realize that the empirical world around him exists because of the general testimony of the Holy Spirit. In Hepp's construction, the general testimony of the Holy Spirit is the domain of common grace. Although it

---

14. Ibid., 47.

15. Even in light of this problem, Van Til exalts Bavinck for the overall direction of his thought. Van Til wrote, "the Christian must stand with both feet upon the bed-rock of special revelation in his study of nature. That is, we believe, the real position of Bavinck, but he has not been fully true to it" (ibid., 51).

seems that Hepp has placed an understanding of common grace upon the foundation of the Holy Spirit, nevertheless, when one examines his position more closely, his position remains in the same dilemma which Kuyper and Bavinck failed to conquer. According to Van Til, his conception of the general testimony of the Holy Spirit is defined by non-Christian conceptions of reason and nature—by modern rational and empirical methods of science. In other words, non-Christian conceptions are defining common grace. Specifically, Van Til claimed that Hepp permitted a methodological construction of the theistic proofs upon a non-Christian view of probable reason, and then placed it in the context of the Spirit's general testimony. For Van Til, probable reason and any testimony of the Holy Spirit (which is absolute) cannot go together.

Has the traditional Dutch Reformed position on common grace really been able to distance itself from medieval scholasticism and a classical theory of knowledge? Although Kuyper, Bavinck, and Hepp attempted to distance themselves from scholasticism and classicism, nevertheless, Van Til believed that they never overcame abstraction. That is to say, although they gave God the strategic place in their system—the starting point and foundation of knowing, understanding, and interpreting all things—nevertheless, they permitted the non-Christian to define the terms they adopted as God's terms. Hence, in the realm of natural and general revelation, God is merely the prelude and the appendix in the structure; rather, according to Van Til, he must be the Being who defines the entire structure. Only in this context can the structure be properly holistic and concrete.

The Denial Position

Perhaps the denial of common grace is the most consistent alternative within the context of Reformed theology. Possibly, it is the only plausible response against the scholastic-classic synthesis with biblical revelation. In fact, Van Til has been identified with such a position by his critics, especially Daane and Masselink in the 1950s. In truth, however, Van Til was more critical of Hoeksema's formulation than any other position within Reformed orthodoxy that he addressed in the late 1940s and the early 1950s. In a famous judicial case in the 1920s which eventually led to his removal from the CRC, Hoeksema denied the basic tenets of the traditional Dutch Reformed view of common grace. He opted for a position which applied the term "grace" only to the redemptive work of God in the sinner. Van Til could not agree. He accused Hoeksema of using a non-Christian conception of logic which denied "the possibility of (a) a certain attitude of favor on the part of God to the reprobate and (b) the ability of the reprobate to do good of a sort."[16] Specifically, Van Til criticized Hoeksema for using a non-Christian view of logic as the basis "to 'harmonize' the revealed and the secret will of God, prayer, and the counsel of God."[17] In Van Til's estimation, Hoeksema's use of a Greek conception of logic reduced the destiny of the elect and the reprobate to a single act of God's will without respect to the activity of God in history. Hence, Van Til believed that Hoeksema's view of the divine will of God leads to absolute determinism; there is absolutely *no significance to a Reformed conception of revelational history.*[18] Moreover, Van Til pointed out that Hoeksema permitted a measure of validity for the medieval scholastic proofs of God's existence; in fact, according to Hoeksema, these proofs stare the non-Christian in the face each day. Since the non-Christian is so depraved, Hoeksema held that the unbeliever will never acknowledge the credence of these proofs. Again, Van Til was disappointed in Hoeksema's position since it admitted that the proofs, built upon the foundation of classical reason, have validity. Only one's depravity prevents their credence for the unbeliever. Hence, Van Til did not find in Hoeksema a clear criticism of non-Christian logic in his critical assessment of the traditional Dutch Reformed understanding of common grace. For this reason, Van Til held that Hoeksema based his denial of common grace on a non-Christian foundation.

Reconstructionists

As Van Til criticized the traditional Dutch Reformed position on common grace and distanced himself from Hoeksema's denial of common grace, he identified his alignment with the work of Dooyeweerd and Vollenhoven. Although he identified himself with their work, nevertheless, he was not very specific about their contribution to his view of common grace. In a vague manner, Van Til suggested that they were the most concrete Dutch Reformed thinkers in the 1950s. By this he seemed to insinuate that they had an integrated interpretation of God's creation, seeing all the creation ordinances subject to God's will. In this construction, the God of the Bible

16. Ibid., 29.
17. Ibid., 27.
18. See ibid., 28, 29.

is the necessary presupposition for a correct analysis of the laws of creation. Moreover, Van Til also mentioned that he appreciated their stress upon man's heart as the center of human activity. Like Kuyper before them, both Dooyeweerd and Vollenhoven maintained that the devotion of one's heart toward Christ or against Christ has an effect upon a true scientific interpretation of the world. In the late 1940s and the early 1950s, Van Til seemed at peace with these notions. Upon the necessary presupposition of the triune God of the Bible and the effects of God upon the creation and man, Van Til reconstructed the Dutch Reformed position of common grace upon traditional grounds. Herein, he maintained that his Reformed brethren must take into consideration the impact of a holistic understanding of biblical, historical revelation as presented in the Reformed confessions for a correct formulation of the doctrine of common grace.

VAN TIL'S POSITION ON COMMON GRACE

Point of Contact and Common Grace

In the marketplace, the subject of common grace and the issue of a common point of contact between the believer and the unbeliever remains a problem when we keep in mind the Reformed doctrine of total depravity. In order to keep a proper balance between common grace, the point of contact, and total depravity, Van Til set forth two ideas which became a point of contention on the part of his critics: 1) "the believer and the non-believer differ at the outset of every self-conscious investigation" and 2) the believer and the non-believer have everything *metaphysically* in common, but nothing *epistemologically* in common.[19] Van Til's critics respond by saying that he cannot be serious; these two points seem to destroy any conception of common grace and a common point of contact while accenting the notion of total depravity. With respect to the first point, his critics may concede that a basic difference between a self-conscious investigation on the part of a believer and an unbeliever exists concerning *an explanation* of the facts, but there is no such difference in the mere *description* of the facts.[20] For example, a Christian and a non-Christian go fishing with each other. The Christian catches a bass. Both parties decide to measure the bass; they agree that it is sixteen inches long. Both parties decide to weigh the bass; they agree

---

19. Ibid., 3, 5.
20. See ibid., 3.

that it weighs three pounds. Both parties look at the bass; they agree that it is grey, and it has two eyes and a mouth. It is evident, therefore, that the *description* of the bass is the same for the Christian and the non-Christian. On the other hand, if they engage in an *explanation* of the fish, then the two positions are not alike. The non-Christian understands the bass as existing in a process of evolution, controlled by the laws of nature in a chance created universe. The Christian holds that the bass is a unique creation of God, which has a distinct purpose in God's created universe. Hence, it should be apparent that the *description* of the bass is the same for the Christian and the non-Christian, whereas the *explanation* is not the same. It is safe to say that most Christians are satisfied with such a distinction. However, Van Til was strongly opposed to this distinction. As we have noted, he held that from the very outset of every self-conscious investigation into the facts, the Christian and the non-Christian differ. Specifically, Van Til maintained that every description is an explanation of a fact—the description of a fact is not a neutral category that exists irrespective of God.[21] As Van Til wrote: "According to any consistently Christian position, God, and God only, has ultimate definitory power. God's description or plan of the fact makes the fact what it is."[22] Since God describes and interprets (explains) the facts, no fact is neutral. Every *self-conscious* investigation into the facts does not separate description from explanation.

Those who have found Van Til's failure to separate description and explanation repugnant have also been hostile toward Van Til's position that the believer and the unbeliever have all things *metaphysically* in common, while they have nothing *epistemologically* in common. Herein, Van Til was consistent with the previous point; every believer and every unbeliever is self-conscious of their view of knowing and interpreting the facts. Specifically, the believer's heart is self-conscious of his dependency on God in order to define, know, and interpret the facts, whereas the unbeliever's heart is self-conscious of his dependency upon his own human autonomy in order to define, know, and interpret the facts. True, the unbeliever may attempt to claim that his position is dependent upon a system not grounded in himself, for example, Plato's demiurge creating the world after independently existing entities in the Form world. Van Til would respond, however, that even Plato's system is a projection of his mind since its basis is not the direct revelation of the living God. In terms of

---

21. See ibid.
22. Ibid., 5.

Van Til and Common Grace

one's epistemological self-consciousness, therefore, Van Til declared that the believer and the unbeliever cannot have any fact in common. The two parties are antithetical in their epistemological self-consciousness. On the other hand, Van Til held that the believer and the unbeliever have every fact in common. What is going on here? This position seems confusing; Van Til seems contradictory! Van Til pleaded on behalf of the distinction between one's epistemological self-consciousness and the realm of metaphysics. In the metaphysical realm, both parties deal with the same God, who alone exists, and the same universe, which is created by God (common point of contact). Moreover, both parties are created in the image of God. For this reason, the believer and the unbeliever can agree that the bass is sixteen inches long and weighs three pounds. In God's created universe, the believer and the unbeliever cannot overlook these metaphysical facts. Even so, in the final analysis, the description of the bass and the explanation of the bass cannot be separated. Alternatively, to put it another way, Van Til held that the unbeliever's understanding of God's metaphysical universe is static; he always operated metaphysically in abstraction. He will agree that the bass weighs three pounds or that $2+2=4$ (which is metaphysically correct), but he will not describe or explain the (epistemological) truthfulness of the bass or the mathematical proposition in the context of a Christian theistic universe (concrete understanding).[23] These Van Tilian phrases become more coherent if we place them more comprehensively within his discussion of common grace.

Van Til and Common Grace

I have already alluded to a number of key elements in Van Til's position on common grace: the authority and sovereignty of God, the Reformed doctrine of total depravity, and the idea of abstraction versus the idea of concreteness. The key in Van Til's view of common grace is, however, a philosophy of history set forth on the basis of biblical revelation and taught in the Reformed confessions.[24] One must not overlook this point; perhaps,

---

23. A neutral view of reason or a classically defined view of reason is not the basis of the metaphysical correctness of the proposition $2+2=4$; rather, the proposition is true only because God has defined the proposition. That is what Van Til declared must be the confession of the Christian.

24. Ibid., v. Of particular interest to Van Til is Romans 1 and 5, 1 Corinthians 15, and the Westminster Confession of Faith (hereafter WCF) 4.2, 6.1, and 6.3.

more than any other subject he addressed, we witness in Van Til's version of common grace a more consistent application of the biblical-theological perspective of his teacher, Geerhardus Vos. Note carefully how Van Til defines the central problem of common grace: "The common grace problem deals with this question: What do entities which will one day be wholly different from one another have in common before the final stage of separation is reached?"[25] Following the structure of Vos's interpretation of Pauline eschatology, Van Til understood that the problem of common grace deals with eschatology (it is not a mere logical construction of God's will—Hoeksema, *et alia*). Specifically, how does the future separation of the kingdom of God and the kingdom of Satan affect the present existence of wheat and tares co-existing with each other? In an eschatological view of history, grounded in God's sovereign covenant of election, it is difficult to draw the boundary between what is presently comprehended and what is not presently comprehended by covenant keepers and covenant breakers. Even so, from the state of pre-redemptive revelation to the consummate state of the eschaton, the final eschatological drama of election and covenant unfolds according to the sovereign purpose of God. In light of God unfolding his will in revelational history, Van Til's main concern was not to provide a lengthy exposition on the "rain falling on the just and the unjust" or whether 2+2=4. Although he addressed these issues, his main concern was to place these issues in the context of revelational history. In this arena, he admitted that "only those who are seriously concerned with interpreting the whole of history in terms of the counsel of God can be puzzled by the question of that which is 'common' between believer and unbeliever."[26] For Van Til, that puzzle comes together by following the basic historical pattern of pre-redemptive revelation, Adam's fall, Christ's redemption, and the final eschaton.[27]

---

25. Van Til, *Common Grace*, 68.

26. Ibid., 12.

27. In terms of the pattern of revelational history, I will focus on pre-redemptive revelation and Adam's fall. As I speak of Adam's fall into sin, I will blend into the discussion redemption in Christ as well as the final destiny of the believer and the unbeliever. For our present discussion, this integration will have to be sufficient; I will not discuss each aspect separately.

Van Til and Common Grace

Pre-Redemptive Revelation

Van Til echoed Vos's concept of pre-redemptive revelation.[28] Herein, we are referring to Adam's original created status in relationship to God's revelation. As Romans 5, 1 Corinthians 15, and the Reformed confessions teach, Adam is the federal head of humanity; he represented all men in his original state. This teaching from Scripture and the Reformed confessions is at the heart of Van Til's view of common grace. To begin, Van Til held that all men, including those who are decreed before the foundation of the world as elect and as reprobate, are represented in Adam when God first created him.[29] Although Van Til did not overlook God's original decree, nevertheless, in the domain of history it is important to understand that God leads the elect and the reprobate to their particular destiny. For Van Til, God's providence incorporates genuine progress, and, thus, *genuine variations* in human relationships, as well as relationships to God and the world, will unfold. In order for these *variations* to exist within the human race, all human beings are represented in Adam's original perfection and holiness, or, to put it another way, all men have a *general* identity in the first stage of Adam's appearance—being perfect and holy. Particularly, Van Til remarked that there is a *sameness* with a *difference*; all men are the *same* in Adam's original perfection, but there is the *difference* of decree between the elect in Christ and the reprobate.[30] Even so, in the original state of perfection, God walked and talked with humanity's representative head—Adam; natural revelation was not separated from supernatural revelation.[31] Adam was not living in two abstract revelations; rather, he was living in one *concrete* situation. Specifically, our representative Adam understood revelation *holistically*. Moreover, "man was originally placed before God as a covenant personality."[32] This covenant relationship with God cannot be separated from God's revelation to man. As Van Til remarked: "To speak of man's relation to God as being covenantal at every point is merely to say that man deals with the personal God everywhere."[33] In the pre-redemptive state, every manipulation or interpretation of the facts is a covenant-affirming

---

28. Cf. ibid., 69; and Vos, *Biblical Theology*, 19–44.
29. See Van Til, *Common Grace*, 30.
30. See ibid., 31, 32.
31. See ibid., 69.
32. Ibid.
33. Ibid., 69, 70.

activity; it is in correspondence to the revelational truth of God's work. Herein, there is *one* holistic, unified interpretation that the facts are from God, through God, and to God.

For Van Til, herein lies the notion of common grace. In this pre-redemptive state, all men in Adam (the elect and reprobate) have a unified understanding and interpretation of the revelation of God and his creation. God's revelation is everywhere; all men have a consciousness within them that God created them in his image and all men have the testimony of God that he is the Creator and sustains all things. In this condition, all men have a common ethical reaction of goodness to the common mandate of God (which some refer to as the cultural mandate); according to Van Til, "they are all mandate hearers and mandate-keepers."[34] God has the *same* favorable attitude to all. Being in union with Adam's original status, mankind has a holistic consciousness of pre-redemptive revelation within them and the testimony of a holistic pre-redemptive revelation to them that continues throughout all the stages of history, even to the final consummation. Van Til calls the continuation of this original status *common grace*. For example, he maintained that the "rain and the sunshine" which envelops all mankind has its root in God's favorable attitude to all in this original state. Moreover, men can agree that 2+2=4, or that a bass is sixteen inches long, because of man's original union with the testimony of holistic revelation given to man's first representative, Adam. Hence, the psychological, ethical, metaphysical, and epistemological conditions of all mankind are represented in Adam's original perfection. A problem occurs, however, at the fall.

The Fall

Once again, following the teaching of Scripture and the Reformed confessions concerning Adam being the federal head of the human race, Van Til held that when Adam fell into sin, *all* men became sinners. All men became objects of God's *wrath*; all became sinners on the same day through the act of a common representative, including those decreed as elect and reprobate.[35] As Van Til stated: "It was *mankind*, not some individual elect or reprobate person, that sinned against God."[36] Herein, there is also a *sameness* with a *difference*; all men are in the *same* state as being objects

---

34. Ibid., 72.
35. See ibid., 30.
36. Ibid., 74.

of God's wrath, but there remains a *difference* in that some are elected in Christ unto redemption and some are decreed to be reprobate. Moreover, man's fall is one of total rebellion; the concrete and holistic interpretation of man in relationship to revelation must remain intact at this point. One cannot separate natural revelation and special revelation as objects against which man rebels (e.g., man cannot rebel against special revelation and leave the truth of natural revelation fully intact) and one cannot separate man's covenant relationship with God from the fall. Hence, after the fall every manipulation and interpretation of the facts is a covenant-breaking activity by a rebellious and depraved humanity.[37]

The Relation of Common Grace and Total Depravity

As Van Til considered the federal headship of Adam in relation to the human race, he carefully noted that Adam represented two states that have profound significance in the providence of God: the original holiness of all mankind and the original sinfulness of all mankind. In light of these two states, Van Til claimed that there will exist *genuine variations* in human relationships as well as relationships with God and the world throughout history. Hence, there is a real conflict in history between common grace and total depravity. Although common grace belongs to the original state of Adam's perfection, nevertheless, it continues in man as he exists in a depraved state.[38] In the negative sense, Van Til held that it is not possible to tone down the doctrine of total depravity.[39] The doctrine has such an effect upon man's evil nature that man makes every attempt to operate unconscious of the original attitude of favor that God bestowed upon mankind, and he also makes every attempt to operate unconscious of the real significance of his sinful direction. On the other hand, in the positive sense, Van Til taught that "common grace is the necessary correlative to the doctrine of total depravity."[40] Herein, one must understand that Adam performed his action of sin against the common mandate (cultural mandate) of God's favor to mankind as a whole. Without the original common mandate, Adam's sin would have operated in a total void; that is to say, his sin would

---

37. See ibid., 70.
38. See ibid., 91.
39. Ibid.
40. Ibid.

have been an offense against nothing. Since man's sin did not operate in a void, all mankind came under the common wrath of God.

For Van Til, however, the correlative relationship between common grace and total depravity has another salient point in the drama of history. In history, through the sovereign work of God the elect will choose redemption in Christ, whereas the reprobate will reaffirm their choice for Satan.[41] God's providential control over history will show that the reprobate, who are totally depraved in principle, will more and more be conformed to the principle of depravity that controls their heart.[42] According to Van Til, "they do this by way of rejecting the common call, the common grace of God. That is to say, they do this by way of rejecting God to whatever extent God reveals Himself to them."[43] Van Til concluded, therefore, that in the historical process in which common grace is correlative to total depravity, we have

> the "relative good" in the "absolutely evil" [non-Christian] and the "relatively evil" in the "absolutely good" [Christian]. Neither the "absolutely evil" nor the "absolutely good" are epistemologically as self-conscious as they will be in the future [day of final judgment]. God's favor rests upon the reprobate and God's disfavor rests upon the elect to the extent that each lacks epistemological self-consciousness [in present history]. In neither case is it God's ultimate or final attitude, but in both cases it is a real attitude.[44]

For this reason, Van Til declared that the unbeliever can be a person who contributes greatly to human culture; he can be a great artist, mathematician, physicist, doctor, mechanic, nurse, or teacher. He can be a person of integrity and honesty by establishing moral law upon a god (like Cicero [106–43 BC]) or upon nature (like Lucretius [99–55 BC]). On the other hand, believers can be seduced by dishonesty; they can be docile in terms of using the gifts God has given them. Furthermore, some believers may base their knowledge solely upon the foundation of the ontological triune God of the Bible, whereas other believers may base their knowledge on the ontological triune God of the Bible and an Aristotelian conception of logic. As you can see, there are *variations* in which God's favor of common grace continues upon all mankind, and there are *variations* in which all mankind

41. Ibid.
42. Ibid.
43. Ibid., 91.
44. Ibid., 92.

Van Til and Common Grace

expresses its depravity. For this reason, Van Til maintained that the antithesis between the unbeliever and the believer was never metaphysical and psychological, but always epistemological and ethical.[45] Metaphysically and psychologically, mankind can never be anything but the image of God, and mankind can never escape the imprint of God upon every inch of the universe and the constitution of his being.[46] All men, even presently, are responsible for the original pre-redemptive revelation of God to mankind.[47]

Even so, in light of the fall, there also exists a real antithesis—an epistemological and ethical antithesis. From Van Til's perspective, one must realize that the antithesis is not referring to the continuation of man's metaphysical and psychological *knowledge* from his original pre-redemptive state. For example, every man knows that he is created by God. In fact, Van Til held that only upon the foundation of man's original union with Adam's pre-redemptive state could there be a discussion of an antithesis. After all, fallen man is rebelling against his pre-redemptive state. Specifically, this rebellion involves the *interpretation* of the facts of revelation which are still in place after the fall. Hence, Van Til was clear that the antithesis is an epistemological and ethical antithesis of *interpreting* the facts; it does not refer to the metaphysical and psychological constitution of man.[48] Van Til was emphatic about this point when he wrote: "The point is that when and to the extent that the natural man is engaged in interpreting life in terms of his *adopted principles then*, and *only* then, he has nothing in common with the believer."[49] Specifically, only when men are "self-consciously engaged in the interpretative enterprise" do the Christian and the non-Christian have nothing epistemologically in common.[50] Moreover, after the fall, the ethical subject, man, acts with an attitude of hostility in respect to pre-redemptive revelation.[51] Following the teaching of the Apostle Paul, Van Til stated that man's ethical hostility operates in his interpretative activity to suppress the truth (pre-redemptive revelation) in unrighteousness (see Romans 1:18). Here, in the context of the interpretative activity, Van Til maintained that a description of the facts is an explanation of the facts.

---

45. See ibid., 86, 196.
46. See ibid., 53–54, 196.
47. See ibid., 88.
48. See ibid., 5, 151, 163.
49. Ibid., 163.
50. See ibid., 151.
51. See ibid., 53.

This interpretative activity is always a holistic enterprise; in this situation, the metaphysical, psychological, epistemological, and ethical aspects are viewed as one exercise. Hence, facts are never neutral. They always exist in the context of man's holistic interpretation of life.

While keeping in mind that Van Til embedded his whole construction in revelational history, let me return to our examples in order to briefly summarize what Van Til is saying. If the unbeliever says that 2+2=4, or if the unbeliever says that a bass is sixteen inches long, then he makes these true statements on the basis of his psychological and metaphysical union with pre-redemptive revelation (a holistic revelation—natural and special). After the fall, this same pre-redemptive understanding continues (common grace), but an attitude of rebellion against the living and true God accompanies the interpretative process. Hence, for the unbeliever, the mathematical proposition and the length of the bass operate in the context of man-interpreted facts and a chance created universe which are epistemologically and ethically antithetical to the continual meaning and purpose of God's revelation (a holistic rejection of revelation—natural and special). Herein, the unbeliever and believer have nothing in common, since the believer interprets factual truth with a heart in obedience to his Creator and with a confession that his Creator is the fountain of all truth.

Hence, Van Til's own reconstruction of the doctrine of common grace was quite different from the traditional Dutch Reformed position. In contrast to Kuyper, Bavinck, and Hepp, he attempted to eliminate the tendency to view common grace in the context of a systematic construction of natural revelation and special revelation. Specifically, natural revelation was viewed as the domain of common grace insights on the part of the unbeliever (through human reason and experience), whereas special revelation was the domain for the illumination of believers (through faith). By analyzing the self-conscious states of man in union with Adam, Van Til was able to understand the reception of the concrete picture of revelation to man (pre-redemptive, common grace) and the rejection of the concrete picture of revelation to man (the fall). For him, the issue has never been that human reason and experience maintain camaraderie with natural revelation in order to preserve or gain common grace insights. Rather, the issue has been that two states of man's historical self-consciousness of God's revelation are placed in a struggle (by variation) against each other until they totally separate in the final eschaton.

4

Antithesis, Common Grace, and Plato's View of the Soul

> There are only two kinds of people in the world, covenant-breakers and covenant-keepers. . . . This distinction, thus baldly stated, indicates the antithesis between the believer and the unbeliever in principle. . . . Any doctrine of common grace or general grace that we hold will surely need to be consistent with this basic point.
>
> —Cornelius Van Til, *The Reformed Pastor and Modern Thought*

Christian academicians seem to agree about the product they would like to see in a graduate from their particular institution. When reading the purpose and/or vision statement from a Presbyterian (Reformed), Baptist, Methodist, Lutheran, Episcopal, Mennonite, Nazarene, or non-denominational evangelical college or university, the reader finds a similar taxonomy of rhetoric. Interestingly, the respective historical roots of these institutions seem to make little difference to the programmatic declaration and, thus, the descriptive language offers a common marketable metanarrative. Specifically, an imitative amalgamation of terminology has emerged across the horizon of Christian education to describe the mission *praxis* of the enterprise. These expressions often include such phrases as the following: "Christ-centered education," "integrating faith and learning (life)," "equipping leaders and servants in a global environment," "impacting, influencing, and engaging church, society, and culture," "bringing justice and compassion to a broken world," and being "agents of renewal and transformation in community, nation, and world."[1]

As these institutions advance the public representation of their college/university, obviously, the purpose and vision of their institution is intended to be integrated into the product they foresee for the school. In fact, it would seem fair to say that any mention of the ecclesiastical affiliation or academic prowess of the school's environment serves only as a means to accent the teleological mission of the institution. Herein exists the implicit eschatological message of the institution's own great commission for its students—be leaders, servants, instruments, and agents of the institution's message of renewal for the world. This activist and geographical view of eschatology comes across as a generic metanarrative characterizing the core of Christian higher education no matter what institution a prospective student considers. Furthermore, where this core belief exists, in most cases it energizes the classroom. Professors seek to apply the purpose/mission statement to their own ends as they blend the Christian message into their own agenda for the natural and human sciences. Meanwhile, these institutions hope that students are riveted to the challenging and passionate call of the professors to become life-changing agents in the world; students are called to make a difference.

As the current establishment of this generic metanarrative becomes further entrenched in academia, perhaps this storyline does not please all who are associated with these institutions. Conscientious dissenters do exist on these campuses, in some cases minority voices that view the current eschatological focus on cultural renewal to be indoctrination into the present popular educational milieu. Moreover, on these campuses marginal voices can be found, those who are genuinely perplexed over the apathetic spirit of leadership with respect to the institution's particular ecclesiastical and theological roots. Indeed, in the public sphere, many of these institutions

---

1. The voice of James Davison Hunter's analysis, argument, and critique concerning the transformation of culture in his book *To Change the World* is timely and appropriate; it needs serious reflection within the halls of the Christian academy.

usually pay lip service to those foundational roots, while in the classroom or on the campus, a student may identify little, if anything, that typifies the historic roots of the institution. In many cases, as a particular academy distances itself from its birth date, it becomes increasingly compelling to those who are shaping the philosophy of the school to seek relevance primarily to the current state of affairs.[2] Clearly, the seduction of being relevant to the changing landscape of life is what leads to our tendency in academia to leave the past behind us.

Not just an interesting cultural phenomenon, the craving to be relevant becomes a crisis within the inner soul of Christian education. In order to attract students and attention, the institution must convey the message that it actively puts into practice the dynamics of the Christian faith. After all, nothing is more hideous than a religion that seems dead and does not have an impact on the world. Meanwhile, some demand that the institution give an account of its historic roots, and how those roots influence the school's progress into the future. In answering to their living constituency (mostly embodied in alumni), most schools endeavor to demonstrate that their current agenda reconciles well with the historical agenda of the institution. Administrations readily attempt to convey that their institutions hold a sacred affinity to the past. However, much ink has been spilled to dissect their claim; most notable are those works that document the failure of institutions to maintain their ecclesiastical, theological, and philosophical roots.[3] For a specific example from within my Reformed heritage, perhaps James D. Bratt sets up my discussion best when he summarizes E. Digby Baltzell's study:

> According to Digby Baltzell's provocative study, *Puritan Boston and Quaker Philadelphia* . . . , nearly a third of the United States' two hundred colleges at the time of the Civil War has been founded "by the heirs of Calvinism" and another third were "indirectly

---

2. Concerning the content in this paragraph, the author is fully aware that there is not a necessary logical consequence here, that is, that the endorsement of this generic metanarrative does not automatically mean that one has surrendered the ecclesiastical and theological roots of the institution.

3. For example, Marsden, *The Soul of the American University*; Marsden, *Reforming Fundamentalism*; Marsden and Longfield, *The Secularization of the Academy*; Burtchaell, *The Dying of the Light*; and Haynes, *Professing in the Postmodern Academy*. Although his thesis can be challenged, Robert Benne's volume *Quality with Soul* has been celebrated as a prescription for the Christian academy to remain faithful to its task. On this note, one can also consult Marsden, *The Outrageous Idea of Christian Scholarship*; as well as Hughes and Adrian, *Models for Christian Higher Education*.

controlled by the Presbyterian church" (248). The prototype of them all was Harvard.[4]

If Baltzell's assessment is correct, then, as the Civil War dawned, nearly two-thirds of the colleges in the United States had roots in the Reformed tradition of Calvinism. At the emergence of the twenty-first century, though, very few of those schools would publicly claim any allegiance to the historic confessional roots of Calvinistic orthodoxy.[5]

Since the Civil War, the themes of modernity have found dominance in many of those schools as a result of an effort by academics to temper, restrain, and conquer the archaic themes of a perceived rigid Calvinism. In a number of those institutions, modernity has flowed easily into the current themes of postmodernity as these worldviews find a voice in the agenda of the institution, whether it be in the school's marketing, its philosophy of education, its curriculum, or the underlying presuppositions of the content within its classrooms. Hence, as historic Reformed orthodoxy has disappeared from those campuses, there seems to be no sympathy for its death. In fact, in acknowledgment of its departure, we hear echoes of the modern world's approach to viewing and understanding the historic past, that is, the dictate that one must view all historical traditions as breathing and living traditions that must be recast to fit the current social, cultural, political, economic, aesthetic, scientific, and moral state of affairs.

Since, with the assistance of Baltzell and others, the demise of the splendid tradition of Reformed higher education has been documented, perhaps a subtle voice can yet be heard which savors the historic confessional roots of Reformed orthodoxy as being relevant for the present academic and cultural environment. Although, to some, such a voice may be

---

4. Bratt, "Puritan Schools," 12. Bratt has brought our attention to the same resource in Bratt, "Reformed Tradition," 126. Cf. Baltzell, *Puritan Boston*, 248. Baltzell's observation receives further credence from Tewksbury, *American Colleges*, 92: "[by 1851] two-thirds of the colleges in the land were directly or indirectly under the control of the Presbyterian Church."

5. The term "orthodoxy" when used throughout this essay will have some different nuances. In most cases, however, whether in reference to Reformed orthodoxy or to Christian (meaning evangelical) orthodoxy, I have in mind an understanding of Christian truth rooted in the infallible Word of God and its interpretation by the era of the Protestant Reformation without being tainted by Renaissance and Enlightenment higher-critical approaches to the biblical canon and ecclesiastical dogmatics. Moreover, the term "orthodoxy" implies being faithful without reservation to the absolute authoritative and self-authenticating Word of God, in which the sole infallible method of the interpretation of Scripture is Scripture itself (see WCF 1.4–5 and 1.9).

Antithesis, Common Grace, and Plato's View of the Soul

an archaic reverberation of the past, to others the rhetoric may be a refreshing innovation, since the historic voice has been silenced so long by the current generic metanarrative. As I attempt to expound this point, my hope is that my example can be broadly applied across the spectrum of Christian higher education. Specifically, those who are part of a splendid tradition in their own heritage of higher education can reflect upon my discourse and apply it to their own legacy. In order to do so, perhaps those who wish to reflect upon my discourse should start with their own historic documents of the Christian faith, and then work back in assessing those documents in light of Scripture, and then apply their reflections to the academy and its curriculum.

THE REFORMED EDUCATIONAL HERITAGE

For those who wish to resist the gravitation toward modernity and secularization, or even the elements of postmodernity, the task of preserving the strength and ability to remain steadfast in the tradition of historic Christianity can be wearisome. As already noted, Reformed higher education within Christendom has dissipated almost entirely since the Civil War. This degeneration has occurred not because the historic ecclesiastical roots of these institutions have been savored, instead, primarily because the agenda of modernity and cultural relevancy has been accommodated.[6] Modernity has trumped historic orthodoxy rather than historic orthodoxy tempering modernity. Specifically, Reformed institutions of higher learning have become secularized since the Civil War because the collective mindset of the institution has stressed common grace arching between orthodox Christian thought and non-Christian thought at the expense of the antithesis. Under the banner of common grace, Reformed Christian educators have adopted the methods and substance of secular thought without clear discernment. They have failed to employ a transcendental analysis and critique that remains faithful to revelational history (Scripture) as

---

6. Bratt and Ronald A. Wells make a salient, succinct analysis of an important observation that George M. Marsden made in his *The Soul of the American University*. Bratt and Wells write, "In academic life in particular, as former Calvin history professor George Marsden has written, secularization occurs not necessarily when religion becomes too little but when it becomes so much and so broad that it is robbed of content" (Bratt and Wells, "Piety and Progress," 161). Although Marsden's observation is not my focus here, the reader must be aware that such a factor is pertinent to a comprehensive study of the deterioration of a Christian institution from its founding principles.

summarized in the ecumenical creeds and the Reformed confessions. Hence, it is not uncommon to find Christian academicians who employ the pious-clad phrase, "all truth is God's truth," to justify a methodology that utilizes the fundamental precepts of rationalism, empiricism, realism, idealism, romanticism, naturalism, materialism, existentialism, structuralism, or poststructuralism, without any clear critique of the foundational premises of those methodologies.

In the history of Reformed thought, its view of common grace can serve both as a stumbling block and as a positive theological rubric. In Calvinistic institutions, this tension between stumbling block and positive formulation has been extremely problematic. When Reformed scholars pay attention to the biblical doctrine of sin, their account of human depravity seems to indicate that the unbeliever cannot know anything correctly while remaining outside of regeneration by Christ's Spirit (1 Cor 2:6–16).[7] The effects of the fall mean that the unbeliever can do absolutely nothing to attain salvation or to interpret God, humanity, and the world correctly (Rom 3:9–20). Every function that constitutes a human being is affected by sin: reason, experience, psyche, and emotions. Nevertheless, the Reformed world admits the obvious—the unbeliever maintains that 2+2=4 just as the believer does. How does this factual agreement fit into the biblical doctrine of sin and its effects? Reformed theology has constructed the concept of common grace to clarify the concord.[8] Simply put, for many the phrase re-

---

7. See Gaffin, "Epistemological Reflections on 1 Corinthians 2:6–16."

8. The Reformed tradition has had a particular interest in the concept of common grace in light of its view of total depravity. If the fall has affected all the faculties of the human, then how can one have any true knowledge at all? In responding to this question, Reformed theology has had its own intramural debate on the subject. For a summary of that debate, especially in the twentieth century, one can consult van Genderen and Velema, *Reformed Dogmatics*, 294–9; and chapter 3 above. In my judgment, principal documents in the discussion within the Dutch Reformed tradition are Kuyper's *De Gemeene Gratie*; Bavinck's "Common Grace"; and Van Til's *Common Grace and the Gospel*. Bratt has included a brief segment from Kuyper's *De Gemeene Gratie* in Bratt, *Kuyper*, 165–201. See also Kuyper, "Common Grace in Science." A brief, but fine discussion accenting the tradition of Old Princeton can be found in Murray, "Common Grace." Perhaps, the present nuances of the discussion on the topic are depicted best in Mouw, *He Shines in All That's Fair*. Although Kuyper claimed that "only the Reformed have clearly perceived the distinction between 'special grace' and 'common grace,'" others have now claimed the notion of common grace for themselves (Kuyper, "Common Grace," 192). For example, Timothy J. Wengert has claimed "common grace" in the older Melanchthon and the Lutheran tradition (see Wengert, "Review"); Raines, "Tools and Common Grace"; Lane, "Dragons of the Ordinary"; Yancey, "Chords That Bind"; Yandell, "Modernism, Post-Modernism, and the Minimalist Canons of Common Grace"; and

fers to the common facts that the Christian and the non-Christian share in God's created world despite the noetic effects of Adam's fall. Sadly, however, while common grace should hold in check the submersion of Christian scholars into secularization since the doctrine of sin should always maintain a prominent position before them, much too often the exact opposite has occurred. Under the rubric of common grace, Reformed scholars have readily fallen right into secular models. Invoking common grace, these thinkers have allowed natural and general revelation to become a shared arena of integration with non-Christian scholars. Invoking common grace, at times the scholar becomes an eclectic collector of non-Christian propositions without serious analysis as long as the secular material can be incorporated into the believer's so-called system of Christian thought. In my judgment, the use of these models by Reformed academicians compromises any coherent, integrated understanding of a discipline in line with historic orthodoxy. By contrast, the work of Van Til stands out.[9]

Van Til maintained that true Christian thinking must begin with the self-attesting Christ of Scripture. In Van Til's estimation, the Christian must never compromise the pervasive revelation of Christ found in the infallible record of Scripture and summarized in the ecumenical creeds of the early church and the Reformed confessions of the Reformation.[10] It is within this theological and ecclesiastical framework that Reformed

---

Johnston, *Rethinking Common Grace*.

9. With respect to the fallen condition of human reason and its spiritual discernment, Calvin's attack upon the philosophers is insightful. In modern academia, his point can be applied across the entire scope of all the academic disciplines. He states: "Certainly I do not deny that one can read competent and apt statements about God here and there in the philosophers, but these always show a certain giddy imagination.... But they [philosophers] saw things in such a way that their seeing did not direct them to the truth, much less enable them to attain it! They are like a traveler passing through a field at night who in a momentary lightening flash sees far and wide, but the sight vanishes so swiftly that he is plunged again into the darkness of the night before he can take even a step—let alone be directed on his way by its help. Besides, although they may chance to sprinkle their books with droplets of truth, how many monstrous lies defile them!" (Calvin, *Institutes*, 2.2.18). If Calvin made this comment in an interview in Christian academia today, one wonders if he would receive an appointment, even in those accredited institutions which stand in the Reformed tradition.

10. One of my favorite statements from Van Til's pen is appropriate here; the quip will enable the reader to see how Van Til viewed the antithesis between Calvin and Aquinas: "Aquinas sought to show the unbeliever that the Christian story is in accord with logic and in accord with fact. Calvin sought to show that 'logic' and 'fact' have meaning only in terms of the 'story'" (Van Til, "Calvin," 8).

scholars should desire to govern every dimension of their discipline from within their identity in Christ. The Christ of Scripture as the ground of the scholar's epistemological self-consciousness defines the parameters of academic interface with the realm of unbelief. With this commitment in place, Van Til set forth a challenging formula for the Christian scholar to use in order to keep his moorings: *antithesis must precede common grace*. By this Van Til indicates that when analyzing the Christian worldview in relationship to a non-Christian worldview, the two systems, holistically conceived, are antithetical to each other. Herein, the *universal* frameworks of two holistic systems of thought are thoroughly distinct and at odds with one another. Nevertheless, although this holistic antithesis exists, such a position does not restrict a non-Christian from affirming a truth in compliance with what has been revealed by God, for example, 2+2=4. In other words, the *holistic* character of one's system of unbelief is antithetical to Christianity, whereas a *particular* element in that system may be a common grace insight, one which can be shared by believer and unbeliever alike. Even as this distinction is made, the Reformed academician must actively take a further pedagogical step—the antithesis must submit all academic material to analysis and investigation so that all elements that emerge as common grace insights are thoroughly examined through the lens of an orthodox commitment to the truth of Christ in Scripture. Herein, a common grace insight can only be called a common grace insight if it is in compliance with the truth of God's revelation.

With this particular component of Van Til's view of antithesis and common grace before us, it is now fitting to present an example of how his formula might be used by the Christian academician in a concrete situation—specifically, in an analysis of Plato's view of the soul. The premise is this: Plato's belief that the soul is immortal is a common grace insight since God's Word also teaches that the soul is immortal. With such an observation before the Christian scholar, careless thinking can lead to errors closely aligned with previously noted stumbling blocks. Some might declare that Plato was enlightened by natural revelation; specifically, they might claim that Plato's observation indicates he acknowledged a biblical truth and was on the correct track toward Christian belief. Herein, Plato may be praised because, as a non-Christian, he gives affirmation to a truth in the Christian belief system. Another popular reaction is exemplified by the scholar who, in observing Plato's common grace insight, will perceive the presuppositional differences between Plato and Christianity for the sake of eventually

Antithesis, Common Grace, and Plato's View of the Soul

qualifying those differences. In particular the distinctions will be contextualized by the Christian academic for the sake of tolerance, support, and encouragement at the table of ideas. Often when this model is employed, the traces of commonly held data on Plato's view of the soul are found in order to be incorporated eclectically into the Christian's system of beliefs so one can attain academic credence. In this way, the ideal of peaceful coexistence between the two camps dissolves the antithesis. Finally, some Christian scholars will take up everything Plato states that seem to be in compliance with a biblical view of the soul without much discernment, and adapt it into the Christian view of immortality. In fact, they may declare that Plato's view of the immortality of the soul is Christian in so far as it goes. On the other hand, Van Til's directive counters these compromised Christian approaches. He instructed the Christian scholar not to surrender the antithesis for the sake of any degree of appeasement. As we proceed, Van Til's edict seems most instructive and challenging in order to maintain a biblical and Reformed conception of the soul.

PLATO'S VIEW OF THE SOUL

Readers of Plato's dialogues must be sensitive to what literary critical scholars refer to as the "Socratic problem," that is, the task of separating which concepts belong to Socrates (470/469–399 BC) and which concepts belong to Plato. Although a number of ideas continue to be subject to speculative analysis, many scholars follow Aristotle's (384–322 BC) lead, maintaining that the doctrine of Forms that appear in the middle and later dialogues belongs to Plato.[11] For Plato the Form world and his view of the human soul are closely related.[12] With respect to knowledge, everything must exist

---

11. See Aristotle, "Metaphysica," I.6, 987a29–b14; 13.4, 1078b12–31. Whether one agrees with Gail Fine's analysis or not, one sees in her work an excellent discussion of the scholarly material surrounding the doctrine of Forms, including the interrelationships among the ideas of Socrates, Plato, and Aristotle on the doctrine of Forms (Fine, *On Ideas*, 20–38, 44–65). Moreover, A. P. Bos has provided an update of the current scholarly discussion on Aristotle's own view of the soul and his rejection of Plato's dualism (Bos, *The Soul and its Instrumental Body*). Concerning the Socratic problem, see Burnet, "Introduction"; Dubs, "The Socratic Problem"; Rogers, *The Socratic Problem*; Ross, "The Socratic Problem"; de Vogel, "The Present State of the Socratic Problem"; Thesleff, *Studies in Platonic Chronology*; Patzer, *Der Historische Sokrates*; Kahn, *Plato and the Socratic Dialogue*; Wallach, "Plato's Socratic Problem, and Ours"; and Prior, "The Socratic Problem."

12. I will not follow Gail Fine's lead on the use of upper-case or lower-case in the term "Form" and the corresponding concepts associated with Plato's Form world. Like

in the transcendent Form world in order to be known and exist in the immanent empirical universe in which human beings dwell. As Plato unpacks his view of anthropology, the human soul is said to be the residence of the knowledge of Forms. In this analogical construct between the objects in the transcendent Form world and the objects in the immanent empirical universe, the soul grasps those objects as it possesses the quality of immortality.[13] Likewise, according to biblical revelation, the Christian religion presents a position that the human soul never dies, that is to say, the soul is immortal. Plato and biblical revelation agree—the soul is immortal. If one believes that biblical revelation is the record of the infallible revelation of the true God of heaven and earth, and that all human knowledge is either directly or indirectly dependent upon God, then in some manner the God of the Bible communicated the truth that the soul is immortal to Plato. Calvin's analysis is insightful at this point.

Calvin held that, as created in the image of God, Plato believed that the soul was immortal because of the "seed of religion" within him, that is to say, the seed of religion "engraved" the immortality of the soul upon his soul.[14] In Reformed language, Plato's belief regarding the soul's immortality was a result of a common grace insight. In this context, Calvin provided excellent insight into the tension between common grace and human depravity.[15] Calvin stated that the soul functions in two basic ways: (1) "ruling man's life" with respect "to the duties of his earthly life"; and (2) "arous[ing]" man "to honor God" in meditating "upon the heavenly life."[16] As Calvin interacted with Plato's view of the soul, he chose to address human depravity with respect to the second point.[17] In light of the fall into

---

Stephen M. Cahn, I have decided to use the upper-case so the reader can easily follow the distinction between a concept in the Form world and that which is not in the Form world (see Cahn, *Classics of Western Philosophy*). Fine maintains that the upper-case was used in order to mark how the entities were viewed as different for Socrates and Plato. Since Fine rejects that premise, she uses only the lower-case (Fine, *On Ideas*, 244–5).

13. Perhaps Plato's most succinct statement about the immortality of the soul comes in the form of a rhetorical question in Socrates's discussion with Glaucon: "Are you not aware that our soul is immortal and never perishes?" (Plato, *Republic*, 608d3–4; cf. Plato, *Phaedrus*, 245c5–9, 245e4–6).

14. Calvin, *Institutes*, 1.15.6; cf. ibid., 1.3.1.

15. The phrase "common grace" which has been used by Reformed theology was referred to as the "general grace of God" by Calvin (Calvin, *Institutes*, 2.2.17; see ibid., n63).

16. Calvin, *Institutes*, 1.15.6.

17. In terms of the functional operation of the soul, one must not conclude that Calvin held that there is a domain within the soul which is not fallen or depraved (first

Antithesis, Common Grace, and Plato's View of the Soul

sin, humanity is corrupt and, thus, cannot perceive clearly and correctly in order to honor God. Nevertheless, Calvin went on to say, there are some "remnants" of God's image in humanity which explain such common grace declarations from Plato's lips. Calvin acknowledged that such assertions appear in the context of the speaker being encompassed by the vices of human corruption. Indeed, the presence of these vices within the soul produces various versions of the soul—some more corrupt than others.[18] Calvin himself acknowledged this degradation of vices among fallen human beings by stating that a better definition of the soul can be extracted from Plato than from the other philosophers of his day because Plato reflected better on the "image of God in the soul."[19] Even so, in the same section of the *Institutes*, Calvin exposed the corrupt aspects of Plato's view of the soul by attacking the latter's alleged view of two souls within a person—a sensitive soul and a rational soul.[20] Hence, as Calvin advanced his common

---

function). In fact, as Calvin presented the nature of original sin, he was extremely clear that depravity and corruption is "diffused into all parts of the soul." Calvin followed this statement by writing, "we are so vitiated and perverted in every part of our nature that by this corruption we stand justly condemned and convicted by God, to whom nothing is acceptable but righteousness, innocence, and purity" (Calvin, *Institutes*, 2.1.8; see also ibid., 2.1.9).

18. Plato recognized that the vices taint the soul as well (see Plato, *Republic*, 439a1–e4).

19. Calvin wrote: "It would be foolish to seek a definition of 'soul' from the philosophers. Of them hardly one, except Plato, has rightly affirmed its immortal substance. Indeed, other Socratics also touch upon it, but in a way that shows how nobody teaches clearly a thing of which he has not been persuaded. Hence Plato's opinion is more correct, because he considers the image of God in the soul" (Calvin, *Institutes*, 1.15.6). Also, it needs to be noted that Calvin would view certain qualities of the remnants of God's image in fallen humanity as positive virtues; he did not view every trait of fallen humanity through the degradation of vices. Indeed, though they are fallen, the Creator endowed some human beings with such virtues as "keenness," "superior judgment," and "learning the arts." According to Calvin, God performed this act upon fallen creatures in order "to display in common nature God's special grace" (Calvin, *Institutes*, 2.2.17). Calvin's point is not to negate what he has written about the depravity of humanity, and it is not to deny that salvation comes solely through the special intercession of the Holy Spirit's work applying the benefits of Christ's redemptive work to sinners. Rather, Calvin is merely bringing to the attention of his readers that God continues to provide virtuous traits (as a special gift of grace) within the fallen human race in order to serve his own providential end for the creation.

20. See Calvin, *Institutes*, 1.15.6. Calvin seems to be referencing Plato—perhaps from Plato, *Republic*, 439d4–6, 439e2–3. (Calvin's reference to Plato's *Republic* comes from the English edition of the *Institutes*; the reference does not appear in the original Latin edition.) The question arises, however, whether Plato is actually referencing two

grace insight into Plato's understanding of the soul, he soon dissolved that insight by applying the antithesis to Plato's formulation.[21]

Before we turn more specifically to that antithesis, we need to direct the Christian academician to the next area of inquiry: does the content of Plato's view of the immortality of the soul agree with the content of the Christian view of the immortality of the soul as disclosed in biblical revelation?[22] In order to answer this question, we must have some competent grasp of the view of the soul's immortality in each system of thought. With respect to Plato, the analysis calls for an examination into the structures of his view of the soul as it functions coherently in his system. Hence, although an empirical comparison reveals that both Plato and biblical revelation teach that the soul is immortal, the task remains to discover whether both present the same understanding of the soul. Without a coherent understanding of

---

souls within a human being in that section of the *Republic*. Rather, it has been viewed by some scholars as two distinct principles, elements, or partitions within the soul, whereas with others it has been argued that Plato's *Republic* presents a "tripartition of the soul" (for an overview of this discussion, see Cooper, "Beyond the Tripartite Soul"; see also Plato, *Republic*, 439e3–4). Moreover, debate continues to surround Plato's view of the functionary categories of the soul or mind (Plato, *Republic*, 511d6–e4) as well as his view that different qualities which compose the soul determine one's status on the human chain of being (Plato, *Republic*, 413c5–414b6).

21. In this same section Calvin returns to a common grace statement, that is, that Plato may be profitable to read in order to understand how the faculties of the soul function. Herein, Calvin maintained that the philosopher may be beneficial to the Christian (see Calvin, *Institutes*, 1.15.6).

22. In recent literature one of the most popular discussions on this topic has appeared in N. T. Wright's *Surprised by Hope*. Wright has been strongly critical of the infiltration of the Platonic view of the soul into Christian thought. In doing so, Wright even questions whether the Bible teaches the immortality of the soul (Wright, *Hope*, 28; see also 36, 80, 160). As Wright feels compelled to free the biblical notion of the soul from Platonism, he can be pressed to distinguish his own interpretation of the soul disclosed in biblical revelation from Aristotle's view of soul. Indeed, a comparison between Wright's view of the soul in *Surprised by Hope* and A. P. Bos's explanation of Aristotle's view of the soul reveals amazing substantive parallels (see especially Bos, *Soul*, 33–68). Moreover, what is the relationship between Wright's notion that Plato presents the soul as a "disembodied entity hidden within the outer shell of the disposable body" (Wright, *Hope*, 28) with David Bostock's analysis that "the belief in a reasonably 'full' mental life after death is common, and from Homer onwards (*Odyssey* ix) all those who have pictured it have pictured the souls of the dead as having the shape of human bodies, and as doing just the kind of things that ordinary living human beings do" (Bostock, *Plato's Phaedo*, 28). Specifically, Bostock remarks that "when the non-philosopher dies, he [Plato] suggests that the soul is not after all *completely* separated from the body, but remains 'interspersed with a corporeal element' (81c4)" (ibid., 28).

Antithesis, Common Grace, and Plato's View of the Soul

how a concept functions within another thinker's system, no judgment can be made about whether that concept is antithetical to one's own system. For introductory purposes, Plato's view of the soul interfaces with his view of the Form world and his contribution to the chain of being.[23] In this context, the soul interfaces with his theory of epistemology—what is referred to as his recollection theory of knowledge, which, in turn, presupposes a cyclical movement of souls. Furthermore, the cyclical movement presupposes his particular construct of reincarnation.

In the *Phaedo*, Socrates faced the immanence of death. In fact, the dialogue presented the day of execution. After discussing suicide with his select group of friends, Socrates entered into a general discussion of his position with respect to death and the immortality of the soul.[24] After all, his friends found him quite amenable to the imminence of death. In their unfolding discussion, Socrates's companions realized that his comfort and peace with death emerged from his system of beliefs. But what are some of the key components that constitute those beliefs?

Socrates maintained that one of the chief aims of a philosopher is to practice for the occasion of death.[25] Death is not the end; rather, for Socrates, the practice for death is directed toward the reward that comes after death. Since Socrates was a philosopher, he had a unique platter of bountiful rewards awaiting him. He would enjoy the companionship of wise gods and good men. Also, in the afterlife he would relish an eschatological state of the good and the realization of greater blessings. In light of these characteristics of the afterlife, R. Hackforth contended correctly, that "at bottom Socrates' faith is in the moral order of the universe, which demands that a good life on earth should have some reward hereafter."[26] Indeed, for Plato, faith and knowledge (reason) are interlocked in Socrates's

---

23. In this study my focus is basically upon Plato's dialogue, the *Phaedo*; my purpose is not to be involved in a critical examination of the changes and progress of Plato's view of the soul throughout his entire corpus, especially found in such other dialogues as *Phaedrus, Republic, Gorgias, Meno, Timaeus,* and *Laws*. In light of the entire corpus, I am also aware that Socrates stated that the nature of the soul cannot be comprehended without an understanding of the nature of human beings (Plato, *Phaedrus*, 270c1–2). For the sake of brevity, Plato provided a microcosm of this construction in the *Phaedo* which is sufficient for our purpose.

24. Plato, *Phaedo*, 63e7–67c2.

25. Ibid., 64a4–6.

26. Hackforth, "Commentary," 42.

belief in life after death.[27] In fact, Plato underlines this point in a statement that Cebes, one of Socrates's friends, makes in the process of the discussion. Cebes states that to believe in the immortality of the soul entails a great amount of "faith and persuasive argument."[28] In fact, as faith and rational persuasive argumentation are intertwined, the dialogue evolves toward one of its central theses, that is, that the soul is immortal, and that the philosopher alone enjoys eternal existence in the Form world without embarking on another cyclical journey back into the empirical world which he just departed.

Socrates, as a philosopher, had strong courage, therefore, in the face of death. In order to construct a portrayal of Socrates's courage, Plato begins with the question of what constitutes death. The answer provided is that death is "the separation of the soul from the body."[29] In order to make his case for defining death in this manner, Socrates begins by noting the philosopher's distinctions between vices and virtues. Simply put, for him, characteristics associated with the body are not good, whereas characteristics associated with the soul are good. More specifically, the body is spoken of as the pleasures of food, drink, and sex, and it includes the desire for, as well as the wearing of, distinguished clothes, shoes, and bodily ornaments. The body is associated with the darker side of moral vices: wants, desires, fears, and various illusions (i.e., passions, will, and emotions). Additionally, the senses are associated with the body, and, thus, they are inferior in acquiring knowledge. In sum, in contrast to human virtue, the body is inherently "evil."[30]

On the other hand, the soul in its pure state is reason functioning without interference from the body. In order to attain this state of purity, the soul must approach the object with thought alone. In this realm of thinking, things exist in themselves, that is, the doctrine of Forms can exist in pure thought (e.g., Justice, Good, Beautiful, Size, Health, Strength). The soul is, therefore, the residence of truth, wisdom, and pure knowledge.

27. Plato does not place Socrates in a vacuum; the belief in the immortality of the soul has long been held in Greek thought. For the most part it is thought that Plato adopted the more recent Pythagorean version, which involved the moral purification of the soul as well as holding to that moral purification through the cyclical view of reincarnation.

28. Plato, *Phaedo*, 70b2.

29. Ibid., 64c4–5; cf. Plato, *Gorgias*, 524b. This definition of death—the separation of soul from the body—was common in Plato's era.

30. Plato, *Phaedo*, 66b6.

Antithesis, Common Grace, and Plato's View of the Soul

Herein, the task of the philosopher is set. Since the philosopher's task is defined by reality, good judgment, and understanding, Socrates points out to his friends that the philosopher alone is equipped for the task of freeing and separating the soul from the body. He is able to attain this objective because in his training he is taught to approach an object of knowledge with reason or thought alone. Being trained in wisdom and reason, he has the ability to free or release his mind from the senses.[31] In doing so, he is able to prevent diseases, contaminations, impediments, confusions, and illusions which the body brings to the soul.[32] Only the philosopher, by means of thought, has this type of access to the soul, the residence of pure Forms. The elite status of the philosopher is exposed: his superior use of reason, thought, intellect, and logic determines his standing as the highest individual on the hierarchical chain of being. Every other human being is in a state of degradation with respect to the philosopher. It is in light of this view of the inner harmony of the soul and the hindrances of the body that Socrates must defend that the soul exists after death.

Socrates's defense deals with more than just a dualistic construct of the body and the soul. Rather, the soul is integrally wrapped in various crucial components of Socrates's worldview as part of a coherent system of belief. So far we have already noticed some of these elements: the body-soul dualism, the superiority of the wise and intellectual soul, the position of the philosopher, and the definition of freedom. As we proceed, our interest is *not* to analyze the strengths and weaknesses of Socrates's arguments or their validity; instead, our concern is to grasp some key components of his arguments concerning the immortality of the soul. In this regard, we will focus on two arguments which are sufficient to illustrate the antithetical nature of his position in relation to the historic orthodox Christian position. These two are his cyclical and his recollection arguments.

Plato set up the cyclical argument in the context of a dialogue between the skeptic Cebes and Socrates. Cebes suggests the position taken by some in his day—that after death the soul no longer exists since it is "shattered [dissipated; disbanded] like breath or smoke."[33] In response, Socrates invokes the ancient theory about the recycling of souls. Socrates inquires of Cebes whether souls of men who have died continue to exist in the under-

---

31. Ibid., 67a1–6.

32. See ibid., 66a1–67b5.

33. Ibid., 70a5. Many scholars point to a similar imagery about the death of the soul in Homer's *Iliad* (Homer, *Homeri Ilias*, ψ:100–101).

world since in that case, the ancient theory states that those souls which arrive in the underworld are from here, and those souls which arrive back here are from there.[34] Herein is the cycle. In addition, this understanding is set up in the context of opposites.[35] Socrates states that opposites come from opposites; specifically, whenever we have a pair of opposites which are on a par with each other, they are generated from each other in a cycle of perpetual recurrence, for example, waking and sleeping, greater and smaller.[36] Life and death are also in the category of recurring opposites. In the construct of cyclical recurrence, Socrates maintains that each process in the cycle must be reversed by its opposite in order to exist. For example, the process of moving from waking to sleeping can only exist if there is a return from sleeping to waking. Likewise, the process of living to dying can only exist if there is a return from dying to living. This process must be cyclical rather than linear. If it were linear, then the soul would enter into a sleepless state, and, life would eventually cease. As we can see, however, life does not cease. For life to continue with respect to the soul, as the soul separates from the body in death, the soul must reenter a body for life. Simply put, it can be said that as the soul enters a body, it becomes incarnate in the body. For Socrates, *every reincarnation is an incarnation.* The cyclical argument of opposites affirms a doctrine of reincarnation as part of Plato's view of the immortality of the soul.

Socrates's recollection argument arises from a connection with his cyclical rotation argument.[37] For Socrates, the recollection argument is fused with epistemology. If learning is the recovery of knowledge possessed in a previous existence (recollection), the soul, the source of true knowledge, must have existed somewhere *before* it was incarnate in a human shape in order to possess understanding. In the flow of the dialogue, the discussion moves from Cebes to Simmias who enters the conversation not as a skeptic, but as one who wants to be reminded about the content of the recollection theory.[38] Socrates comes to his assistance with the example that when a person sees, hears, or perceives one thing, that person not only knows the

---

34. Plato, *Phaedo*, 70c7–8.

35. Scholars often point to Heraclitus's (535–475 BC) fragment 88 and his argument of opposites as background to Socrates's argument here (see Heraclitus, *Fragments*, 88).

36. Plato, *Phaedo*, 70d9.

37. Ibid., 72e3–7.

38. Calvin in an antithetical manner attacked Plato's view of recollection (see Calvin, *Institutes*, 2.2.14).

object being perceived but also thinks of another such object. For example, Socrates uses the imagery of a lyre. Seeing a lyre, it would be customary for a person also to imagine a boy playing a lyre. This image of the boy *playing* a lyre would be something recollected since at the moment the object that is seen is only the lyre in *isolation*.[39] In the recollection of an object, then, the object is perceived not only in isolation but also in relation to its function—the person perceives both the lyre and the tune from the lyre.

With this illustration before Simmias and his companions, Socrates turns to the crux of his argument; he speaks of the intersection of the doctrine of Forms and the common statements of knowledge. Herein, he employs another illustration: as two people talk about whether two sticks are equal, one sees them as equal, and the other does not see them as equal. Socrates points out that people can only speak of sticks being equal if they know what Equal is in the Form world. Consequently, Equal stands behind the senses as something different from the judgment by the senses of two things equal to each other. Equal in the Form world and equal things perceived in the sensual world are not the same.[40] Clearly, we have knowledge of equal in the sensual world, so Socrates argues that we had to have a prior knowledge of it. In other words, Socrates argues that a person must possess the knowledge of Equal before ever applying it to equal objects. Only by prior contact with the Form world would an individual know what equal is. The general principle is, therefore, that all human learning is acquired by means of recollection. We have this knowledge before birth; it is lost, and it is reestablished by the senses—recollected.[41] The conclusion of Socrates's argument is quite simple for our purposes: if the Forms exist before one's birth, then one's soul exists before one's birth. For Plato, through Socrates's argument, the existence of the Form world is a necessary part of the proof for the immortality of the soul.

Another critical component of Plato's cyclical recurrence is his view that the immortality of the soul is dependent upon an intimate connection with other biological creatures, such as insects, birds, and donkeys. In Plato's construction, a soul that is polluted by the impure elements of the body (e.g., eating, drinking, and sexual gratification) gravitates to a continual existence on earth.[42] Explicitly, in the cycle of reincarnation, inferior souls

---

39. Plato, *Phaedo*, 73c4–73d10.
40. See ibid., 74c4–9.
41. Ibid., 75e.
42. Ibid., 81b.

polluted by the human body depart from the body in death but hang around graveyards waiting for a biological creature to enter. Indeed, these souls pay the penalty for their life of vice; they must wander around "monuments and tombs," waiting to dwell in another living creature that corresponds to their moral conduct while dwelling in a human body in their prior life.[43] Obviously, in Plato's understanding, some animals and insects have souls. Meanwhile, as these souls dwell in such creatures, they wait for a human being to be born in order to reenter a human body. (Hence, the cycle of the soul functions in the following manner: the soul released through death lingers around graves → it enters a biological creature → it enters into another human body.) When the soul enters another human body, it enters at the same level of the vice it practiced when it departed its previous human body. For example, a person who was a glutton in a previous life returns as a glutton. However, the chain of being is not fixed, so the person returning to life can move up or down the chain of being:

Chain of Being

Philosopher: Form world: live like a swan

↑

Top: practiced popular & social virtue: those who lived in moderation & justice (without philosophy) = reincarnated as bees, wasps, ants

↑↓

Middle: injustice, tyranny, theft = reincarnated as wolves, hawks, kites

↑↓

Bottom: gluttony, violence, drunkenness = reincarnated as donkeys

For Plato, the goal is to move to the status of the philosopher where the cycle ceases. Only the philosopher lives forever in the afterlife, free from returning into the body—a state that Plato compares to that of another creature, a swan.

REFORMED ORTHODOXY RESPONSE

In view of Reformed orthodoxy's historic creeds and their understanding of the teaching of the soul in Scripture, Plato's view of the soul is a departure. Reformed orthodoxy would not agree that Scripture teaches the immortality of the soul as dependent upon the cyclical motion of the soul between the Form world and the empirical world (reincarnation). As well,

43. Ibid., 81d1.

Antithesis, Common Grace, and Plato's View of the Soul

Reformed orthodoxy would not concur that human knowledge is a recollection of knowledge from within the Form world, encountered as the soul makes contact with the Form world in its revolving cycle of perpetual motion in and out of bodies. Simply put, the interrelationship between the Form world and the immortal soul is not the Archimedean point on which the Bible predicates the immortality of the soul. For this reason, Plato's *holistic* construct of the immortality of the soul is *antithetical* to the *holistic* teaching of the immortality of the soul found in Holy Scripture.

The Bible teaches that male and female were created with an immortal soul (Gen 1:26-28; 2:7; 2:21-23). Reformed orthodoxy has clarified Scripture's teaching about the immortal soul. For example, the Vallérandus Poullain Confession made the following statement about God's image: "And therefore He made him [man] after His own image and likeness, giving him, to wit, a soul which is a spirit, as God Himself is, and also immortal, albeit it hath a beginning."[44] Pollanus's (1520–1557) last phrase is important; theologians have maintained that an essential attribute of God is that he is immortal. On the other hand, although an immortal soul is said to be an essential characteristic of human beings, it must be noted that this immortality is given by God. God's nature alone is immortal (1 Tim 6:16), whereas the human soul's immortality is derived from God's creative activity. In order to clearly distinguish between the Creator's immortality and the creature's immortality, Calvin states that "the term 'soul' [is] an immortal yet created essence"—it is characterized as "immortal spirit."[45] When viewing human beings as image of God, it is the spiritual soul that clearly distinguishes them from the brutes—the engraving of the divine and immortal essence which gives life to a human body (Ps 16:10; Matt 10:28; Luke 16:22-23; 2 Cor 5:6, 8; Heb 12:9; 1 Pet 1:9).

The human fall into sin and its penalty of death, to be sure, raises the issue now as to how this "immortal spirit" is to be viewed at the moment of death. As Reformed exegetes reflected upon this subject, a position emerged that maintained continuity with historic orthodoxy: at the moment of death, the soul immediately separates from the body and continues consciously to live either as a recipient of Christ's blessings or as an object of God's wrath (Eccl 12:7; Luke 16:23-24; 23:43; Acts 7:59; 2 Cor 5:1-8; Eph 4:10; Phil 1:23; Heb 12:23; 1 Pet 3:19; 4:6).[46] On the basis of such bibli-

---

44. J. Dennison, *Reformed Confessions*, 651.
45. Calvin, *Institutes*, 1.15.2.
46. This position on the state of the soul after death was definitely found in Calvin.

cal texts as those just listed, Calvin was convinced that the soul's immortal essence continues to survive in the intermediate state between the death of the body and the final resurrection of the body. Calvin is cautious, however, about reading too much into the intermediate state; he warns the church to remain within the domain of Scripture's teaching. For example, Calvin states, "Scripture goes no farther than to say that Christ is present with them [believers upon death], and receives them into paradise . . . that they may obtain consolation, while the souls of the reprobate suffer such torments as they deserve."[47] Indeed, Calvin maintains that the soul continues a conscious existence of life after death (Luke 16:14–41). In other words, the soul continues to live in the intermediate state between temporal death and the final resurrection of the body. The secondary standards of the Reformed tradition give testimony to this biblical truth. For example, chapter

---

Although it is not my focus, it is still worth noting that the Protestant Reformation did not have a united position on the state of the soul after death. In fact, Calvin scholars point out that his first major theological treatise was *Psychopannychia* which attacked the Anabaptist view that the soul is in a state of sleep between death and the last judgment (Calvin, *Psychopannychia*, 414–90). Calvin was alarmed with the Anabaptist position since he thought it was affecting the positive advance of the Reformation among the evangelicals in France. Regarding the historical circumstances and current debate on this dispute, one can begin with Quistorp, *Calvin's Doctrine of the Last Things*, 55–107; Balke, *Anabaptist Radicals*, 25–38; Calvin, *Treatises Against the Anabaptists and Against the Libertines*; and Williams, *Reformation*, 897–912. In terms of my own focus, I find it interesting that Williams falls into the trap of which I have given warning for those who do not employ the transcendental critique. Williams maintains that Calvin holds to a Platonic view of the soul (Ibid., 901; Williams does not stand alone on this viewpoint [see Babelotzky, *Platonischer Bilder und Gedankengänge in Calvins Lehre vom Menschen*]). Quistorp is not as careless as Williams in his assessment. Quistorp recognizes that Calvin noted respect for Plato and Aristotle's view of the soul while at the same time clearly maintaining that the scriptural teaching on the soul is antithetical to these philosophers (Quistorp, *Calvin's Doctrine of the Last Things*, 71–72; see Calvin, *Psychopannychia*, 420). With respect to our own subject matter, Calvin admits that the insights by Plato and Aristotle about the soul (common grace) surpass certain points by those who claim to be followers of Christ (Calvin, *Psychopannychia*, 420). Hence, even within the antithesis-common grace paradigm it can be maintained that certain particular insights by non-Christians can surpass the insights by Christians but only as those insights occur within the true parameters of the teaching of biblical revelation. On this crucial point it may be well to have Calvin's statement before us: "Plato, in some passages, talks nobly of the faculties of the soul; and Aristotle, in discoursing of it, has surpassed all in acuteness. But what the soul is, and whence it is, it is vain to ask at them, or indeed at the whole body of Sages, though they certainly thought more purely and wisely on the subject than some amongst ourselves, who boast that they are the disciples of Christ" (Calvin, *Psychopannychia*, 420).

47. Calvin, *Institutes*, 3.25.6.

Antithesis, Common Grace, and Plato's View of the Soul

32, section 1 of the WCF states, "The bodies of men, after death, return to dust, and see corruption: but the souls, which neither die nor sleep, having an immortal subsistence, immediately return to God who gave them."[48]

Furthermore, theologians in the Reformed tradition have readily maintained that the human body must be viewed as an integrated whole with the soul. Bavinck summarizes the position: "And precisely because the body, being the organ of the soul, belongs to the essence of man and to the image of God, it originally also participated in immortality."[49] Bavinck's position that the image of God includes the immortality of the body and the soul in the original state stimulates questions. In order to remain within our own context, however, those questions will remain mute. Rather, we note merely that Bavinck's position accents the antithetical distinction between the biblical view of immortality and Plato's view of immortality. After all, Bavinck acknowledges that Christians had been too accepting of Platonic nuances about the immortality of the soul.[50] Under the direction of biblical revelation and the confessional standards, Bavinck demonstrates the teaching of Scripture to be in strict contrast to Plato, that is, for Bavinck the body is not inherently mortal and evil.[51] Specifically, as disclosed in NT revelation, the immortality of the soul is never to be separated from the

---

48. See the Heidelberg Catechism Q&A 57; also consult the following secondary standards in J. Dennison, *Reformed Confessions*: "William Farel's Summary (1529)" (ibid., 105); "Waldensian Confession of Mérindol (1543)" (ibid., 456); "Large Emden Catechism (1551)," "Q&R, 182" (ibid., 627); "Vallérandus Poullain (1551), Death" (ibid., 651); "The Forgiveness of sins; The Resurrection of the body, And the life everlasting" (ibid., 657–658); and the "Rhaetian Confession (1552)" (ibid., 669).

49. Bavinck, *Reformed Dogmatics*, 2:560. In terms of Reformed orthodoxy, Bavinck's position is not original with him, for example, it is definitely implied in Francis Turretin's discussion on Adam and Eve's original "state of innocence" (Turretin, *Elenctic Theology*, 1:569). G. C. Berkouwer began his discussion about the immortality of the soul with Bavinck (see Berkouwer, *Man*, 234–78).

50. Bavinck, *Reformed Dogmatics*, 4:591. Warfield expressed the same concern about those in the church who gave greater affinity to Plato than Scripture on the immortality of the soul and the state of the body (see Warfield, "Immortality," 346–7).

51. See Bavinck, *Reformed Dogmatics*, 2:554–62, 4:591–2. On this point, Bavinck is clearly in agreement with Augustine; it is worth noting that Augustine has provided one of the strongest criticisms of Plato's view of the soul and the body in the early church (see Augustine, *The City of God*, 4:280–3). Here, in reference to Plato and the Platonists, Augustine wrote: "For when anyone approves the substance of the soul as the highest good and denounces the substance of the flesh as an evil, surely he is carnal both in his pursuit of the soul and in his avoidance of the flesh inasmuch as it is through human vanity and not divine truth that he holds this view" (ibid). See also Bavinck's further insights in Bavinck, *Reformed Dogmatics*, 4:600.

resurrection of the body as patterned in the resurrection of Christ's body. In view of the fall into sin, Bavinck forcefully affirms his point regarding the body and soul "violently torn from the soul by sin, it [body] will be reunited with it [soul] in the resurrection of the dead."[52] Plato's conception of immortality, of course, incorporates no such relationship between the body and the soul.

As we are confronted with Bavinck's position, we could become suspicious as to whether he affirms a traditional understanding of the intermediate state. We even note that he is more reticent to speculate about that condition of existence than Calvin was. In fact, Bavinck admits that, in his view, the Bible is mostly mysterious and silent about the intermediate state. Even so, Bavinck affirms that Scripture teaches that the soul continues to exist as an immortal subsistence after physical death (Luke 16:14–41).[53] Bavinck wishes to make clear that though the living eternal soul continues to exist after physical death, the intermediate state is not, however, the final state. In this "interim period," Christ "is not content with the redemption of the soul, but effects also the redemption of the body."[54] What was not completed for Adam and Eve in the garden will be completed in the final consummation. Hence, for Bavinck, the final condition of the intermediate state is the full-orbed projection of Adam and Eve's destiny as described in Scripture and reflected in the Heidelberg Catechism: "That I, with body and soul, both in life and death, am not my own, but belong unto my faithful Savior Jesus Christ" (Q&A 1; cf. Q&A 26, 37, 57–58, 125; Rom 12:1–2; 1 Cor 6:12–20; 1 Thess 5:23). What belongs to believers in Christ's redemp-

---

52. Bavinck, *Reformed Dogmatics*, 2:559. See also the Heidelberg Catechism Q&A 37 and 11. I mention here 37 prior to 11 to emphasize the believer's eternal state first and those under eternal judgment second (see also Q&A 57–59).

53. See Bavinck, *Reformed Dogmatics*, 4:600; and Bavinck, *Our Reasonable Faith*, 557–8. Hodge does not approach the intermediate state with the same caution as Calvin and Bavinck; he places before his reader clear parameters about what the Scriptures teach on this doctrine (see Hodge, *Systematic Theology*, 3:724–30). Likewise, see Berkhof, *Systematic Theology*, 674–6, 679–94; and Francis Turretin, *Elenctic Theology*, 3:571–4. Although a strong antithesis can find testimony in the Reformed tradition distinguishing between the biblical notion of immortality of the soul and the Platonic view of immortality of the soul, this contrast does not mean that Christianity must surrender the term "immortality" because of some scholars' contention that the term must be viewed as Greek. Even though Oscar Cullmann does not stand in the Reformed tradition, he has challenged scholars with his assessment that the term "immortality" is Greek, whereas the Christian idea of immortality is *resurrection* (see Cullmann, "Unsterblichkeit der Steele und Auferstehung der Toten").

54. Bavinck, *Our Reasonable Faith*, 558.

tion is grounded in one's state of existence prior to the fall, and what was designed in the pre-fall state was predicated upon the final eschatological existence in Christ's total redemption for all believers of Christ's bride.

Scholars who make it their practice to explore the Christian landscape of higher education will find it difficult to prove that the deterioration of a once outstanding orthodox institution has been the result of that body's stressing the antithesis between Christian thought and non-Christian thought too much. Rather, I would suggest that the secularization of any such institution occurs because the epistemological, metaphysical, ontological, and ethical truth of the integrative and progressive infallible revelation of the triune God of the Bible has been compromised under what Reformed thought refers to as common grace. In reality, as I have attempted to make clear, a particular concept can only be a common grace insight if it agrees with the truth of the inner fabric of progressive biblical revelation. Unfortunately, too many Christian academicians, for the sake of their own conceptual tolerance toward adopting non-Christian thought, have justified their activity under an incorrect representation of the rubric of common grace. Often this misrepresentation follows a popular pattern. Christian academicians adopt into their discipline principles from non-Christian thought, and, while doing so, they synthesize those principles of choice into the distinct methodological structure of their discipline. At this point, such an academic journey is taken with minimal reflection upon a biblically informed, Christ-centered epistemological approach to their discipline. To be sure, perhaps the Christian academician will note this neglect at some point and will act. In consequence, the academic will take the step of baptizing the secular principles and methodology with abstract and isolated proof-texts from Scripture.

Possibly this scenario is too simplistic, but, in my judgment, the truth is in its simplicity. In my estimation, this picture illustrates a dominant trait of the descent of any institution from a Christian education grounded in historic orthodoxy. With abstract biblical proof-texts in hand, without any true integration of their discipline with progressive biblical revelation, such Christian academicians simply justify a methodology that uses selected precepts of rationalism, empiricism, realism, idealism, romanticism, naturalism, materialism, existentialism, structuralism, or post-structuralism without any significant critique of the Archimedean premises of the methodology of their choice. Out of this state of affairs, in combination with the current obsession that Christian higher education must be socially and culturally relevant, it is not surprising that the dominant controlling ethos of Christian higher institutional life has become a critical-social hermeneutic, that is, a method of interpreting the fallen creation by means of a generic metanarrative of impact, renewal, and transformation of social and cultural realms and norms for the sake of a socio-academic construct of Christ's kingdom. After all, it is thought, since the evolving movement of history and culture is so *distant* from the history and culture portrayed in the biblical narrative or the ecclesiastical creeds, the most that can be employed from the Bible and the creeds for the current age is a set of abstract principles which direct and justify a social/cultural agenda for the academic enterprise.

The deterioration of the historic roots of Christian orthodoxy upon the campuses of Christian learning is straightforward. Christian academicians isolate individual concepts and methods of choice from non-Christian thinkers and adopt them into their own Christian worldview.[55] In contrast, the directive that needs to be followed is that every concept and method presented by a non-Christian thinker must be subjected to a holistic critical analysis within the structure of the thinker's own system. As concepts and methods are scrutinized and subsequently placed alongside a holistic philosophical understanding of the content of the revelation of God's Word, then the non-Christian system under investigation is exposed for what it is—an antithetical system at odds with the truth of God's Word. As demonstrated in our Platonic illustration, only after doing this analysis is the Christian academic in the position to truly evaluate the common grace concepts presented by the non-Christian. Recognizing the antithesis running through any common grace insight, the Christian academic can approach the particular concept grasped by the non-Christian and correctly comprehend and commend it within the scope of the revelation of God's truth. In our presentation of Plato's view of the immortality of the soul, we acknowledged that although Plato understood the soul as immortal (a

---

55. Obviously not all Christian academicians arise in a context where they are interacting mainly with non-Christian academics. Some arise within the halls of Christian academia. Herein, the young Christian mind must be made aware that the Christian mentors within those halls may be the product of the scenario that I am outlining here. Christian mentors may already be tainted by non-Christian concepts and methods which have come to expression in the mentor's own Christian perspective of a particular discipline. Hence, in my judgment, all Christian educators, in whatever stage of life they find themselves, must be willing to apply constantly the transcendental critique to their own thought in order to place themselves in service and subordination to the sovereign wisdom of Christ.

Antithesis, Common Grace, and Plato's View of the Soul

common grace insight) this conception placed within the holistic structure of his thought emerges as one antithetical to the biblical position of the soul's immortality.[56] Indeed, *we cannot pursue the truth unless we begin with the truth.*[57]

This essay is intended to encourage those who may be marginalized in academia because of their commitment to the historic roots of the theological and ecclesiastical identity of the institution in which they serve. I have attempted to suggest a way to conduct rigorous academic teaching and scholarship in a manner that will not surrender commitment to God's Word and the historic roots of one's tradition. Concerning my own commitment to the Reformed tradition, I have found enlightening the directive of Van Til, which is submissive to God's Word and the exposition of that Word as summarized in the ecumenical creeds and the Reformed secondary standards. Inside the framework of this paradigm, I have found myself, within the frailty of a fallen mind, sufficiently equipped to engage any system of secular thought. In fact, when a biblical transcendental analysis is employed with respect to the encyclopedia of thought, the contemporary socio-cultural world will never have the endowment to set the agenda of Christian academia. Rather, the full-orbed message of the gospel always sets the agenda for interacting with culture—entreating conformity and service to Christ through repentance and faith. Such language may seem archaic and foreign to the pluralism embodied within the present halls of the Christian academy. Nevertheless, some within those corridors wish to preserve the historic roots of the Christian religion as grounded in the self-attesting Christ of Scripture. If you count yourself among these, then allow your voice to be heard from your seat in the academy—not from

---

56. The approach here is candidly and forcefully summarized by Calvin (Calvin, *Institutes*, 2.2.18). Specifically, allow me to remind the reader that Calvin's analysis is found in footnote 46.

57. What is mysteriously missing as one reads Anthony Diekema's (Emeritus President of Calvin College) model of the "Socratic Covenant" is the a priori objective truth as found in Holy Scripture. The inscripturated Word is the truth of God *already* given to a fallen world. Specifically, the Bible is the only infallible rule of faith and obedience (see the Westminster Shorter Catechism Q&A 3). Rather than guarding and defending the truth which God has already established in his creation, Diekema's nine points of the "Socratic Covenant" emphasize the guardianship of academic freedom as being the academic's *pursuit* of the truth (see Diekema, *Christian Scholarship*, 101–3). Herein, the freedom to pursue the truth is not conditional upon the truth already established in God's Word; in other words, the freedom to pursue the truth is not grounded upon a corresponding and coherent view of epistemology which maintains that all pursuit after the truth must be found directly or indirectly in conformity with biblical revelation.

those seats where even Michel Foucault (1926–1984) would have to endure nausea as the powerful elites and masses drown you out, but, in the imagery of Christ, from your designated chair of humility (cf. Luke 11:43; 20:46; Matt 16:24–25; 1 Pet 2:21–25). Just perhaps, those who have ears might hear and, thus, Christian education committed to historic orthodoxy will survive as a unique beacon rather than as just another species of the broad secular educational genus. Why should it not be that every institution within Christian academia would participate in the posture of the Queen of Sheba before the encyclopedic wisdom of Solomon, the pre-figure and type of the encyclopedic wisdom of Christ (see 1 Kgs 10:4–5; 2 Chr 9:3–4). Confronted with the picture of the eschatological glory of Christ's wisdom in the temporal life of Solomon, the spirit of Sheba fully dissipated and was immersed solely and absolutely in the eternal wisdom of the Christ of Scripture.

5

Van Til and Classical Christian Education

> The "threat of peace" to Christian thinkers comes more persistently from Platonic Aristotelian sources than from any other.
>
> —Cornelius Van Til, "Plato"

As a professional educator for over thirty years at the secondary, collegiate, and graduate levels, I have paid close attention to day school educational models implemented by families and congregations in the OPC. Through these years I have experienced great joy meeting parents who desire a Christian education for their covenant children, families who have taken seriously the application of the biblical injunction to raise children in the "discipline and admonition of the Lord" (Eph 6:4 my translation; cf. Prov 3:7). In most cases, the parents in these homes have become convicted that our triune God insists on the education of his covenant children taking place in the context of his covenantal Lordship. I have witnessed such parents turning to three dominant alternatives for the education of their children: (1) a Christian day school that follows closely the templates of a liberal arts curriculum; (2) a Christian home school curriculum that employs an eclectic approach to materials, tailoring them to the particular interests of the parents for their children; and (3) a *classical* Christian day school or home school curriculum that incorporates the *trivium* (grammar, rhetoric, dialectic), *quadrivium* (arithmetic, geometry, music, astronomy), and modern liberal arts into the child's education.[1] I wish to analyze this third alternative, one that has become increasing popular among OPC parents.

Obviously, different households find this modern edition of classical Christian education attractive for various reasons. Some point to the failure of the state to educate in the public schools, while others will point to the lack of quality education even among Christian day schools. Still others, although they acknowledge the lack of quality education in both public and Christian settings, focus their attention more on the troubling modern secular influences found within many local Christian day schools. Hence, classical Christian education emerges as a striking alternative. Educators and parents are attracted to the depth, breadth, and rigor of the classical Christian model, characteristics truly missing in the typical educational models of our day. Some parents discover that they are unable to afford the costs of a classical Christian day school while others discover that such a day school is unavailable in their community and, thus, they turn to a classical Christian home education. In these particular homes, the father and/or mother may only trust a guarded range of materials as appropriate. In terms of their covenantal responsibility, they may be thinking as follows: what the parents place before the child will be exhibited in the life of their child.

In addition to the feature of avoiding ineffective schools or modern secular influences, educators and parents are often attracted especially by the curriculum of the classical Christian model. Some have the opinion that the curriculum immediately elevates the student into an elite circle with respect to the quality and quantity of information presented, comprehended, and processed. For example, depending upon the approach taken, a student in this educational model may acquire a fairly comprehensive knowledge of Greek and Roman mythology, the fundamental tenets of Aristotelian logic, the basic principles of persuasive argumentation and communication from classical rhetoric, the qualities of social and political virtue embodied in the pursuit of the good and of happiness, and perhaps, a reading understanding

---

1. The *trivium* is often traced back to the sophists and Isocrates (436–338 BC), whereas the structure and interplay of the educational disciplines known as the *quadrivium* are often traced back to the sophist, Hippias of Elis (later fifth century BC), although the latter term is said to have been coined by Boethius (476–524 AD).

of Latin and/or Greek. To be sure, as a college professor, I can say that a student educated in such a way has a broader and deeper wealth of knowledge in the liberal arts than most students who enter higher education. However, this background does not result necessarily in a discerning Christian educated student. In fact, the classical Christian model of educating our covenant youth is not inherently Christian at its foundation and core. Nevertheless, often when I make this point to parents who use the classical Christian model, I sense their immediate shock and tension. They wonder why anyone would wish to question this pursuit of knowledge grounded as it is in the classical age—that world which served as the backdrop for our Savior's entrance into history and set the established protocol for the Apostle Paul's education. After all, did not that ancient pristine world hold that truth and certainty of facts actually could be attained? Was not this the purer time, prior to the dawn of modernity, when atheistic Darwinian evolution corrupted the interpretation of science and creation, when classical political democratic ideas began to be held captive by socialist and Marxist ideologies, when the moral autonomy and relativity of the individual was seen to transcend moral responsibility to others? Moreover, is not the classical model even further removed from the evolution of modernity into postmodernity, in which multiculturalism, political correctness, deconstruction, and absolute relativity rule the landscape? Indeed, many believe the framework defined by the classical era and its revival from the medieval period through the Renaissance, Reformation, and into the nineteenth century provides a safe haven for parents and their covenant children, a place untainted by modern secularism and humanism and, yet, offering a quality encyclopedic education. This understanding, however, must not be assumed without proof. Is it true that classical Christian education escapes secularism and humanism? In order to address this question adequately, the current generation of OPC parental educators would do well to reflect seriously on the work of Van Til about education.

VAN TIL'S VIEW OF ANTIQUITY

Although the OPC rightly cautions its members about raising men on pedestals, OPC history also acknowledges that God has used certain individuals to shape the identity of orthodoxy as found in our denomination. Specifically, Van Til's apologetic method emerged over the years as the dominant apologetic motif within the denomination.[2] What, then, is at the core of Van Til's apologetic? Simply put, Van Til maintained that there can be no compromise with the self-attesting Christ of Scripture as mapped out in biblical revelation and summarized in the ecumenical creeds of the early church and the Reformed confessions. Given that foundation, how did Van Til assess the perspectives of Greek and Roman antiquity in light of this uncompromising principle? *He viewed them as our enemy and not as our friend.*[3]

This harsh pronouncement might lead evangelists for classical Christian education to react in the following manner: "How could anyone object to the quality of classical Christian education; it takes the best of two worlds—the Greek/Roman world and the biblical world—as an integrative and synthetic environment in order to provide the most comprehensive and well-rounded education for our children." Undoubtedly, such Christian educators are not naïve about the secular and pagan worldviews of the Greeks and Romans; their ire is raised, however, at the allegation that their educational design is as grounded in pagan synthesis as that of those Christian educators who synthesize post-Enlightenment models with Christian thought.[4] Nevertheless, like most Christian education today which baptizes post-Enlightenment models of their disciplines with biblical concepts and ideas from the biblical text, Christian classical educators baptize Greek and Roman models such as grammar, rhetoric, logic, mathematics, political theory (natural law), and education with biblical material in order to construct their educational world.

---

2. The path for Van Til's apologetic to become an identifying dominant trait in the OPC was not an easy one. He had his critics as the new church was formed, but perhaps the defining moment for Van Til's apologetic came within the OPC when his position triumphed in the context of the "Clark Case" during the 1940s. See Muether, *Van Til*, 80–88, 96–114, 162–75.

3. In order to drive home Van Til's position, it may be helpful to provide a serious concrete example. Van Til wrote, "Platonism itself, and not merely the excrescences that have grown out of it, is an enemy of Christianity. Its [Platonism's] chief service in preparing the world for the coming of Christ was, we firmly believe, a negative one" (Van Til, "Plato," 44).

4. At this point, some readers may claim kinship with Douglas Wilson's view of "antithetical classicism" as a thorough and true classical Christian education model and, therefore, tune out Van Til's concern about a classical synthesis with Christianity. Although Wilson claims to be committed to Van Til's apologetic, I do not see a clear working out of that method with respect to his understanding of classicism. I will expand on this point later in footnote 35.

Van Til and Classical Christian Education

How can we understand Van Til's antagonism toward classical thought? We can begin by noting some key elements in his philosophy of education. One of those emerged when Van Til found himself a principle player in a movement during the late 1930s and into the 1940s to transform Calvin College into a Christian university. Although this renovation never materialized, Van Til's main concern during the conception of the project was identifying clearly *the method* of understanding, interpreting, and teaching the academic disciplines. Van Til voiced his apprehension in an article, "A Calvin University," which appeared on November 9, 1939, in the CRC publication, *The Banner*. In that article Van Til explains that even if the finances are available to make the transition to a university and even if the entire faculty confesses serious commitment to the Reformed faith, these measures were not sufficient to begin a Christian university. Although it goes without saying that these two measures would be necessary, Van Til asserts that a far more important step must be taken before such a university could become a reality: the academicians must endorse a biblical "method" as summarized in the Reformed confessions in order to engage "current scientific methodology."

Van Til's analysis of the current scientific landscape was insightful and most penetrating, yet, his scrutiny of the utility of modern scientific method earned criticism among many Reformed academics. Van Til writes, "In my humble judgment the current scientific method is based upon the assumption of the truth of a non-Christian conception of reality and can in consequence never conclude that Christianity is true unless it is prepared to deny its own principles."[5] In this he presented Christian educators with a severe challenge. He was maintaining that if one begins with the assumption that the facts (reality) stand on their own—that the facts are "neutral" and "objective" to the observer—then, on the basis of such a presupposition, one can never conclude that Christianity is true. Why? Because *there can never be a separation of facts and the interpretation of those facts*. If the facts are neutral and objective entities, then the interpretation of those facts also stands in the realm of neutrality. Hence, when the current scientist maintains that one can come to know the facts projected upon the mind like a blank piece of white paper without any prejudice, the scientist has already removed the God of the Bible from the picture of reality; thus, an integration of the facts of reality with an understanding and interpretation of the God of the Bible is impossible. In this construct, Van Til specifies

5. Van Til, "A Calvin University," 1040.

correctly the biblical view of the human person in God's image—human beings are incapable of observing facts without interpreting those facts. In light of the fall into sin, one either complies with God's interpretation of the facts or complies with Satan's interpretation of the facts. This antithetical approach to knowledge and interpretation was exactly the dilemma that confronted Adam and Eve in the garden. Upon Satan's suggestion, Eve approached the forbidden fruit as a neutral category; she determined that she could place the fact or meaning of the fruit within the framework of neutrality without undermining the integrity of God's Word—replicating the exact approach Satan had used. Satan had posited that Eve could easily look upon the fruit as an objective fact, concluding that nothing with respect to looking at that fruit demanded death. Then, because she accepted Satan's interpretation, and rejected God's interpretation, Eve failed to reach an eschatological glorious end. Because of her disobedience, she received God's judgment of death.

Van Til's writing in the late 1930s regarding the formation of a Christian university pertained specifically to modern scientific method, but, clearly, his own particular method of analysis transcends the modern era. Given that the God whom we worship is the same yesterday, today, and forever, the method of critiquing the products of human thought is the same in every era. Van Til always approached human culture in the same manner—he advanced the thesis that culture is shaped by the simple *antithesis* defined by God himself in Genesis 3:15; that is to say, the history of human culture is the battle between the seed of the woman (promise/grace/Christ) and seed of the Serpent (judgment/wrath/Satan).[6] Van Til was emphatic that any effort to understand and dissect human thought must begin with a philosophy of history that has at its core this antithetical conflict—the kingdom of God versus the kingdom of Satan. There is no middle or neutral ground; there is absolutely no compromise of the truth revealed throughout the full course of biblical revelation as summarized in the Reformed confessions. Hence, only two trees growing side by side can be observed as God unfolds his providence from the fall into sin until Christ's second coming—the tree of unbelief and the tree of belief. Indeed,

---

6. Van Til does speak of the unity of human culture. He does so, however, not as a monistic construct, but as God's one unified sovereign providential plan with respect to the history of human culture. As the fall into sin has revealed itself in that plan, two absolute antithetical *principles* have emerged that control the inner life of humanity: those "who serve and worship the creature, and there are those who serve and worship the Creator" (Van Til, *Dilemma*, 35–36).

Van Til and Classical Christian Education

each tree has its own root (one grounded in a lie and the other grounded in the truth), but each will also send out various branches and offshoots, that is, diverse systems of unbelief and belief that come forth from each particular root.[7] For our purposes, the same tree that brought us the modern scientific method of Van Til's concern in 1939 also brought us the world of unbelief in classical antiquity. In fact, when analyzing a particular subject, Van Til often would go back to the Greeks in order to uncover the roots of the unbiblical perversion of that subject, and then trace the thread of that thought forward into its manifestations in modern thought. He commonly began such an analysis with Parmenides/Plato/Aristotle as the main stem, the villains of antiquity, and then advanced to Kant as the central villain of the various branches of modern thought.[8]

What are some of the crucial problems that Van Til delineated in the classical world's understanding of knowledge and reality? In order to address this question it is important to note a principle point of Van Til's view of knowledge. He states, "It is God's interpretation that determines the nature of all created being. Consequently if man's interpretation of any created being is to be a true interpretation its truth lies primarily in its analogical correspondence with God's interpretation."[9] For example, a human being's interpretation of a tree (being) is true only as that interpretation corresponds (analogically) to God's (Being) interpretation of the tree. God

---

7. Van Til provides an excellent summary of his view on the antithesis in an address given for the National Union of Christian Schools Convention in August 1932. The address appears in print—in my view a must read for every Reformed Christian educator. See Van Til, "Antitheses."

8. I would encourage and challenge every Christian educator to read Van Til's analysis of this point. He traces what he called, "the Platonic-Kantian principle" in a brief and succinct manner in his 1930 address to the National Union of Christian Schools Convention in Holland, Michigan (Van Til, "The Education of Man," 44–52).

9. Van Til, "Plato," 40. Hear Van Til's description of analogical knowledge: "The system that Christians seek to obtain may, by contrast, be said to be *analogical. By this is meant that God is the original and that man is the derivative. God has absolute self-contained system within himself.* What comes to pass in history happens in accord with that system or plan by which he orders the universe. *But man, as God's creature, cannot have a replica of that system of God.* He must, to be sure, think God's thoughts after him; but this means that he must, in seeking to form his own system, constantly be subject to the authority of God's system *to the extent* that this is revealed to him. For this reason, all of man's interpretations in any field are subject to the Scriptures given him. Scripture itself informs us that, at the beginning of history, before man had sinned, he was subject to the direct revelation of God in all the interpretations that he would make of his environment" (Van Til, *Theory of Knowledge*, 16).

alone, the Being who is the Author and Creator of facts such as a tree (being), already knows exhaustively the interpretation of the tree. On the other hand, according to Van Til, human beings are not on the same level as God in knowledge and interpretation—human beings do not possess exhaustive and comprehensive knowledge and interpretation of reality as God does. Simply put, "God's thought alone is original and absolute, while human thought is derivative and finite."[10] Hence, the human "personality must believe that complete comprehensive interpretation exists in absolute personality [God] and that this comprehensive interpretation of God furnishes the only basis for man's interpretation as far as that interpretation goes."[11] Alternatively, to put it more strongly, "I cannot in any genuine sense be a Christian unless I believe in a God who alone interprets to me."[12] For this reason, Van Til maintained that if one does not begin with the presupposition that in God's Being the interpretation of all created things is identical to God's knowledge of beings than one is destined to end up in serious trouble regarding one's knowledge and interpretation of God and created beings. In the post-fall era, Van Til notes that this problem clearly has emerged: "Ever after the entrance of sin into the world man has assumed that there is no God in whom being and interpretation of being are identical."[13] As a result, corrupt sinful hearts are compelled to reject the knowledge and interpretation of reality in correspondence with God's knowledge and interpretation of those objects. The Greeks provide significant examples of this fraudulent activity. With this judgment in mind, let us explore some salient points in Van Til's analysis of the Greek rejection of a biblical view of analogical knowledge and interpretation grounded in God's Being.

First, since the Greeks rejected the God of the Bible, they approached the objects of the universe with an independent and individual mind. According to Van Til, the Greeks thought that it was reasonable to ask the question, What is the universe? (What are the facts?) before they asked, Where does the universe come from? (Where did the facts come from?).[14]

10. Van Til, "The Education of Man," 43.

11. Ibid.

12. Ibid., 55. In another place Van Til clearly puts his case before us: "God knows or interprets the facts before they are facts. *It is God's plan, God's comprehensive interpretation of the facts that makes the facts what they are*" (Van Til, *Christian Apologetics*, 27). Later in the same source, he succinctly states: "It is this plan of God that makes all created facts to be what they are" (ibid., 33).

13. Van Til, "Plato," 40.

14. Ibid., 40–41.

Van Til and Classical Christian Education

Van Til pleads with us to examine carefully this paradigm which has had such a profound influence on Western thought's approach to created reality, including methods employed by academic disciplines. For Van Til, the serious flaw in this paradigm emerges when applying it to God's person. If God himself followed the prescription that the Greeks did, then God could deny his own being in order to gain knowledge and interpretation of the facts; that is to say, denying his own existence, God could employ the empirical method in order to discover the true meaning of facts and their origin. For Van Til, such a procedure is ridiculous and impossible, for God, the Creator of the facts, is the integrally linked and inseparable interpreter of the facts as well. In examining the paradigm in relation to God's being, Van Til shows the absurdity of the empirical method of research, the method which has characterized scientific research from the Greeks into our present era.[15] Clearly, to remove God at any point (especially the starting point) or in any way from the activity of scientific research is to forfeit honest knowledge and interpretation of the data of phenomenon.

Despite Van Til's profound insight, however, almost all Christian educators approach the various academic disciplines by looking empirically at the facts and then trying to understand their unity as well as their origin. Yes, the Christian educator may be truly conscious that the God of the Bible exists, but, under the pious code of natural revelation, such an educator will declare it imperative to begin studying on the same footing as the natural man (in this case, the Greeks)—viewing the natural world as a neutral environment on which we should have a common agreement, then using the faculty of human reason as we discuss and argue the origin of our natural environment. In Van Til's judgment, the natural theology found in Roman Catholicism, Arminianism, and less-than-consistent Calvinism arose upon the foundation of this pagan starting point.[16]

---

15. Ibid., 40.

16. The dominant players associated with Van Til's criticism and analysis of natural theology are Thomas Aquinas (Roman Catholicism), Bishop Joseph Butler (Arminianism), and the so-called "Old Princeton School" of Archibald Alexander, Warfield, and the Hodges (less-than-consistent Calvinism). Van Til's criticism of each of these players is based primarily upon their failure to apply the biblical doctrine of sin (total depravity) consistently to the faculty of human reason and its knowledge and interpretation of the creation. Sadly, many committed to classical Christian education know more about Dorothy L. Sayers's views on the subject of education than Van Til's views on the subject. Van Til would consider Sayers not Reformed, but in the line of Aquinas. This observation should become obvious in a comparison of Van Til's view of analogy with the position formulated by Sayers. On the topic of analogy, Sayers builds upon Aquinas's classical

In his analysis of the Greek rejection of a biblical view of knowledge and interpretation, Van Til directs us, secondly, to the problem of abstraction in Greek thought. Again, when the principle of *concrete* analogical knowledge in the person of the God of the Bible is not known and given assent, then the relationship between the human subject and the object is bound toward *abstraction*. Specifically, many Greek intellectuals came to hold that the human subject looked at brute facts within the creation as diverse and *particular* objects, and therefore, a *universal* object was needed to explain the *particulars*. Even these Greeks recognized that the diverse objects in the creation necessitated a single object of origin and explanation. Van Til refers to this in his own writings as the "one and the many problem" which has continued to plague Western thought: what is the *one universal* thing that explains the *many particular* things in our natural environment? Observing the various attempts of thinkers in the non-Christian world (including the Greeks) to provide solutions to this problem, he notes that none have brought final resolution. By contrast, Van Til keeps reminding us that the "one and the many problem" has its resolution only in the triune God of the Bible, that is, the three persons (many) in one God (one) whose self-contained and self-sufficient Being (one) has exhaustive knowledge and interpretation of all things (many).

What answers did the Greek intellectuals offer? Among the pre-Socratics there arose Thales's position, that all is water, or Heraclitus's position, that all is fire. If water and fire were universal elements that existed in all things (particulars), then all the particulars in the universe could be explained respectively by these two universal elements. Van Til notes correctly that with the God of Scripture out of the picture, an *impersonal* universal entity or law must explain the relationship between the universal and particular. Since water and fire do not possess any personality, the Greek is left with an impersonal explanation of the universe—a further abstraction. According to Van Til, this elucidation is what must occur when God's concrete Being is not acknowledged as the ground for knowledge and interpretation of beings in the universe—human beings live and interpret their existence from the perspective of an impersonal universe. Certainly, although today's scientific explanations of the natural environment have advanced beyond the thought of antiquity, the underpinnings

---

foundation and, then, she places analogy from that foundation into the context of human language as metaphor and human experience. She is beginning with human experience and not God (see Sayers, "Image of God").

Van Til and Classical Christian Education

of an impersonal universe are still present with us. As Van Til wrote: "The method of abstraction as employed by the Greeks, and as employed by the 'scientific method' today, is the only method that a sinner, who has declared his independence from God, could follow in his thinking."[17] Hence, looking back, the Greeks are not our educational hope for reviving the integrity of the method of science, rather they are our enemy.

Though many may concede this point, some might wonder whether Van Til goes too far when suggesting the failure of abstraction in Greek thought. Could it be that he overlooks the positive contribution of the moderate realism found in the evolution of thought from the era of Homer to the latter era of Plato/Aristotle? Obviously, in this evolution many of the elements of Greek mythology are discarded in favor of a more common-sense view of reality. Specifically, some argue that Christians are indebted to Plato and Aristotle for formulating a world of common sense more to the Christian's liking. Once again, however, Van Til is unimpressed. Van Til refuses to bow to any system of thought that places the "common" in the world of sense experience outside the domain of the sovereign plan of God, that is, the unfolding providence of God in history.[18] The common world of experience can only be truly understood and interpreted within the fabric of the historical revelation of the God of the Bible.[19] Plato and Aristotle presented their understanding of realism independent of Scripture's God. Their perspective declared that the God of Abraham, Isaac, and Jacob is not necessary to understand the universe. Hence, a third salient point emerges in Van Til's rejection of Greek thought: he notes that for both of these towers of Greek thought, the particulars and universals were set within the context of *form-matter*. In their construct, anything that existed in the empirical world had its essence (what made it what it was) in the realm of Forms. For Plato, the realm of the Forms (the essence of things that appear to us in this world) was in a transcendent world beyond empirical observation. In other words, anything that exists in the empirical world of appearance has its replica in the transcendent invisible Form world.[20] On the other hand,

---

17. Van Til, "Plato," 42.
18. See chapter 8 below.
19. In discussing the position of the historical plan of God's providence in the context of education, Van Til finds kinship with Augustine. Van Til writes: "For Augustine God's interpretation is prior even to the existence of the spatio-temporal universe. It is made according to God's plan. Would one interpret reality, would one interpret anything, one must find in it the plan of God" (Van Til, "The Education of Man," 53).
20. Throughout Christian thought, many have drawn the analogy between Plato's

for Aristotle, the realm of Forms was in the immanent world of the objects surrounding us; that is to say, the essence of a thing (form) is within the thing itself (object)—or, to say it precisely, the form is in the object. Often, Plato's form-matter distinction is characterized in modernist's terms as being an idealist construct although in Plato's day it was a realist construct, whereas Aristotle's form-matter distinction is characterized as being a realist construct in his time and in our time.

Even so, Van Til does not dismiss Plato's thought as insignificant, and yet, he makes his relatively positive observation of Plato's realism in typical fashion, that is, he places the common grace contribution of Plato's realism within the antithesis between Christian and non-Christian thought. After all, for Van Til, antithesis should always be the foundation for the Christian's analysis of the common grace insights coming from the unbeliever. He writes the following:

> To maintain the "objective" character of truth [Platonism] is indeed worth much. It has no doubt restrained men from deeds of despair and led them on to earnest endeavor in the various fields of human research. Plus Platonism has no doubt contributed its positive bit to the preparation of the world for the coming of Christ. But this relative good that we may find in Platonism should not blind us to the fact that Platonic realism or modern idealism is basically opposed to the Christian scheme of things. Platonism itself, and not merely the excrescences that have grown out of it, is an enemy of Christianity.[21]

In other words, while Plato's view that real objective facts appear before all humanity does not conflict with a positive preparation for the reality of Christ and his work in history, Plato's independent construct of a form-matter view of reality made his position a foe to biblical truth. Van Til rightly understood that anyone who wishes to construct the Christian system upon the foundation of Plato/Aristotle has to accept their form-matter

---

Form world and the Christian view of heaven, as well as between Plato's construct of the empirical world and the Christian view of the created universe. Nothing is further from the truth; for Plato the Form world is an extension of the material universe which maintains Plato's notion that matter is eternal. After all, the Demiurge, Plato's creator god, creates the material universe of appearance on the basis of the matter that has always existed in the Form world. A close examination of Plato's view of creation is antithetical to the biblical presentation. Again, in the context of our educational discussion, consult Van Til, "The Education of Man," 44–49.

21. Van Til, "Plato," 43–44.

abstraction, which then serves as the foundation for constructing a natural theology upon which a theological superstructure is built. In this regard, Van Til primarily took issue with Roman Catholic medieval scholasticism. As Van Til notes:

> Rome, to be sure, takes its philosophical instruction from the Lyceum rather than from the Academy; yet in Aristotle there was so much of Plato that Plato, almost as much as Aristotle, speaks to us in Roman Catholic theology. The *natural theology* of Rome is little else than Platonico-Aristotelian philosophy in theological garb.[22]

Instead of following a method that begins with the Plato/Aristotle's abstraction like Rome, Van Til declares that "Christian philosophy should follow the method of concretion, the method of implication into God's interpretation."[23] A method of concretion, for Van Til, means that solely within the self-sufficient and self-contained God of the Bible can be found the true and exhaustive knowledge and interpretation of the facts—a unified integrative unity in God's person, on which the human being is absolutely dependent for any knowledge at all. For Van Til, this truth should never be surrendered or compromised among the covenantal children of Christ. If it is compromised, the pagan element will already be in the house of belief. Van Til criticized such compromise without timidity; as we have observed, he not only accused Roman Catholicism but also Arminianism and less-than-consistent Calvinism with this exact conciliation. He points out that these systems in some degree surrender the sovereign person of God, through viewing God and man as "partners in an effort to explain a common environment. Facts then are not what they are, in the last analysis, by virtue of the plan of God; they are partly that, but they partly exist in their own power."[24] In this common environment (matter in the form-matter paradigm) in which the empirical approach of abstraction of the Greeks is viewed as a legitimate starting point, the faculty of human reason is said to be liberated in the partnership between human beings and God. Further, as Van Til notes, "by 'reason' is meant the reason of man as the determiner

---

22. Ibid., 44.

23. Ibid. Elsewhere Van Til wrote: "But what, then, do we mean by education? *Education is implication into God's interpretation.* No narrow intellectualism is implied in this definition. To think God's thoughts after him, to dedicate the universe to its Maker, and to be the vice-regent of the Ruler of all things; this is man's task. Man is prophet, priest, and king. It is this view of education that is involved in and demanded by the idea of creation" (Van Til, "The Education of Man," 40).

24. Van Til, *Theory of Knowledge*, 12.

of the possible and the impossible by means of 'logic,'"[25] especially the laws of logic found in Aristotle's construct. From this starting point, even the truth of the full-orbed revelation of God must be tested by the laws of reason and logic. In other words, human reason enters into a partnership with God, judging what is to be believed and not believed within the Christian worldview. This authority given to human reason, even from within the confines of Christendom has been from its foundation in the renaissance of the classical era a strong contributor to the secularization of the West.

VAN TIL APPLIED TO THE TRIVIUM

In these salient points demonstrating how Van Til viewed classical thought as our enemy instead of our friend, the reader can plainly see from Van Til's perspective that the attributes of God's person can never be separated from the unfolding *plan* of God's revelation executed in history. On this, Van Til's thinking was not only grounded in Calvin's theological perspective and the Reformed confessional statements on providence and creation, but it also reflected the thought of Bavinck as well as the teacher whom Van Til confessed had the most profound influence on him, Vos. Too often those who claim expertise in Van Til's thought overlook his declaration that a biblical philosophy of history grounds his theory of knowledge, in other words epistemology must be founded on the unfolding supernatural self-revelation of God in history in its two *forms*—natural and special.[26] As

---

25. Ibid., 17.

26. One will be strained to uncover whether Frame and Greg L. Bahnsen (1948–1995), two premiere exegetes of Van Til's apologetic in the eyes of many, have comprehended Van Til's position that a biblical philosophy of history is fundamental and foundational to his epistemology. This essential point to Van Til's theory of knowledge is mysteriously missing in their comprehensive presentations, and it points to a serious flaw in their analysis of Van Til (see Bahnsen, *Van Til's Apologetic*; and Frame, *Van Til*). Furthermore, it is imperative for the educator to digest Van Til's analysis here on the two forms of revelation—in his words, "Any revelation that God gives of himself is therefore absolutely voluntary. Herein precisely lies the *union* of the various forms of God's revelation with one another. God's revelation in nature, together with God's revelation in Scripture, form God's one grand scheme of covenant revelation of himself to man. The *two forms* of revelation must therefore be seen as presupposing and supplementing one another. They are aspects of *one general philosophy of history*" (Van Til, *Christian Apologetics*, 66; italics mine). In the same document, Van Til concludes his section on the philosophy of history with these words, "Here, then, is the picture of a *well-integrated and unified* philosophy of history in which revelation in nature and revelation in Scripture are mutually meaningless without one another and mutually fruitful when taken together" (ibid., 68; italics mine).

Van Til and Classical Christian Education

Van Til maintained an integration of history, revelation, and epistemology in his philosophy of Christian education, let us apply his understanding to the classical model of the trivium, especially to the area of rhetoric as it relates to preaching. In other words, we will analyze what consequences arise when the classical area's approach to rhetoric is incorporated into understanding and interpreting the biblical text as part of the preaching ministry of the church.

It is important to recognize that the teaching of rhetoric has generated controversy from the beginning. As a sophist himself, Isocrates exposed the corruption of other teachers of rhetoric in Athens in his famous treatise *Against the Sophists*. According to Isocrates, the sophists were not concerned with the "art of persuasion" (rhetoric) as a discipline that was integrated with truth. In fact, for these rhetoricians all was conducted under the façade of deception. Rather than to articulate the facts and the truth, the goal in their use of language was only to persuade others of an opinion, no matter what the facts or the truth might be. For the rhetoricians under Isocrates's attack, truth was a relative matter, whether applied to the classroom, to the courtroom, or to political discourse. Surely, most Christians would gravitate not only toward Isocrates's criticism, but also toward Plato's judgment of the sophists' view of rhetoric as horrendous.

Most scholars hold that Plato was opposed to the discipline of rhetoric in light of its abuse by the sophists. Still, Plato undeniably used his own form of rhetoric, both in the oratory of the principle figure of his dialogues, Socrates, and in the general written communication of his dialogues. Christians are likely to find Plato's dialogues *Phaedrus* and *Gorgias* appealing, considering that in those dialogues he focuses on the sophists' lack of concern for the truth. In Plato's worldview, rhetoric must be integrated with truth; otherwise, justice, natural rights, and the common good are suspended in an unreal world in which chaos and irrational law reign. Unlike the sophists (with their parallels to postmodern thinking), Plato (with his parallels to modernity in which the certainty of truth can be ascertained) presents a possibly more attractive model to Christians today.[27] Furthermore, for Plato the ethical components of goodness and justice govern

---

27. One needs to proceed in this discussion keeping Van Til's assessment of Greek thought close to the heart—that, although Plato's realism is an advance in Greek thought and prepares the Greek world better for the Christian gospel (common grace), its abstract construct of viewing truth and reality outside the domain of understanding and interpreting all things upon the foundation of the Being of Scripture's God is antithetical to biblical truth.

the understanding and interpretation of reality and truth with regard to the "art of persuasion." In other words, if rhetoric is to be used correctly, *it must serve the true components of virtuous goodness*, and this necessary link between rhetoric and virtue becomes an extremely strong paradigm in the classical world, one which will have lasting effects upon the Christian church.

The position of virtue within the *trivium* is an attractive quality for classical Christian educators. In some settings of antiquity, the students learned grammar by constructing brief literary pieces pertaining to Greek or Roman stories handed down through time. In this way, grammar was no isolated investigation of the rules of language; rather, its components were taught in a larger context of mining the past (history) for stories embodying the *virtues* of either Greek or Roman culture. Clearly, within the *trivium* the specific discipline of history was not found, but history served the task of grammar—and, under the rubric of grammar, young students received the rules of language and inculcation into virtues of the past. These young students were responsible for embracing moral examples of good virtue while rejecting immoral examples as they examined the heroic figures of the past.

The curriculum incorporates the same method into the discipline of rhetoric. Having progressed to the stage of oratory, a student would not make a personal presentation related to individual experience, but instead a speech about mythological or historical stories of the past. The purpose in this exercise (which involved learning and reciting stories, often from memory) was for students to acquire skills of oration and a knowledge of the past, while also having incorporated in themselves the qualities of virtue found in the accounts.[28] Moreover, in such a construct, dialectic (logic), the third subject of the *trivium*, was designed as a method of presentation and argumentation in which the rules of reason serve virtue and good rather than vice and evil.

Our brief sketch of the relationship between the *trivium* and ethics raises a serious issue—the placement of the discipline of history in a subservient and subordinate position in these academic disciplines. This secondary location is borne out when we see that history appears as a formal discipline neither in the *trivium*, nor in the *quadrivium*. Moreover, as we have seen, when the discipline is employed, it serves grammar, rhetoric,

---

28. See Quintilian, "*Institutes of Oratory*," 371.

Van Til and Classical Christian Education

and dialectic, offering examples of moral virtue.[29] History serves ethics; as the Greek teacher of rhetoric, Dionysius (30 BC) stated: "History is [moral] philosophy teaching by examples."[30] Whether Christians wish to admit it or not, this classical notion of history has made dominant inroads into the exegesis and analysis of biblical revelation. Too often in the history of the church and in the life of individual believers, the historical narrative of the biblical text *dissolves* into moral ideals that end up having little more distinctiveness as guides to Christian living than the qualities of moral goodness found by applying the ethics of the "Plato-Kant principle" to human life. Caught between the ideas of Greek/Roman culture and teachings of the church regarding understanding, interpreting, and applying the biblical text, Christians at times have seen historical narratives and historical figures in the Bible as best understood and applied merely as moral lessons of either aspiration or degradation. Drawing attitudes from the cultural heritage of Western antiquity, Christians have difficulty breaking free from the shackles of a moralistic construct of history, especially when attempting to understand the biblical narrative for our lives.[31]

It is imperative to apply Van Til's assessment of classical thought at this point: the classical construct of the *trivium* is a serious abstraction of the concrete existence of God's Being and his plan disclosed throughout the history of revelation. This construct is built upon the foundation of human autonomy apart from the organic unity of the two forms of God's

---

29. Classical Christian educators admit freely that one of the reasons that they are attracted to the classical era is that they wish to recover the moral virtues of that era (see Leithart, "Classical Schooling," 5). Usually what this entails is finding abstract virtues in the classical era which can be found to have a parallel in Scripture. Again, there seems to be little, if any, reflection upon the structure of biblical ethics as an antithetical paradigm to the various classical paradigms of ethics.

30. Quote appears in Greidanus, *Sola Scriptura*, 9n25.

31. Charles Swindoll, whose writings have been popular among Reformed Christians provides an excellent example of this problem. His principles of application of the Israelites and the Red Sea are Greek; one would be pressed to find anything that resembles the gospel of Jesus Christ in the principles he proposes. He states confidently his moralistic hermeneutical principle toward the text: "Old Testament experiences have modern-day lessons. They pass on timeless truths from which we can learn." Then, he maps out the four "timeless truths" from the exodus: (1) "It takes tight places to break lifetime habits"; (2) "When hemmed in on all sides, the only place to look is up"; (3) "If the Lord is to get the glory, then He must do the fighting"; and (4) "'Red Seas' open and close at the Lord's command, not until" (Swindoll, *Moses*, 67–68). The church must grasp that this type of exegesis and application paralyzes the essential message of the gospel on the landscape of God's redemptive activity in history.

revelation. Human beings are seen as the authority responsible for constructing the *trivium* within the domain and limitations of the empirical world while no manifestation of God's historical activity in the creation is acknowledged. Human activity (truly secular history) serves grammar, rhetoric, and dialectic, usually to teach moral virtue. In this classical liberal arts education, the self-attesting Christ of God's historical revelation is virtually meaningless, with Christ serving as an appendix in the biblical narrative or a biblical story. Christians following this approach may become experts in the classical paradigm, and, in the tradition of Aesop's *Fables* seek to grasp and apply the *moral* of the story and, then, view Christ as consummating the story as the *moral* example to imitate.[32] How can we counter such a paradigm? We must look to the core of Van Til's apologetic to find not only the Creator-creature distinction, but also the redemptive-historical understanding of revelation. For Van Til, neither the knowledge of the facts, nor interpretation of the facts, nor the creation of the facts can be separated from the *plan* of God. Van Til declares that the facts are never separated from the self-disclosure of the triune God in his providential history, centered in the person and work of Christ.[33] In a very brief

---

32. Sadly, many Christians who attempt to remain faithful to orthodox Christianity fail to realize that it is this exact paradigm which has characterized liberal Christianity and modernism since the Enlightenment. My observation here is not new. In his inauguration lecture on May 3, 1915, as Assistant Professor of New Testament Literature and Exegesis at Princeton Theological Seminary, J. Gresham Machen warned his audience that critical modern theology was separating the factual events of history recorded in Scripture from the ideals of pious living, that is, principles of modern piety trump the factual activity of God in history. Machen declared, "The separation of Christianity from history has been a great concern of modern theology. It has been an inspiring attempt. But it has been a failure" (Machen, "History," 1).

33. To substantiate this understanding of Van Til, we need to look no further than the context of Van Til's survey of Christian epistemology. Immediately he tells us: "We shall have to approach the matter of a Christian world-and-life view from an historical point of view." He then continues: "As Christians we have a very definite philosophy of history. For us history is the realization of the purposes and plans of the all-sufficient God revealed through Christ in Scripture. And if this is the case we are naturally persuaded that in history lies the best proof of our philosophy of human life. The core of our system of philosophy is our belief in the triune God of Scripture, and in what he has revealed concerning himself and his purposes for man and his world" (Van Til, *Christian Epistemology*, xiii). With respect to the historical nature of biblical revelation, Van Til not only echoes the thought of Vos, but also the thought of Machen. Machen opened his inauguration lecture with these profound words: "The student of the New Testament should be primarily an historian. The centre and core of all the Bible is history. Everything else that the Bible contains is fitted into an historical framework and leads up to an historical climax. The Bible is primarily a record of events" (Machen, "History," 1).

Van Til and Classical Christian Education

essay on Christian education, Van Til drives his point home; he provides a profound glimpse of the Creator-creature distinction in discussion of key figures (Adam, Noah, Abraham, Moses, and Paul) in the history of redemption, an analysis in which Christ as prophet, priest, and king is at center stage in the task of Christian education.[34] Van Til fixed his attention on the centrality of Christ in any subject that he addressed, including education. Hence, regarding ethics, nothing surpasses Christ's death and resurrection as the foundation and power to live an ethical life which pleases our God (Rom 6:1–14; Gal 2:20; Col 3:1–17). Likewise, we must not fall into classical abstraction with respect to the ten commandments given at Sinai, that is, we must not view the ten commandments (law) in isolation from grace—the gospel grounded in Christ (Exod 20:2 can never be separated from Exod 20:3–17). When Christians applaud the mere listing of the ten commandments on a billboard (Exod 20:3–17), they are actually applauding the removal of the ten commandments from the full biblical context and intent on the part of God; in effect, they are endorsing the removal of the gift of grace from the moral law. After all, at the giving of the law at Sinai, the reality of Christ's death (passover) and resurrection (exodus) is spiritually foreshadowed, that sole reality which offers the power to live an ethical, godly life in conformity to God's law. In the redemptive plan of God, the moral life only has true meaning within the domain of Christ's death and resurrection in history.

In biblical revelation, therefore, history is not subservient to ethics (a classical pagan notion); rather, ethics is subservient to history, or, more specifically, ethics has its compliment in the accomplished *historical* work of God's plan as completed in his divine Son. Indeed, human beings have no release from the bondage of sin and corresponding freedom unto eternal life without Christ's central redemptive-historical work. Life in Christ through his Spirit is absolutely and solely the gift of grace; our reconciliation comes solely from the power of Christ's death and resurrection. Can the Christian find such a truth in classical pagan literature? No—nor can it be found in any construct of the *trivium* in classical education.

Christians cannot risk remaining blind to this reality in Christ and seeking the godly life by starting with moral goodness based on the ethics found in the tradition of the "Platonic-Kantian principle." Sadly, too

---

34. See Van Til, "God." Interestingly, Van Til incorporated the same redemptive-historical figures (Adam, Noah, Abraham, Moses, and Paul) into the basic outline of his book addressing the subject, "Who is Jesus Christ?" (see Van Til, *The Great Debate Today*).

many Christians try to maintain a synthesis, with one foot in the classical world and one foot in the Christian world. Van Til's warning on this is worth the attention of every Christian educator: the consistent outworking of the classical to modern "Platonic-Kantian principle" of knowledge, interpretation, and ethics will not land our covenant children in Christ (see 2 Kgs 1:6). In God's providence, the history of the nineteenth century verifies this profound truth in the circumstances of key players who demonstrated where a consistent application of the classical worldview will end: Karl Marx (1818–1883) as a political philosopher, an atheist; Auguste Comte (1798–1857) as an advocate of modern scientific positivism, an atheist; Max Weber (1864–1920) as father of modern sociology, an atheist; Sigmund Freud (1856–1939) as a key founder of modern psychology, an atheist; Friedrich Nietzsche (1844–1900) as contributor to the rise of nihilistic existentialism, an atheist; and Charles Darwin (1809–1882) as proponent of biological evolution, a strong opponent to Christian theism.[35] Their world is one of consistent autonomy, which ends in condemnation without Christ. Even so, it is also telling that God has preserved his church and his people despite their compromising throughout history their sole allegiance to the kingdom of Christ by synthesizing the world of classicism with Christian truth. Only by God's grace and the power of his Spirit have true Christians been able to resist the dominant implications of their error. Undeniably, we can acknowledge with gratitude that, in God's unfolding plan in history, Christ always preserves his church despite the continuing weakness of the flesh. However, recognizing Christ's faithful promise to his church does not justify flirting with a compromise between the full-orbed truth of the kingdom of God and the classical world of the Greeks and the Romans (Matt 16:18).[36]

---

35. In my judgment, on this point we can see the evidence that Douglas Wilson fails to understand and apply Van Til's ideas; Wilson maintains that "classical culture and education" had a type of sanctifying presence in the West from "the Reformation down through the middle of the nineteenth century" (Wilson, "Antithesis in Education," 25). On the contrary, Van Til understood the demise of the nineteenth century as being rooted in the secular and pagan elements of autonomy carried forward from the classical world. To Van Til, those pagan elements were not divorced totally from prominent thinkers of the Reformation or of the centuries that followed.

36. Most Christians who live in this compromise will find themselves in a lifelong struggle with the biblical teaching of salvation by sovereign grace; as they do, they will always struggle with the dynamics of salvation by faith and/or by works. This struggle is already implicit in any incorporation of the ethical motif of the common good that is grounded in the classical era; this so-called objective moral standard of good works

Van Til and Classical Christian Education

Christian educators must understand, therefore, that nothing inherent in the classical disciplines of the *trivium* (grammar, rhetoric, and dialectic) brings biblical ethical transformation for a human being. In fact, in perhaps the clearest critique of classical rhetoric found in Scripture, the Apostle Paul declares to the Corinthian church that he knows nothing among them "except Jesus Christ and him crucified" (1 Cor 2:2 my translation). Paul makes the *antithesis* clear: regarding his use of rhetoric in preaching and rhetoric as viewed by the Greeks, he does not come before the Corinthians with "persuasive speech of human wisdom," rather he comes with the demonstration and power of the Spirit (1 Cor 2:4 my translation). Indeed, Paul used the rhetorical device of preaching to proclaim the gospel, but his method of rhetoric was grounded in the plan of God as revealed in the work of his Son, specifically his death and resurrection which was applied to sinful hearts by the Holy Spirit.[37] For Paul, rhetoric and its relationship to ethics had to be grounded in the redemptive-historical activity of God in Christ. Paul found no such understanding in Greek and Roman thought. Likewise, Van Til's grasp of this biblical truth is revealed when he tells us that the method of education must be grounded in the self-contained and self-sufficient God of Scripture whose ontological triune Being knows the facts, interprets the facts, and creates the facts in accordance with his sovereign plan in revelational history. For those who truly embrace and understand a biblical view of covenant consciousness with their God, this starting point must never be compromised in the educational content and curriculum which the teacher places before the student (see Deut 6:4–9; 7:6–11; 1 Kgs 10:3–5; 2 Chr 26:1–4). No matter the era, the discipline, or the curriculum, the sovereign plan of God grounded in the self-attesting Christ of Scripture must infiltrate thoroughly the whole academic process from beginning to end (Rom 11:36).

---

paralyzes such believers in their assessment of others as well as their assessment of themselves.

37. One may wish to consult further an application of history, rhetoric, and ethics to the history of Reformed preaching. See W. Dennison, "Biblical Theology and the Issue of Application."

PART 2

Redemptive History and Apologetics

6

The Christian Apologist in the Present State of Redemptive History

> The Commander-in-chief sits enthroned in glory now. He has given [his people] his word to direct them. He has given them his Spirit to enlighten and to quicken them. They have put on the whole armour of God in order to do battle with the powers of darkness.
>
> —Cornelius Van Til, "The Christian Philosophy of Life"

As Christ's church lives out her pilgrimage in the sovereign plan of the triune God of the Bible, we face this question: should her present status in that plan include a significant role as a defender of the truth of orthodox Christian thought? Typically, apologetics involves engaging a non-Christian, or a non-Christian worldview, by building deductive and/or inductive arguments in order to demonstrate the authenticity of the Christian religion. In fact, the Christian apologist generally fails to focus on the church's present position in redemptive history. Although aware that he is operating after the close of the canon of Scripture, at a time when the miraculous evidence for Christianity has ceased, the typical apologist makes no self-conscious effort to understand his task in the context of the progressive providential plan of God. Indeed, the average apologist goes into the marketplace equipped with three basic tools: the laws of logic, capable of convincing any rational creature of the evidences for Christianity; Christian revelation, capable of compelling surrender from any autonomous creature; and stories of personal experience, capable of melting the heart of any unbeliever. The goal of that apologist, then, is to defend the historic truth of biblical religion—to present and win arguments in hope that the unbeliever might become convinced of the Christian faith.

A different and richer view of the apologist's task emerges, however, when that task is shaped by a commitment to the self-attesting Christ of Scripture and brought into conformity with the progressive revelation of God in history. This version of apologetics focuses on where the church stands in revelational history. It acknowledges that with respect to the metaphysical, psychological, epistemological, and ethical elements of the apologetic task, a change has occurred in history—Christ has arrived and has been exalted. The "fullness of time"—the fullness of redemptive history—has come in the person and work of Jesus Christ (Gal 4:4). The gracious promise of God that a federal head would ratify a new covenant has been fulfilled. The eternal Son has come into history as one born under the law in order to bring the transition of the eschaton into the life of his bride, the church (Gal 3:15–19, 29). The church has now moved into the period when the justifying grace of God in Christ has dissolved the divide between Jew and Gentile, slavery and freedom, male and female (Gal 3:28–29). By virtue of the birth, ministry, death, resurrection, and ascension of Christ, the kingdom of heaven has already arrived—the eschaton is *now* (Mark 1:15; Luke 4:16–21; 4:43; 1 Tim 4:1; Heb 1:1; 1 John 2:18). At the same time, although the eschaton has *already* begun (2 Cor 5:17; 6:2; Gal 4:4; Eph 2:2–3, 12–13; Phil 2:15; Titus 2:12), it has *not yet* been consummated; that is to say, its completion remains in the future (Rom 8:18; Eph 1:21; 2:7; 2 Tim 3:1; 4:1).

Apologetics must take into account the truth that the church/believer now lives in two aeons or worlds: the age/world to come and the present evil age/world as defined in the construct of Paul's eschatology—which itself is in harmony with the canon of the New Testament. Further, although her present pilgrimage takes place in the tension of the two ages, the church is only a member or citizen of the age to come—not a member or citizen of the present evil age (Phil 3:20). The covenantal flock of Christ has

The Christian Apologist in the Present State of Redemptive History

citizenship in heaven where she enjoys her exclusive identity in union with Christ (Rom 6:1-14; 1 Cor 1:30-31; Gal 6:14-15; Eph 2:1-10; Col 3:1-4). Significantly, in Paul's eschatological structure, the age to come is defined by its federal head, the last Adam, that is, the glorified person of Christ. By contrast, the present evil age is defined by its federal head, the first Adam, that is, the fallen person of Adam, who was caught in the web of seduction by the god of this age, Satan (Rom 5:12-21; 1 Cor 15:20-23; 2 Cor 4:4).

This eschatological structure leads to crucial implications for believers facing the apologetic task. To begin with, the apologist stands not on earth pointing the unbeliever to heaven, where Christ is; rather, the apologist stands in heaven—in the *age to come*—pointing the unbeliever to heaven. In apologetics, the believer begins with his identity in Christ, as one who is part of Christ's bride located in the heavenly places, and then he defends full-orbed Christian theism from this glorified position. The apologist's foundation for addressing the unbeliever must not be a neutral appeal to reason (logic) or temporal experience (empirical data) because the apologist, through Christ's Spirit, is already draped in the glorious atmosphere of Christ's presence in heaven. The apologist's faculties of reason and experience have been transformed, and, when he defends the sacred faith as one conditioned by the mind of Christ, he is speaking to those who are conditioned by the mind of rebellion against the Creator. Believers and unbelievers do not share common cognitive processes of reasoning and experiencing. The Christian apologist's mind translates all things through union with Christ—his cognition is shaped by the heavenly places—whereas the unbeliever's mind is blindly, stubbornly, and arrogantly suppressing the truth about God (Rom 1:18-21), translating all things through a grid of obedience to the evil one. The former binds reason and experience to a heavenly existence; the latter binds reason and experience to a temporal and earthly existence. After all, as the WCF speaks of all our human faculties being affected by the fall, clearly, all those faculties are transformed by our redemption in Christ. Christians who fail to acknowledge this point will continue to live in a world of classical synthesis, patching together secular Greco-Roman thought with Christian revelation. (As Van Til has demonstrated, such an amalgamation is found in Roman Catholic thought, Arminianism, and less-than-consistent Calvinism.) The ideologies of antiquity and the redemptive religion of the Bible are antithetical; thus, Christian apologists only succeed in compromising their heavenly life in Christ when they attempt to win unbelievers to the gospel through sewing together the teachings of Jesus with the teachings of Socrates—this type of synthesis allows secularism to invade the holy realm of heaven (1 Cor 6:19–20; 2 Cor 10:5; Rev 21–22).

Truly, nothing is the same since Jesus came, and, having ascended into the heavenly places with Christ through faith, the believer can now view all things through new glorified spectacles. The eschatological event of Christ shapes the apologist's interpretation of all reality, as he is a citizen of heaven on a pilgrimage in the creation. Unmistakably, in this state of grace, the apologist can give no assent to carnal philosophical doctrines such as Aristotle's view of reason or John Locke's (1632–1704) view of experience. Such theories are not credible analogues to the truth in the eschatological mind of Christ Jesus.

The apologist's task is a defense (*apologia*) of the final state of heavenly life, a state into which he has already entered through Christ; he is in defense of the eschaton. For this reason, the apologist must begin not with an earthly conception of reason and experience in line with the unbeliever's own ideas; rather, he must begin with an imperative: protect the sanctity (*hagiasate*) of the covenant Lord in his heart. It is the hope that the Spirit of God has placed in the believing apologist that he defends (1 Pet 3:15). Peter places the corpus of this hope before the believer:

> Blessed be the God and Father of our Lord Jesus Christ, who according to His abundant mercy has begotten us again to a living hope through the resurrection of Jesus Christ from the dead, to an inheritance incorruptible and undefiled and that does not fade away, reserved in heaven for you, who are kept by the power of God through faith for salvation ready to be revealed in the last time. (1 Pet 1:3–5)[1]

In a hostile world of suffering and persecution, the apologist defends his hope: *the gospel*—the "already" eschatological redemption and the "not yet" resurrection of the body that Christ's past resurrection secured. With the context of this passage before us, we should note that if "reason" is the best translation for the term *logos* that appears in 1 Peter 3:15, the point stated earlier about the believer's use of reason is confirmed; that is to say, this faculty must operate according to a sanctified covenantal devotion to the Lord and a comprehensive faith in the accomplished redemptive work of Christ. Herein, Peter's thinking can be supplemented with that of the author of

---

1. All Scripture quotations in this chapter are from the NKJV unless otherwise indicated as my translation.

The Christian Apologist in the Present State of Redemptive History

Hebrews, that is, the apologist should complete his task by exuding a faith that embraces the God who has spoken through his Son in these last days (Heb 1:1–3), a faith that rests upon Christ as the source of "things hoped for, the evidence of things not seen" (Heb 11:1).

Oddly, apologists often have used 1 Peter 3:15 to justify their technical, academic defenses of the faith in a seminary curriculum. They often see Peter's call for believers to "always be ready to give a defense to everyone who asks you a reason for the hope that is in you" (1 Pet 3:15) as an imperative for all believers to engage in such a technical defense. I have never been convinced of this interpretation of Peter's text, and my skepticism has been reinforced by passages in the New Testament where the word *apologia* and its cognates are used—especially in Luke's account of the gospel and the Acts of the Apostles. If we focus on the biblical theology of Luke-Acts, a distinct pattern of defense emerges, one much different from the one proposed by many academic apologists.

First, in Luke 12:11–12, we note that Christ is speaking to his disciples (12:1); he is warning them about those who deny him and those who blaspheme the Holy Spirit (vv. 9–10). He then states, "Now when they bring you to the synagogues and magistrates and authorities, do not worry about how or what you should answer [verb form: *apologēsēsthe* from *apologeomai*], or what you should say. For the Holy Spirit will teach you in that very hour what you ought to say" (12:11–12). The verb form of *apologeomai* is the subjunctive, aorist middle, 2nd person plural. In v. 11, Luke presents a phrase that has the following construct: *mē* ("not") + aorist subjunctive = prohibitory subjunctive. The idea here is this: his phrase refers to action that has not yet begun. Specifically, the action of the disciples in providing an answer during persecution that has not yet begun; hence, when the time of persecution arrives, they are not to worry because their response will be contingent upon the presence and words of the Holy Spirit (pointing to post-Pentecost). Moreover, as we add the middle voice here, we note that the disciples will speak receiving the active directive of the Holy Spirit.

Second, we turn our attention to Luke 21:14, where once again Christ is speaking to his disciples. Note the context in 21:12: Christ informs the disciples that they will be persecuted as they are delivered to synagogues and prisons—brought before rulers and kings; he then charges them, "Therefore settle it in your hearts not to meditate beforehand on what you will answer [verb form: *apologēthēnai* from *apologeomai*]; for I will give you a mouth and wisdom which all your adversaries will not be able to contradict or resist" (21:14–15). In this case, the verb form is the infinitive, aorist passive, communicating that the disciples will be passive, while the Lord will be the active transmitter of their wisdom.

Note the pattern: Christ delivers a sincere and serious prophecy that the disciples will face suffering and persecution after he departs from them. Christ also promises to secure them in their trial. He promises that the Holy Spirit will provide them with an answer, a defense, for the gospel that is within them. In fact, both passages in Luke advise no prior preparation for what they are to say, for example, no rehearsed answers or prearranged academic talking-points. Rather, the presence of Christ through his Spirit will be sufficient. We must be careful here. Christ is not saying that the disciples should go before their persecutors with a blank mind (a spiritual *tabula rasa*). Rather, he is saying that the Spirit will lead them in a defense that will grow out of what Christ has placed within them. Their defense will arise from the wise directive of the Holy Spirit as a testimony to the gospel that has taken root in their hearts. In other words, except by the Spirit of God, no one can say, "Jesus is Lord" and then defend all that phrase means. It is just such a confession and defense that Christ promises to give his disciples as they face their future persecutors.

The pattern here involves prophecy and promise: Christ prophesied trial for his disciples, and Christ promised grace to persevere through that trial. We must not overlook the movement here in the history of redemption as espoused by Luke. These prophecies by Christ took place prior to his death (Luke 12:11–12; 21:12–15), and they pointed to a period demarcated by the first resurrection (Christ's resurrection) and the final resurrection (the church's resurrection). Therefore, Christ promised to preserve his disciples even after he left them at his ascension. The disciples would then enter into the era of the church, an era characterized by suffering and persecution, in synagogues as well as in prisons; a time when kings and rulers would abstain from nothing in their efforts to prevent the furtherance of the gospel. This harassment was the reality of living in the apostolic age—and, more broadly, it is the reality of living between Christ's ascension and his second coming. In this final era of the history of redemption, what is Christ's gracious gift to the disciples and the church? It is his continual existence in the midst of his people through the release and abiding presence of the Holy Spirit. Christ's Spirit is the gift of grace to the disciples to secure them and the church for the final day of Christ's glory.

The Christian Apologist in the Present State of Redemptive History

What role does this gift of the Holy Spirit play when persecution takes place? The Spirit provides a credible defense, that is, an answer for the gospel in the midst of hostile opposition. Is this answer a trained academic defense? No, it is one defined by the events of the gospel—God's work of redemption in the historic accomplishment of his Son. The Christian's answer is grounded in the work of Christ, what true believers have come to know in their hearts and confess with their lips about the gospel of Jesus Christ (cf. Rom 10:10). The activity of the triune God in history is the content of our defense; we (covenant people/church) do not first look to the temporal constructs of reason and experience to mediate that activity. Rather, as Christ is seated on the right hand of his heavenly Father, he sends his Spirit who mediates the apologetic answer in the midst of suffering and trial, while the apologist is positioned in faith-union with Christ in heaven. The believer's faculties of reason and experience have been enveloped by the aroma of glorification, and from this glorified status of union with Christ, believers can respond through the Spirit to the attacks of unbelievers; thus, believers can eschatologically declare with the Psalmist: "The Lord is on my side; I will not fear. What can man do to me?" (Ps 118:6; cf. Rom 8:31–39). Through his Spirit, Christ will not forsake his promise. We can rely on this promise to the disciples and the church because of the testimony of Christ's letter to us from the pen of Luke. Christ makes the oath of promise, fulfills the promise, and records that fulfillment (in Luke-Acts) as a testimony to his covenant faithfulness. Let us turn to that page of revelational history.

Luke shows us Paul, Christ's disciple chosen to be the Apostle to the Gentiles (Acts 22:1; 24:10; 25:8; 26:1). In the midst of hostile opponents—from the Jews and the Romans who bound him in Jerusalem (Acts 22:1) to Ananias, the high priest, and the Roman governor Felix (Acts 24:10) to Festus (Acts 25:8) and to King Agrippa (Acts 26:1)—Paul gave a defense to his accusers for his proclamation of the gospel of Christ. There is no mistake about the testimony Paul delivered: Paul's life was radically transformed by the appearance of the ascended Christ to him on the Damascus Road (Acts 9:1–9). Paul's conversion was unique; it was a distinctive revelation of the exalted Christ that transformed one who had persecuted Christ and the church into one designated to be *the* Apostle to the Gentiles. Such a conversion and missional calling has never been duplicated, and it never will be in its full revelatory significance in the history of the church. Therefore, we must be careful not to misuse Paul's testimony as a justification for the kind of personal testimonies popular in the church today. For many evangelicals, Paul's rehearsal of his conversion before his accusers (Jews/Romans in Acts 22:3–21; Agrippa in 26:2–27) validates the idea that all who get converted should give their personal testimony before the congregation or before those in the marketplace. As a result, too often evangelicals allow subjective, self-gratifying, and self-authenticating personal testimonies center stage, seeing them as apologetic evidence for the work of Christ in the midst of the church.

Clearly, elevation of personal testimonies is not the point of this passage about Paul in Luke's narrative. Non-Christian religions (e.g., Islam, Judaism, Buddhism, and Hinduism) and systems of thought (e.g., Marxism, Socialism, and Democratic capitalism) also push personal testimonies to the fore in order to use converts as evidence that their position is true. In that case, how do we determine which personal testimony is authentic? Which one is evidence of the truth? On what basis should one believe the personal testimony of the convert to Christ over against the convert to Buddhism? Undoubtedly, this opens a host of questions that cannot be addressed here. However, it is imperative to see that, in the context of redemptive history, Paul's conversion is not analogous to the modern-day Christian's salvation experience, and, therefore, it does not play the same role in Paul's apologetic answer as personal testimonies do in the evangelical's defense of Christianity.

When we place Paul's conversion in its appropriate position in the organic flow of redemptive history, some important facts become apparent. As the Lord appeared to Abram to confirm his covenant to him, calling him out of the midst of pagan Gentile religious worship (Gen 12:7), likewise, Christ appears as the light of the world to Paul, calling him out of an apostate Jewish religion in order to return him to the Gentile world in fulfillment of the Abrahamic covenant (Acts 9:3; 22:6; 26:16). This unique relation to a past historic revelatory appearance of the Lord in covenant to his chosen servant both anchors and propels Paul's gospel to the nations—the Gentiles (Gen 12:7; 17:5; Acts 1:8; 9:15; 26:16–17). The distinctiveness of Paul's conversion and ministry is further evinced in his persecution and imprisonment. Here, the pointed words of Christ come to assure Paul of his unique status in the history of redemption: "Be of good cheer, Paul; for as you have testified for me in Jerusalem, so you must also bear witness at Rome" (Acts 23:11).

Furthermore, Christ's appearance to Paul on the road to Damascus not only directs us back to the Abrahamic covenant, but also opens up the

The Christian Apologist in the Present State of Redemptive History

revelatory theme of Christ as the light of the world: he appeared to Paul as light—this pushes us to reflect upon the fact that Christ came into the world to overcome the darkness of sin and evil. Christ's appearance as light impels us back to the original creation, in which God separated the darkness from the light (Gen 1:3–5; first day). Indeed, in the original creation the light brought resolution to a dark universe. In Paul's conversion, Christ's grace penetrated Paul's heart of darkness, which hated and persecuted the church. Yes, Christ revealed himself in the light—a light so glorious and so marvelous that it brought blindness to this new elect servant so that he could understand that no eye has seen what Christ has laid aside in glory for those whom he loves. Indeed, when sight was restored to Paul, he was completely absorbed with viewing the world through eyes that had been to glory, eyes that had seen the risen Savior in all his splendor, eyes that were part of someone transferred into the new eschatological creation.

Moreover, this Christ revealed in light points us to the Old Testament pillar of fire—Israel's light in a dark and desolate wilderness, the presence of Christ that redeemed them, directed them, and defended them. And we cannot forget the other unique appearance of the Lord in light to a chosen one—Moses, who was chosen by the Lord to secure for Israel redemption out of bondage, who encountered the Lord in the midst of a burning bush that would not be consumed. Furthermore, while Paul was the designated Apostle to the Gentiles, the Lord made clear that Paul was also called to the lost sheep of Israel (Acts 9:15; 26:17).

This religious transformation in Paul turned his prior life completely on its head. Previous to this conversion event, Paul's faculties of reason and experience were shaped by his identity as a Pharisaic Jew born as a Roman citizen. Applying the rational and experiential presuppositions of his Jewish-Roman identity, Paul could neither accept Jesus as the promised Messiah, nor accept Jesus as Lord over all. How much less, then, could he define himself solely in terms of a heavenly citizenship! On the Damascus road, however, his identity-based presuppositions were entirely truncated by the revelation of the exalted Christ. Paul's life was freed from the bondage of Jewish and Roman unbelief. Paul's reason and experience were transformed by the event of redemptive revelation present in his conversion. He was given understanding of his position in the progressive revelation of the gospel, starting with Abraham and leading on to the Gentile world in the apostolic age. The redemptive revelation enveloping his conversion made him a participant in God's revelatory activity in the past; that is to say, he was drawn in to participate in God's promises to Abraham as well as God's prophetic word for the Gentiles. By contrast, as a Pharisaic Jew, he had been merely a spectator, unable to experience Old Testament revelation as his own.

Furthermore, through the revelation of the Christ of heaven, Paul became a participant in the domain of heaven's glory, when previously he had been a spectator of that glory who could savor his citizenship only in a kingdom of this world. God did something unique in the event of Paul's conversion, and the event had a particular place in God's progressive revelation, demonstrating that Paul's conversion is not a model for Christian conversion. Rather, it was a distinctive event that served the Father's purposes as his Son ushered in "the fullness of time" (Gal 4:4). In that qualitatively new time, God captivated the earth with the gospel. The Lord used Paul's status as a Roman citizen to fulfill Christ's prophecy that Paul would be God's chosen servant to the Gentiles, kings, and Israel. Nonetheless, Paul was simultaneously destined for a life of suffering leading to imprisonment and then death (Acts 9:15-16; remember Paul's destiny must always be tied to Acts 1:8). Indeed, we must note the irony here. Although Paul's mind, heart, and life resided in the heavenly places with Christ during his earthly journey (Eph 1:2; 2:6; Phil 3:20; Col 3:1-4), his Roman citizenship assured the fulfillment of his Savior's prophecy, that is, that he would suffer for the gospel as his Lord took him and the gospel to the "end of the earth" (Rome). When Paul appealed to his Roman citizenship, rather than utilizing a two kingdoms doctrine for the sake of his ministry and the church, he was undermining his Roman citizenship for the purpose of promoting his sole, real, and final citizenship in faith-union with his Savior who now sits at the right hand of his heavenly Father. Paul perceived that his journey as a Roman citizen was death, but he knew, in light of his citizenship in Christ's heavenly glory, that he would not die. There is no boasting in an earthly domain; there is only boasting in Christ.

We have gone from the prophecy and promise of Christ to Paul's apology in the midst of his opponents and then back to Paul's conversion experience. Perhaps, we need to connect the dots more clearly. Paul is the paradigm Luke uses to exposit Christ's words of prophecy and promise—Christ's prophecy that his disciples would suffer and be persecuted in the hands of kings and rulers, and Christ's promise that in this era of redemptive history the Spirit would provide a defense before his and his disciples' enemies. Christ's promise is fulfilled in Paul before Ananias, the

The Christian Apologist in the Present State of Redemptive History

high priest; Felix, the Roman governor (Acts 24:10); Festus (Acts 25:8); and King Agrippa (Acts 26:1). But what is the defense that Christ's Spirit supplied Paul in the midst of persecution and suffering? It is much richer than a personal testimony; Paul's conversion, apology (defense), and testimony are grounded in the historical revelation of God as embodied in the gospel of Jesus Christ. Christ's self-revelation to Paul on the Damascus road incorporates the profundity of the original creation, in which light is the resolution to darkness; indeed, the light of Christ is the only resolution to the darkness of sin as initiated by Adam's fall. Further, Paul's conversion incorporates the appearance of the Lord in covenant for the sake of the nations, a pattern of revelation that points us back to the Abrahamic covenant, when the Lord promised to bring out of Abraham's seed (Christ) the light which would extend to all the nations. Moreover, Paul's conversion points to Mosaic revelation. It incorporates the appearance of the Lord in redemptive history as a consuming and blessed light that redeems, directs, and defends. Herein lies the full-orbed gospel that convicted and converted Paul on the road to Damascus; it is the gospel that he came to know and love and declare before his persecutors. In this incredible testimony of sovereign grace, Christ turned him from being the persecutor to being the persecuted. In fact, in the providence of God, Luke shows that the Apostle Paul, rather than any of the disciples that Christ addresses in Luke's gospel, served as the paradigm of the Spirit's defense and answer in the synagogues and before kings and rulers—a defense that extends to the eschatological church existing in the period between Christ's first and second coming.

With that foundation, let us turn to Peter for his amplification of the nature of the church's apologetic task. In the present eschaton, a promise from Christ to his church remains—a promise embedded in the life-pattern of suffering and hope. Peter embraced this promise when he taught the apostolic church that their life would be characterized by suffering even after the apostles' death (1 Pet 3:14). According to Peter, as long as the age to come and the present evil age collide, evil people will attack the righteous who find their life in the goodness of the Lord (1 Pet 3:10–17). During this age of militant conflict, faithfully defending the Word of God will always involve a tension between suffering and hope. To be sure, suffering in the hands of the church's accusers is a painful, agonizing, and gruesome experience. Nevertheless, it is in this historical moment that the Christian apologist finds the greatest comfort—faith-union with Christ in the heavenly places. From what better position could the Christian apologist present a defense to the pain-ridden, sinful world? Even as he endures persecution and assault for the sake of the gospel, he is enveloped with the goodness, holiness, righteousness, justice, and peace of Christ's heavenly eternal glory.

With the apologist's identity established in Christ, what is his procedure for combatting his accusers? The apologist begins by cleaving to the abounding blessings in Christ (1 Pet 3:14). In 1 Peter 3:15, Peter tells us to "sanctify the Lord God in your hearts." In the original Greek this phrase says, "But sanctify (consecrate) Christ as Lord in your hearts." Sanctify here means to "set apart" or to be "holy for sacred purposes." Christ the Lord is set apart; the name and person of Christ the Lord are holy for a sacred purpose. Set apart for what? Holy for what purpose? Clearly, the holy setting apart is for the suffering believer's defense, *apologia*, answer, and testimony before accusers. Peter's imperative means that Christ must be set apart as Lord because he is the foundation, starting point, and peaceful counselor in the apologetic situation. This Christ—in whom the believer already shares the inheritance of his accomplished redemption—only this Christ compels us always to be ready to give the reason for the hope that is in us. There is, however, a notable difference between Christ's word for the disciples facing opposition in the apostolic era and his word for the body of the church facing opposition in the post-apostolic era. For the apostles, Christ's Spirit immediately intervened with a defense and answer before their adversaries, whereas the post-apostolic church is given an imperative to provide a defense and to answer their adversaries. Nevertheless, in both eras the Spirit of Christ apologetically operates for the sake of Christ's church. The Spirit of Christ has settled within the hearts of believers, and he will continue to function as a comforter and aid to them as they voice their defense before accusers in the form of a testimony to the accomplished redemptive-historical work of God in Christ revealed in the canon of Scripture (1 Pet 1:11–12; 1:3).

Undoubtedly, as the Holy Spirit empowers the apologist, his voice should go forth with meekness, humility, and fear. Is this fear of man? No, it is the fear of God. The believer should have absolute reverence for the Lord of blessing and judgment in the marketplace. And when the apologist's Christ-centered hope is placed before his persecutors, he must not deviate from the message of truth that is grounded in Christ so that his "good conduct" (v. 16; cf. 2:12 same Greek word) will shame unbelief. By contrast, if the apologist's defense vilifies or slanders the unbeliever so that the apologist spitefully abuses him with a spirit of vengeance, then the

The Christian Apologist in the Present State of Redemptive History

apologist has turned to evil, neglecting the imperative to conduct himself "in Christ" (v. 16).

Can the believer ever be ready perfectly to defend his heavenly life in Christ? Surely not as long as apologetics is necessary, on this side of resurrection-glory! Peter's life offers encouragement for the believer who will often fail to set Christ apart as Lord. Peter denied his Savior when interrogated before Christ's sacrificial death, but as the Holy Spirit invaded his heart, the tremendous weight of guilt was released by his gracious and redeeming Savior. Later on, Peter stoutly faced a martyr's death because of the hope that Christ put in him. The work of Christ in the past assured Peter of his blessed inheritance in the future. This hope in Christ, shared by all believers, is so powerful, so assuring, so convincing, that it is the *apologia*—the defense of the believer in the marketplace. The believer is impregnable when he defends the hope of Christ since his life is encompassed by what Christ has done in the past, what Christ is doing in the present, and what Christ will do in the future (cf. Pss 27:1–3; 118:6; Rom 8:31–39). This blessed hope, grounded and centered in the believer's union with Christ in heaven, is what the apologist takes into the hostile world of ideas; moreover, the Spirit of Christ accompanies his voice. Given the position of the apologist in the history of redemption, we have every reason for confidence, strength, and stability, as we depend on Christ's heavenly preservation in the continuing tension of the two ages. Indeed, we stand beside the enthroned Son at the right hand of the Father.

7

The Eschatological Implications of Genesis 2:15 for Apologetics

> Christ has assigned to his followers the task of breaking down the works of darkness everywhere. . . . And as they are on their daily search-and-destroy mission, this mission must begin with the daily cleansing of their hearts.
>
> —Cornelius Van Til, "The Christian Philosophy of Life"

What does eschatology have to do with apologetics? In terms of the traditional arrangement of the theological rubrics, it would seem that eschatology has nothing to do with apologetics. Eschatology is the last discipline of the theological encyclopedia, and it discusses subjects that relate to Christ's second coming. Apologetics is usually discussed in relationship to the first theological rubric, the doctrine of God, under the concept of theism.

In the twentieth century, however, many Reformed exegetes came to grips with the fact that the theological rubrics are intertwined with the eschatological revelation of God. For example, they came to understand that the glorious doctrines of soteriology are draped in the eschatological

The Eschatological Implications of Genesis 2:15 for Apologetics

person and work of Christ, especially the efficacious power of his death and resurrection. In other words, Christ's death and resurrection form the core eschatological event in redemptive history, and as such are the ground, source, and power of every believer's eternal union with Christ through the Holy Spirit (Rom 6:1–14; 2 Cor 4:11—5:8; Gal 2:20; Col 3:1–4). There would be no election, effectual calling, regeneration, faith and repentance, justification, adoption, sanctification, and glorification without that event.

We have come to realize, therefore, that Christ's eschatological kingdom has begun (Matt 4:17; Mark 1:15; Luke 4:43). We are in the *eschaton* looking forward to its consummation (2 Cor 6:2; Heb 1:1–4; 1 John 2:18). Moreover, we are seated already by faith in the heavenly places with Christ even as we remain pilgrims on earth (Eph 1:3; 2:6; Col 3:1–2; 1 Peter 1:1). From this heavenly perspective, every theological rubric must be shaped, including the doctrine of God and apologetics. With respect to apologetics, we *defend* the holy presence of Christ and our present union with him in the heavenly places against every evil advance in opposition to him and his kingdom.

A biblical text on the pre-redemptive state (pre-fall) of historical revelation has stimulated my thinking in regard to the eschatological dimension of apologetics. The text is Genesis 2:15: "Then the Lord God took the man and put him in the garden of Eden to serve and to guard it."[1] In my judgment, as eschatology is intertwined into the inner fabric of the history of revelation, this text will introduce and highlight some profound implications for apologetics.

FROM CHRIST TO THE GARDEN

The recent work of Gregory K. Beale and Meredith G. Kline (1922–2007) has provided an insightful and stimulating interpretation concerning the garden of Eden.[2] Their basic thesis is that the garden is a creational representation of the heavenly temple or sanctuary of the Lord, which later will come to expression in the construction of the tabernacle and the temple in Israel's

---

1. Except where indicated, Scripture quotations in this chapter are my translations.

2. Although his interest is not apologetics, my essay is stimulated by the thoughts of Beale from his lectures, "Already and Not Yet Eschatology and the Temple." More recently, three publications by Beale have appeared that relate to the themes in those lectures: (1) "Garden Temple"; (2) *The Temple and the Church's Mission*; and (3) "Eden, the Temple, and the Church's Mission in the New Creation." See also Kline, *Kingdom Prologue*, 85–87.

history as these objects point us to the person and work of Jesus Christ, the true tabernacle/temple of the Lord (John 1:14; 2:19–22). Moreover, the eschatological vision concerning the new heaven and earth recorded in the book of Revelation presupposes this revelatory pattern (Rev 21–22). In fact, in terms of God's knowledge of his eternal decrees, he knows the beginning from the end, and he knows the end from the beginning. God's knowledge is so comprehensive that he can foreknow a certain event in time and space, and know everything from that event retrospectively (past) and prospectively (future). Since God knows the beginning from the end, let me begin with God's revelatory vision to John about the new heaven and earth (Rev 21–22) and then return to the garden in Genesis.

God's eschatological revelation of the new heaven and earth comes to John in the form of a city—the New Jerusalem (Rev 21:2; cf. 21:10, 14, 16, 19, 21, 23; 22:2).[3] Interestingly, the city of John's vision does not contain any description of a typical geographical landscape, for example, the various sections of an urban environment or the aesthetic surroundings, such as mountains, plains, forests, and even a sea (21:1 notes that there is no more sea). Rather, the appearance, construction, and dimensions of the New Jerusalem are visualized as a temple-city (cf. Rev 21:16 and 1 Kgs 6:20; also Rev 21:18–21 and Ezek 40–48). Specifically, this temple imagery is grounded in God's final revelatory presence in his creation—the true tabernacle/temple, Jesus Christ (Rev 21:3–8, 22–27; 22:5). God's infallible interpretation of John's vision verifies this connection.

God immediately directs our attention to "the tabernacle of God," which dwells with his people (21:3). This tabernacle is a clear reference to Jesus Christ (John 1:14; Rev 21:3, 6–7, 22–23). Herein, God is connecting the dots in the text; he composes an integrative picture that connects the new heaven and earth, the New Jerusalem, and the tabernacle to his presence in his Son, Jesus Christ. God's integrative picture is grounded, however, in his historic progressive revelation. For example, just as the tabernacle/temple in the Old Testament points to Christ, likewise Christ points us to the imagery of the New Jerusalem in the form of a temple-city. In John's vision, the order is *reversed*: in the Old Testament we move from tabernacle/temple to Christ, while in John's vision we move from Christ to temple-city.

---

3. If one wishes to examine Revelation 21–22 more extensively, I would recommend Beale, *Revelation*, 1039–157.

The Eschatological Implications of Genesis 2:15 for Apologetics

God reverses the order in John's vision because the new temple-city begins with Christ's finished work (21:6); all things are now viewed from the perspective that he is the beginning and the end (21:6; 22:13). Specifically, we are in the midst of a new heaven and earth in which Christ's finished work is the beginning of the new creation. If we use creational language, Christ is the origin as well as the source of all existence and life for the temple-city. The Lamb, who has been slain, and the Redeemer, who has been exalted, is the Creator of all things new and good! In terms of redemption accomplished, Christ's activity for the new creation is seen to be for sinners who have been brought into the eternal and final glory of their Savior (21:23–24). Those redeemed sinners are said to reside in the temple-city as the Lamb's bride—the church (21:9, 12–13). Keep in mind, we are not presented with a city in one place and a separate temple in another place; rather, the city is a temple (21:22). The temple-city is the place of the glorious presence of God in his Son, and it is the place where he shines his glorious presence into the faces of his people—the church (cf. 2 Cor 4:6).

Furthermore, not only is the new heaven and earth pictured as Christ's temple-city, but it is also pictured as Christ's garden-city (Rev 22:2). As the eschatological Christ is the source for the new temple-city, likewise he is the source of the new garden-city (22:1). This pattern of God's revelation to John is written clearly upon the pages of the history of revelation. In the garden of Eden, God's presence dwells with his servant, Adam. After the fall, God's presence dwells in the midst of his people in the tabernacle, then in the temple. As we examine closely God's revelation to John (Rev 21–22), the images transmitted to him are of places that reveal God's presence in the midst of his people: Christ, city-temple (tabernacle/temple), and city-garden (garden of Eden). John's vision is not about a generic garden or a generic city; rather, God is communicating life in the garden-city and the temple-city. More specifically, God is communicating life in the garden-city and the temple-city as life in Christ.

Again, one needs to note that the order in John's eschatological vision is *reversed*; in the sequence of history the movement is from garden to tabernacle/temple to Christ; in John's vision the picture pans from Christ to tabernacle/temple to garden. In God's progressive revelation in history, Christ is the consummation of the presence of God; moreover, Christ is the all-comprehensive presence of God in the eschatological life of his bride.

We realize now that an integral understanding of the fabric of God's revelation can be comprehended from its end rather than always starting at the beginning of the story. Specifically, we have moved from the end (new heaven and earth) to the beginning (garden), noting that the integrative revelatory relationship of the presence of God in Christ, the tabernacle/temple, and the garden is consummated in Christ's coming in history and his exaltation in glory. As God's revelation to John has moved from Christ to the garden, let us now direct our attention to the temple imagery in the garden with its eschatological end in mind.

THE TEMPLE-GARDEN AND GENESIS 2:15

As God performs his creative activity, the garden becomes the place of his localized presence in the midst of the creation, where he enters into covenant communion with man, who alone is made in his image (Gen 1:26–27; 2:7–8; cf. Ezek 28:13; 31:8–9; Isa 51:3). Adam is placed immediately in the visible and created replica (the garden) of God's heavenly sanctuary as that sanctuary manifests the glorious presence of God (cf. Ezek 47 and Rev 21–22). The hithpael form of the Hebrew word *halak* ("to walk back and forth") in Genesis 3:8 further impresses the sanctuary idea upon us. There *halak* is used to describe God's presence as he walks in the garden; likewise, in the same manner, *halak* is used to describe God's walking back and forth in the future tabernacle/temple sanctuary (cf. Lev 26:12; 2 Sam 7:6). In the tabernacle/temple as well as the garden, God's walk is a special revelation of his glorious presence in covenant union with his people. Biblical revelation makes a clear connection between the heavenly sanctuary, the tabernacle/temple, and the garden. In terms of the revelatory imagery, Adam should be viewed as the first priest in the Lord's garden-temple (sanctuary). This observation will be solidified by turning our attention to Genesis 2:15: "Then the Lord God took the man and put him in the garden of Eden to serve and to guard it."

Typically Genesis 2:15 has been viewed as an extension of the cultural mandate found in Genesis 1:26–28. Specifically, Genesis 2:15 is thought to teach that Adam is fulfilling the cultural mandate as a gardener; he is dressing, tilling, tending, cultivating, and keeping the garden. Recently, closer attention has been given to the words *'abad* and *shamar* in Genesis 2:15, especially as those terms appear together elsewhere in the Old Testament. Beale has observed correctly that when the two words appear in the same context, they never refer to the gardening task (unless Genesis 2:15 is the

The Eschatological Implications of Genesis 2:15 for Apologetics

only instance in the entire Old Testament for such a reference).[4] Rather, when *'abad* ("serve") and *shamar* ("keep, guard") appear together, Israel is told to serve the Lord and to keep his Word (Deut 10:12–13; 1 Chr 28:8–9). This same idea is taught when the people are instructed to keep God's Word and *not* to serve other gods (Deut 30:16–17; Josh 23:6–7; cf. also 1 Kgs 9:6). For our purposes, however, there is a second manner in which *'abad* and *shamar* appear together; the terms appear together in reference to the duties of the priest to serve the Lord and guard the tabernacle/temple (Num 3:6–8; cf. also the duties of the Gershonites, Kohathites, and the Merarites in Num 3:17—4:49).

If we remain consistent with God's revelatory pattern, then the connection should be evident. In John's vision, the temple-city and the garden-city are correlative revelations. Likewise, the use of *'abad* and *shamar* with respect to the tabernacle/temple and the garden-temple of Eden show that they are correlative revelations. In this revelatory pattern, *'abad* and *shamar* are priestly terms when they appear in the same context; they are not gardening terms. Hence, as the priest serves as a guard of God's presence and his Word in the tabernacle/temple, likewise Adam, as the first priest, serves as a guard of God's presence and his Word in the garden. In fact, one of the important priestly duties of Adam and the Levites is to guard the garden and tabernacle/temple from any intruder—the unclean who would attempt to penetrate the sanctuary (Num 18:7; cf. also Num 3:38).[5]

Adam failed in his task as priest in the garden-temple; he permitted an unclean intruder to invade the premises. Adam, as priest, failed to serve (*'abad*) the Word of God and to guard (*shamar*) the holy and glorious presence of his Creator from that evil trespasser, Satan. To put it another way, Adam failed in his defense (*apologia*) of the Lord's sanctuary from the Serpent's evil advance. Hence, as federal head of humanity, Adam not only failed as the first priest, but also failed as the first apologist.

In my judgment, there is a clear connection between *shamar* (to "guard") and its synonym, to "defend" (*apologeomai*) in the garden-temple. Simply put, to *guard* the presence of God in the garden-temple from any

---

4. Beale, "Eschatology and the Temple," session 2.

5. I am fully aware that Genesis 2:15 can be used to demonstrate the constitution of man as prophet, priest, and king in accordance with the teaching of the Heidelberg Catechism Q&A 32. For the purpose of this essay, however, I am concerned with only the priestly function, although it will be apparent that the prophetic office and its service to God's Word will constantly be placed before us. However, an outline or discussion of Adam's office as king is not the design of this essay.

intruder is also to *defend* the presence of God in the garden-temple from any intruder. The instrument for such a defense is faithfulness to the Word of the Lord. However, as Adam failed his apologetic task, he, along with the woman, accepted the rebellious presuppositions of the invader who questioned the truth, integrity, and authority of God's Word. Satan convinced them that they were their own reference point for knowing good and evil, being like God himself (Gen 3:1–5). In their act of rebellious sin, they exchanged the truth of God for a lie as they worshiped and served the creature rather than the Creator (Rom 1:25). Hence, they surrendered their status of fellowship and communion in the intimate presence of their Lord for the sake of fellowship and communion with the embodiment of evil. As a consequence, God cast them out of his garden-sanctuary; they were no longer fit for his presence.

GENESIS 2:15 AND APOLOGETICS

Genesis 2:15 has profound implications for apologetics. First, God created and placed Adam in the sanctuary of his created universe. In the garden-temple, Adam is immediately placed in God's presence. A crucial observation must be grasped here: Adam is not placed in the garden in order to begin reading natural revelation as he makes his way to special revelation. Neither is Adam placed in the creation in order to proceed by means of deductive and inductive logic from theism to the triune God of the Bible. As God places Adam in the garden, God does not design Adam so he would move intellectually from comprehending God naturally to comprehending God more fully. Rather, Adam is immediately in the presence of the personal God who made him; here God reveals himself clearly in this pre-redemptive state. If a movement is to be observed here, it is not with Adam moving rationally and empirically to God, but with the sovereign Lord condescending to Adam.

The true, personal, triune God has condescended in covenant bond to his servant. Immediately, Adam is encountered with God's supernatural and self-authenticating existence as the Lord's presence envelops Adam's existence in the garden-temple. Herein, the eschatological nature of the garden-temple comes into view. If we comprehend the retrospective process of revelation that we have outlined from the city-temple (Revelation) back to the garden-temple (Genesis), we must note that Adam's apologetic state in the garden-temple is eschatological. The eschatological reality of

The Eschatological Implications of Genesis 2:15 for Apologetics

being in the presence of the Lord forever (New Jerusalem) is forecasted in history as a present reality to Adam as the Lord's presence envelops the garden-temple. For this reason, it should be noted that to unfold the biblical doctrine of eschatology is to unfold the biblical doctrine of apologetics.

Second, Adam's task is to guard or defend the sacred presence of God from any intruder or invader into his created sanctuary, the garden-temple. Here is the core of Adam's priestly and apologetic task; he is to guard and defend the sanctuary of the Lord from unclean things. As the Lord places Adam in an apologetic setting, he defines his apologetic task; it is to keep every intruder and invader out of his presence. Herein, the eschatological dimension of Adam's task becomes evident. In order to grasp this dimension of his task, however, one must think in terms of the eternal realm of God's eschatological glory. In the new heaven and earth, do unclean intruders and invaders reside in the eternal glory of the Lord's presence? Absolutely not; in God's eternal residence nothing unclean will be in the presence of the Lord—only those cleansed by the blood of the Lamb of God are permitted there. Hence, the eternal eschatological realm is injected upon Adam's apologetic commission in the pre-redemptive state in history. Adam is to maintain and secure the purity of the garden-temple from any contamination (cf. Ps 84:10).

As God defines Adam's apologetic task in the garden-temple, there is absolutely nothing that suggests, or even hints, that Adam is to begin his defense with natural revelation, natural theology, or generic theism. Rather, according to Genesis 2:15, Adam is to perform his apologetic task by defending and serving the Lord and his Word; he is to live by every Word that proceeds from the mouth of the Lord. The eschatological dimension of God's revelation determines the *method* of the apologetic task: he must start with God, and he must end with God; or it can be said that he must start with God's Word, and he must end with God's Word.

Third, if we connect Adam's fall into sin (Gen 3:1–7) with his stated task in Genesis 2:15, we note the pitfalls of his apologetic performance. Adam's breakdown is defined simply as a failure to guard and defend the sacred presence of God (garden-temple) from an unclean intruder (Satan). In other words, if Adam and Eve had adhered faithfully to God's Word, the invader would have been repelled from God's presence. Instead, the Word of the Lord was compromised, surrendered, and forfeited. Once this was done, Adam and the woman were doomed for failure. After all, Satan understood the situation well; if Adam and the woman would buckle under his seductive words, he could succeed in contaminating God's sanctuary and presence.

Indeed, Adam and Eve buckled; they exchanged eschatological glory for eschatological judgment. Instead of remaining faithful to the absolute authority of the Lord's Word, Adam and the woman allowed Satan to define the discussion; they surrendered to the "neutral" claims of Satan's reason. He seduced them to think of a world in which the Lord God is not the Lord God, and, thus, he convinced them that they needed to experience the empirical world outside the presence of the Lord. Alternatively, to put it another way, Adam dropped his armaments against the intruder for the empirical experience of life outside the presence of God. Instead of savoring the presence of the Lord, Adam wished to experience the lying world of Satan (cf. John 8:44).

For Adam and Eve, God and the truth of his Word no longer defined what was rational and irrational; rather, they felt comfortable to turn such definitions over to the invader. Specifically, Satan presented Adam with a world in which his reason was autonomous in blatant rebellion against the truth of God's Word. Once Adam capitulated to Satan's summons, his security against the enemy was gone. That is, Adam relinquished the Word of God as the starting point and finishing point of his apologetic. He failed his apologetic task across the eschatological spectrum.

GENESIS 2:15 AND CHRIST, THE APOLOGIST

In contrast to the first Adam, the last Adam upheld the eschatological dimension of the apologetic task. Keep in mind that as we move prospectively, the garden-temple points us to the tabernacle/temple in Israel's history, which in turn points us to the true tabernacle-temple of God, the Lord Jesus Christ (John 1:14; 2:19–22; Rev 21:3–7). Where the first Adam failed in his priestly and apologetic task to serve the Lord and his Word while guarding and defending the Lord's presence, the second Adam succeeded. Moreover, the second Adam is fully equipped as priest and apologist to deal with the stipulations of Genesis 2:15.

As Immanuel, he is the actual presence of God, whose own ontological identity as the Word of God provides him with the guard and defense against any intruder or invader of his being (Isa 7:14; Matt 1:23; John 1:1, 14). His effectual defense is seen at the beginning of his ministry when he confronts the intruder (Satan) in the wilderness (Matt 4:1–11; Mark

The Eschatological Implications of Genesis 2:15 for Apologetics

1:12–13; Luke 4:1–13). Although the wilderness confrontation with Satan is primarily about Christ's faithful reenactment of Israel's failure in the wilderness, the event also points us back to the garden. Just as God's enemy intruded and invaded the residence of God's presence in the garden-temple, now Satan attempts to intrude and invade the ontological presence of God in the eschatological Son of God. Just as Satan seduced the first Adam, he attempts to seduce the second Adam to act with respect to an autonomous rational and empirical world outside God's presence. Moreover, Satan challenges the second Adam to compromise, surrender, and forfeit the Word of God. But the second Adam *is* the Word of God!

As the Word of God, Christ is equipped ontologically to be *the* apologist who can recite the Word of God as part of his own essence against the onslaught of Satan. He will not be seduced to pursue a rational and empirical world outside his own ontological presence. The self-attesting Christ as the Word of God is sufficient to guard and defend his own ontological divine presence from Satan's evil intent. Specifically, Christ's own epistemological self-consciousness goes into effect; he uses the Word of God to repel each advance by his enemy. By beginning and ending with the Word of God (his ontological identity as well as his performance in Word and in deed), Christ's initial defense against his archenemy undermines Satan's malicious plot to divert him from the cross. Hence, in his initial confrontation with Satan, the eschatological Adam fulfills the apologetic task. He protects his own divine presence by faithfully adhering to the eschatological method of defense—beginning and ending with the Word of God. In Christ, therefore, we have entered into the realm of eschatological apologetics for the sake of guarding, protecting, and entering into the divine presence of the triune God forever!

Furthermore, Christ's initial apologetic act against Satan is consummated at the cross. As Christ makes his way to the cross, he protects the presence of the Lord within himself. He accepts freely the path his Father has ordained for him as revealed in the Word of God (Matt 16:21; 26:42; John 20:9; Heb 5:8). When we follow Christ's path to the cross, we must not overlook that his apologetic faithfulness directs him to suffering and death. In fact, like Christ, those who faithfully adhere to his apologetic mission may expect suffering, and the possibility of death in this world (e.g., Stephen, Peter, and Paul). Death came to Christ, and, perhaps, we may come to the same end.

Interestingly, the failure of the first Adam in his apologetic task brought the state of death, whereas the success of the second Adam in his apologetic task delivers him to the cross. However, the act of the first Adam was grounded in pride and sin; the act of the last Adam was grounded in servitude and righteousness. The path of death secured by the first Adam was destruction; the path of death secured by the eschatological Adam was life. Hence, Christ's faithfulness to the apologetic task destroys the works of the devil in order to secure a place for his elect in his presence.

For this reason, the believer's apologetic must comprise the central message of the cross and the resurrection to be effectual. It is the actual event that destroyed the works of the devil (Acts 17:1-4, 18, 31-32). As the church operates faithfully within the confines of this apologetic task, the Lord may provide the fruits of her faithfulness. Just as Christ's faithfulness was rewarded as his Father raised the Lamb of God from the dead for the sake of his elect, likewise, the Lord may reward the church for her faithfulness by raising those who are spiritually dead to life (his elect). Indeed, just as Christ is vindicated by the Spirit to life in his resurrection (1 Tim 3:16), likewise, the unbeliever is vindicated by the Holy Spirit as he is transformed from death to life (Rom 6:1-14; 8:9-11). Herein, the eschatological work of the Holy Spirit ushers the unbeliever into the presence of the eschatological sanctuary, Jesus Christ!

GENESIS 2:15, THE CHURCH, AND THE HOLY SPIRIT

As we consider the work of the Holy Spirit to convict, convince, and persuade sinners about the gospel, we return to the book of Revelation and the imagery of the Bridegroom and the bride (21:2, 9-13; 22:17). Christ and his bride are present in God's vision to John concerning the new heaven and earth. They play an essential role in the revelatory pattern of God in Christ, the tabernacle/temple, and the garden. Just as we have seen with the previously mentioned revelatory pattern, we may project the eschatological Bridegroom and bride into the garden-temple in Genesis. The marriage of the man and woman in the garden is the initial eschatological picture of the eternal marriage of Christ and his church; the eschatological future is thereby projected into the pre-redemptive state.

In the garden, the woman was created immediately to dwell in the presence of her husband just as Christ's bride dwells eternally in his presence. Moreover, from the beginning it was God's intent to have the man

The Eschatological Implications of Genesis 2:15 for Apologetics

and the woman dwell in his presence as the man and the woman depict his bride. Hence, as we consider the original priestly and apologetic task of Adam, his task has been enriched and expanded.

Thus far we have established that apologetics is to guard and defend the presence of God by the Word of God; but in God's eschatological revelation to John, God's presence also includes his bride—his church! Adam's task to guard and defend the presence of God by his Word also included himself and his wife (the church in the garden). For this reason, since eternity is pictured as the wedding feast of Christ (Bridegroom) and his church (bride), and this eschatological dimension is revealed in the garden, apologetics is also the defense of the bride and Bridegroom against their intruders and invaders.

In order to combat the enemies of the church and the gospel, the eschatological work of the Holy Spirit is paramount. One function of the Spirit's eschatological work is that the church and the believer are now the dwelling place of God's presence. The body of the believer is the temple of the Holy Spirit; the believer's body is the place where the presence of Christ dwells by his Spirit (1 Cor 3:16-17; 6:19). As the Spirit dwells in the body of believers in Christ's church, the apologetic task is defined by the fact that the apologist is placed immediately in the sanctuary of the Lord. He is engulfed by the revelation of Christ's exalted glory in the heavenly places as the Holy Spirit dwells in him. Encompassed by the revelation of Christ in the heavenly sanctuary, the apologist is not instructed to begin with an abstract concept, for example, reason, experience, feeling, or inner faith. Rather, consistent with the teaching of Genesis 2:15, *the apologist begins in the eschatological realm of the "fullness of time." In this realm, the apologist is to serve, guard, and defend the purity of Christ's holy presence in the heavenly places and his union with his church from any contamination by faithfully adhering to the Word of God.*

As God revealed to John, Christ's eschatological work cannot be separated from his church; the Bridegroom and the bride are part of her epistemological self-consciousness. In this eschatological situation, the apologist has no recourse; he must guard and defend the church and the believer against the continual seductions of Satan's advances to defile God's holy presence. Although already conquered and defeated by Christ, Satan will fight until his final destruction. But the church is equipped for his advances; as she continues to live as a pilgrim bride, she is the presence of Christ in this world. As such, she is not permitted to allow anything to defile the

Spirit's holy presence of Christ; this includes the things her members see, the things they hear, and the thoughts they entertain.

Specifically, Christ's bride is to defend and guard herself in the marketplace by living the Word of God. Once again, we see that apologetics begins and ends with the Word of God, thus maintaining a true eschatological method. Blending our notion of apologetics with Van Til's definition, we could say that *apologetics is the vindication of the presence of Christ and his church against the various forms of the non-Christian philosophy of life that constantly attempt to invade and intrude that presence.*[6] And as the church is engaged in the marketplace, she has a confidence never enjoyed before in redemptive history. The second Adam has fulfilled the apologetic task of Genesis 2:15; the self-attesting Christ has already won the apologetic battle. In this context, Christ provides the presence, witness, and testimony of the Spirit to his bride to sustain his victory in this world.

EPILOGUE

Over the years, my interest in apologetics has been the issue of prolegomena; I have been concerned about the starting point of a Christian apologetic method. This essay continues to elaborate upon that concern, especially in association to the apologetic method of Van Til. Those familiar with Van Til's method will recognize that this essay reflects upon two of his most salient points: the self-attesting Christ of Scripture as his starting point and the Word of God as the tool of apologetic engagement.

Taking Van Til's own acknowledgment that Vos was his most influential teacher, I have attempted to push Van Til's biblical apologetic deeper into the fabric of God's revelation. In other words, I want to understand how God and the historical revelation of himself shape the foundation (prolegomena) and method of Christian apologetics. For example, Vos and other Reformed exegetes have exposed the rich eschatological nature of God's revelation. It seems to me this understanding of revelation can only enhance and enrich what Van Til has placed before us. In terms of the self-attesting Christ of Scripture, the eschatological nature of revelation has actually placed the apologist and his method in the presence of God's sanctuary. He is actually placed in the presence of his glorious and holy

---

6. Van Til defined apologetics as "the vindication of the Christian philosophy of life against the various forms of the non-Christian philosophy of life" (Van Til, *Christian Apologetics*, 17).

The Eschatological Implications of Genesis 2:15 for Apologetics

Savior, who testifies about himself in Holy Scripture. Being in covenant union with the exalted Christ, the Christian apologist begins his defense and ends his defense with God's Word. After all, he is in the presence of, and he is in union with, the Word of God who has become flesh. He does not begin with reason and then appeal to God's Word, and he does not begin with God's Word and then finish with personal experience. Rather, God's Word is the starting point and the ending point; Christ, as the Word of God, is "the Alpha and the Omega, the Beginning and the End, the First and the Last" (Rev 22:13 NKJV)!

As this essay attempts to solidify Van Til's apologetic in the historical revelation of God, pastors and laity in the church may be very curious about the next step, especially since I have closed by discussing the church and the work of the Holy Spirit. Such a concern is legitimate. Pastors and laity want to see what an eschatological apologetic looks like, that is, how the defense of Christ's presence by the Word of God comes to expression in the marketplace.

Everyone in Christ's true church realizes that Satan and his forces continue each day to attack Christ's sacred presence. Indeed, I realize that we must move beyond prolegomena issues. Next, we need to investigate how the Word of God provides the substance for the transcendental critique against all vain imaginations raised up against the knowledge of God. For pastors and laity, it becomes necessary to show how the transcendental critique exposes the folly of unbelief (eschatological judgment) for the sake of preserving the sanctity of the presence of Christ and his bride. Let us press forward in this discussion.

8

A Reassessment of Natural and Special Revelation

Here, then, is the picture of a well-integrated and unified philosophy of history in which revelation in nature and revelation in Scripture are mutually meaningless without one another and mutually fruitful when taken together.

—Cornelius Van Til, *Christian Apologetics*

On the first day of creation, God created light, and separated the light from the darkness:

> Then God said, "Let there be light"; and there was light. And God saw the light, that it was good; and God divided the light from the darkness. God called the light Day, and the darkness He called Night. So the evening and the morning were the first day. (Gen 1:3–5)[1]

---

1. All Scripture quotations in this chapter are from the NKJV unless otherwise indicated as my translation.

A Reassessment of Natural and Special Revelation

How do we generally understand God's creation of light, as natural revelation or special revelation? We tend to understand it as natural revelation. Now let us observe the dawn of the new creation:

> All things were made through Him, and without Him nothing was made that was made. In Him was life, and the life was the light of men. And the light shines in the darkness, and the darkness did not comprehend it. There was a man sent from God, whose name was John. This man came for a witness, to bear witness of the Light, that all through him might believe. He was not that Light, but was sent to bear witness of that Light. That was the true Light which gives light to every man coming into the world. He was in the world, and the world was made through Him, and the world did not know Him. (John 1:3–10)

Later in John's gospel, the Light in John's prologue speaks to us. Our Savior, Jesus Christ, affirms: "I am the Light of the world. He who follows Me shall not walk in darkness, but have the light of life" (John 8:12; cf. Rev 21:23).

At the dawn of the new creation, the Light of life (Jesus Christ) came into the world. How do we understand Christ's redeeming work? Is it natural revelation or special revelation? Generally, we understand Christ's redeeming work as special revelation.

It seems that the distinction is clear: God's creation of light on the first day is an expression of natural revelation, whereas God's sending of the divine Light, Jesus Christ, to usher in the new creation is an expression of special revelation. For many Christians, this is where the boundaries and limits of natural revelation and special revelation are set. Natural revelation is a distinct and separate revelation, consisting in God's imprint upon the created universe; special revelation is a distinct and separate revelation, consisting in the divine accomplishment and verbal communication of redemption. Further, though distinct, the two revelations are complementary, never contradictory. Using this model, Christians seem efficiently to distinguish natural revelation and special revelation. R. C. Sproul, a preeminent expositor of this common model, has argued that natural (or general) revelation "evidences that a supreme being has created the universe, but we do not see that the being is triune, nor do we see a plan of redemption anywhere in the created order."[2] According to Sproul, for humanity to see that the supreme Creator of the universe is triune (Father, Son, and Holy

---

2. Sproul, *Defending Your Faith*, 74.

Spirit), and for us to see God's plan of redemption in Christ, we need special revelation.[3]

It seems appropriate to examine these rigid boundaries between natural and special revelation to determine if they have biblical support. In this respect, Van Til provides us with an insightful way forward.

VAN TIL'S PHILOSOPHY OF REVELATION

Van Til questioned whether nature reveals nothing about God's grace.[4] In his book, *Christian Apologetics*, he writes: "Saving grace is not manifest in nature; yet it is the God of saving grace who manifests himself by means of nature."[5] In other words, Van Til held that God displays his saving grace upon the landscape of nature; saving grace is not identical with nature, but saving grace is brought about on the natural terrain of created history. For this reason, Van Til did not speak of two distinct and separate revelations, one natural and one special. Rather, he understood revelation to be a *single unified complex* constituted by two *forms*, a natural form and a special form. Van Til writes the following:

> Any revelation that God gives of himself is therefore absolutely voluntary. Herein precisely lies the union of the various *forms* of God's revelation with one another. God's revelation in nature, together with God's revelation in Scripture, *form* God's *one* grand scheme of covenant revelation of himself to man. The two *forms* of revelation must therefore be seen as presupposing and supplementing one another. They are aspects of *one general philosophy of history*.[6]

Perhaps an example from one of Van Til's favorite Bible stories, Noah and the flood, will help clarify Van Til's philosophy of revelation.[7]

---

3. Ibid.
4. Van Til, *Christian Apologetics*, 66.
5. Ibid.
6. Ibid. Italics are mine. Here Van Til is following the line of Bavinck, who wrote, "Scripture, though it knows of established natural order, in the case of revelation makes no distinction between 'natural' and 'supernatural' revelation. It uses the same terms for both. . . . In its origin all revelation is supernatural. God is always working" (Bavinck, *Reformed Dogmatics*, 1:307).
7. See Van Til, *Christian Apologetics*, 67–68.

A Reassessment of Natural and Special Revelation

In the flood, God executed his wrath upon unbelief; he used nature—the flood—to wipe the reprobate from the earth. At the same time, God displayed grace to Noah and his family; he protected them from judgment by providing them with safe residence in an ark that Noah was instructed to construct from natural materials. Certainly, God's covenant of grace is a covenant of salvation. By Noah's safe passage through the flood of judgment, God's covenant was continued for the sake of all mankind and all living creatures (Gen 8:21; 9:9–11).

Not only did God use the natural objects of water and wood to mediate his wrath and grace, God also used a natural object to signify his covenant promise. God chose the rainbow to be a sign that he would never again destroy all flesh with a flood (Gen 9:12–15). The rainbow—a natural object—is not saving grace, but it *is* a sign of God's saving grace to Noah. In Van Til's language, the natural rainbow is "a limiting notion."[8] The rainbow, as a natural sign of covenant promise, is insufficient in itself; it exists in expectation of Christ's redemptive fulfillment. Hence, Van Til used the story of Noah to show that saving grace is "mediated through nature." In fact, the entire Old Testament testifies to the fact that nature *serves* "the purposes of redemption. The forces of nature are always at the beck and call of the power of differentiation that works toward redemption and reprobation."[9]

When Van Til stressed the unified character of natural revelation and special revelation, he also insisted that we must locate the unity of these two forms in (A) the triune God of the Bible; and (B) God's "one unified comprehensive plan for the world."[10]

First, concerning (A), nowhere in the Bible is God pictured *deistically*. The Bible never depicts nature as if it is unfolding according to predetermined, impersonal laws set by an out-of-touch supreme being. Simply stated, the Bible is not in agreement with Aristotle's conception of God as the unmoved mover. By extension, the Bible is equally opposed to Aquinas's dualistic construal of revelation, according to which God should be thought

---

8. Ibid., 68. Bavinck states, "The covenant that after the flood was made with Noah and in him with the new human race is a covenant of nature, yet no longer natural but the fruit of non-obligatory supernatural grace" (Bavinck, *Reformed Dogmatics*,1:311).

9. Van Til, *Christian Apologetics*, 68. Interestingly, Jonathan Edwards (1703–1758) conveyed the same idea in the eighteenth century, that is, that creation serves redemption. Edwards wrote: "This seems to have been one reason why God made the world by Jesus Christ, viz. that the creation of the world was a work that was subordinate to the work of redemption" (Edwards, *Miscellanies*, 289).

10. Van Til, *Christian Apologetics*, 78.

of in an Aristotelian manner when viewed through natural revelation and in a trinitarian manner when viewed through special revelation.[11] In contrast to Aquinas and those who share his dualistic view of revelation, Scripture as well as the WCF tells us that the natural revelation of creation is the product of the Father (Gen 1:1), Son (John 1:3; Col 1:16), and the Holy Spirit (Gen 1:2; cf. WCF 4.1). The entire creation bears the blueprint of the triune God. Hence, imbedded in the Bible's account of creation is the idea that no one can interpret or understand the world or the making thereof unless one views reality through the trinitarian lens of Scripture.

Second, concerning (A), nowhere in the Bible is God pictured *pantheistically*. In other words, the Bible never reduces the reality of the natural world so as to exalt the supernatural. For example, in 1 Corinthians 10:4 Paul states that the rock that God used to provide water for the Israelites in the wilderness "was Christ" (Exod 17:6; cf. Pss 95:1; 114:7–8). What does Paul actually mean here? Is he really identifying the natural revelation of the rock with the supernatural revelation of God in Christ? If Moses touched the rock, would he have touched Jesus? Should I put my faith in the rock in the same way I have put my faith in Christ? Are natural revelation and special revelation identified such that the very being of God is identical with a natural phenomenon? Does the Bible teach *supernatural pantheism*?

Not at all. Instead of teaching supernatural pantheism, Paul is using an ontological revelational metaphor. The rock from which water came in Exodus 17:6 points to the reality of Christ as the everlasting Water of Life (John 6:35). The rock is not God incarnate. Rather, the rock is a natural sign that directs the covenant people of God to the Living Water who will not allow his people to thirst—the incarnate Christ. Yet again, we can see that the Bible never speaks of natural revelation without bringing it together with its compliment in special revelation; the two forms of revelation, natural and special, are organically united.

To exposit (B), it is helpful to turn to Van Til's writings once more. Van Til held that natural revelation and special revelation must be viewed

11. Perhaps, the contrast here between the biblical account of revelation and Aquinas's account can be seen in the way Guido de Brès intended to open article 2 of the Belgic Confession. The opening phrase presently reads, "We know Him by two means," which refers to creation (natural revelation) and Scripture (special revelation). As it presently reads, many find in this phrase a construction that fits with Aquinas's understanding of revelation. However, in the original draft de Brès wrote, "we confess to know Him as such by two means," which stresses the organic union of natural revelation and special revelation, rather than a sequential movement from one revelation to a second (Aquinas) (see Berkouwer, *General Revelation*, 275).

A Reassessment of Natural and Special Revelation

from within the spectrum of God's "all-comprehensive plan for the created universe."[12] To repeat a previous quotation from Van Til, "the two *forms* of revelation [natural and special] must therefore be seen as presupposing and supplementing one another. They are aspects of *one general philosophy of history*."[13] For Van Til, natural revelation and special revelation are brought together on the landscape of history, as providentially realized by God. To put it another way, we can only speak about the two forms of revelation within the context of revelational history.

Perhaps, the following statement by Van Til is more enlightening: "He [God] has planned the end from the beginning."[14] The earmarks of Vos are clear in this remark by Van Til. Van Til held that God's plan for the creation should be examined from its endpoint, not its starting point. Stated a bit more robustly, we should understand and interpret the beginning of creation by starting with its endpoint. In the vernacular of biblical eschatology, Van Til started from our present stance in the eschatological kingdom of Christ and worked back to the beginning of the creation. In Van Til's view of history, the two forms of revelation as well as the discipline of apologetics are unified and shaped by eschatology.

To examine more closely Van Til's unified understanding of natural revelation and special revelation, let us reflect again on the concept of *light*. We can never understand fully the creation of light on the first day of creation unless we understand the eschatological Light of the new creation—Jesus Christ. In fact, Jesus Christ brings the light of the original creation into existence (John 1:3; Col 1:16). Furthermore, Jesus Christ, the special

---

12. Van Til, *Christian Apologetics*, 76. Again, Edwards would agree—creation serves redemption. Moreover, Edwards sees providence in this vein: "And that work of God's providence to which all other works of providence, both in the material and immaterial part of creation, are subservient, is the work of redemption. All other works of providence may be looked upon as *appendages* to this great work, or *things* which God does to subserve that grand design" (Edwards, *Miscellanies*, 284).

13. Van Til, *Christian Apologetics*, 66.

14. Ibid., 76. Van Til comments further: "It is not that we are merely brought into existence by God, but our meaning also depends upon God. Our meaning cannot be realized except through the course of history. God created man in order that man should realize a certain end, that is, the glory of God, and thus God should reach his own end" (Van Til, *Defense of the Faith*, 40). Edwards also seems convinced that we need to understand the beginning from its end: "The work of redemption may be looked upon as the great end and drift of all God's works and dispensations from the beginning, and even the end of the work of creation itself; yea, the whole creation. It was the end of the creation of heaven: the preparing that blessed and glorious habitation was with the eye to this" (Edwards, *Miscellanies*, 284).

revelation of God, is the pattern for the natural light of natural revelation in the original creation.[15] At the same time, the light of the original creation is a pointer to Christ as the Light of the new creation.

Let us go one step further: as light gives resolution to the darkness in the original creation, likewise, Christ as the Light of the world gives resolution to the darkness in the new creation (Gen 1:1–5; cf. John 3:16–21). The eschatological coming of Christ, as the divine Light, sets the pattern for the light in the original creation. *The eschatological work of Christ's redemption in the new creation (special revelation) is written upon the fabric of the original creation (natural revelation).* The end determines the beginning. For this reason, the natural revelation of the original creation is inherently eschatological. Written upon the very fabric of the original creation (natural revelation) is a telegram to all humanity saying they must see the special revelation of Christ in the natural aspects of the world. A person cannot understand the one form of revelation without the other; or, to put it another way, one cannot interpret Genesis one without John one. In fact, the eschatological pattern for which Van Til argued is this: *starting with John one, we must interpret Genesis one.*

On the basis of such a biblical construct of revelation, the believer possesses a unique, epistemological self-conscious response to modern naturalistic science. One should never look at natural phenomena outside the eschatological reality of Christ. Furthermore, no natural phenomenon can be understood correctly outside the integrated work of God's plan for the creation. We can say it like this: if there is no new creation, there can be no original creation. Any understanding of the original creation that does not bring the new creation immediately into view is reductionist. Such a reductionistic understanding abstracts the original creation out of the integrated fabric of supernatural revelation.

PAUL'S VIEW OF REVELATION IN ROMANS

Van Til's philosophy of revelation is helpful in addressing some challenging texts found in Romans 10:18, 8:12–30, and 1:18–25. Let us begin with

---

15. Edwards was emphatic about his point: "That the recovery of the world from confusion and ruin is by Christ, who is the wisdom of God and the brightness of his glory and the light of the world; and that the first thing that was done in order to the recovery of the ruined world, was the giving of Jesus Christ to be the light of the world to put an end to its darkness and confusion" (Edwards, *Miscellanies*, 284–5).

A Reassessment of Natural and Special Revelation

Romans 10:18 and make our way back, mainly because Romans 10:18 presents us with a major problem, which, if we can solve it, might shed light upon Romans 8:12–30 and Romans 1:18–25.

In Romans 10, Paul is speaking of the propagation of the gospel in the world. He places before his audience the truth that both Jew and Greek are in need of salvation, and, hence, whoever calls upon the name of the Lord will be saved (10:11–13). Herein, Paul identifies some obvious questions: Who will call on him in whom they have not believed? How shall they believe in him of whom they have not heard? Similar questions are often heard within the church: How can a person be saved if they have never heard about Jesus? How can a person be responsible before God if they have never heard about Jesus?

Have we not all wrestled with these questions? Is it fair for God to send someone to hell if they have never heard of Jesus or of his gospel? After all, we might cry out, such persons never had a chance to be saved! Paul goes further: "How shall they hear without a preacher?" (10:14); "How shall they preach unless they are sent?" (10:15a). Indeed, the church can say the gospel has gone forth into many areas of the world (fulfilling Isa 52:7), but, as the gospel goes forth, many have heard but have not obeyed the gospel. Like Isaiah, the apostolic church can raise the same question: "Lord, who has believed our report?" (Isa 53:1). Paul follows his questions with a clarification: "So then faith comes by hearing, and hearing by the Word of God" (10:17). In other words, saving faith and obedience to the gospel are a result of effective listening to the Word of God.

Still, we may continue to wrestle with the point that many in the world have not heard the gospel; they have not had a preacher come to them to instill faith in Jesus Christ. So, are we to be satisfied that the gospel has been preached to many people but not all people? Are we to be content that the gospel has been received in faith or rejected by many people, but not all people? To those who are stuck here, contrasting the "many" *versus* "the all," Paul's next question may be a bombshell (v. 18): "But I say, have they [all] not heard?" Paul answers: "Yes, indeed [all]," and then proceeds to quote Psalm 19:4: "Their sound has gone out to all the earth, And their words to the ends of the world." Paul says that the communication of the Word of God concerning the gospel of Jesus Christ has been preached to the ends of the world. Paul makes his case by quoting Psalm 19:4, asserting that everyone on the face of the earth has heard the gospel.

According to Paul, Psalm 19:4 is a reference to the universal propagation of the gospel through the preaching of the Word of God. Why, we might ask, are many amazed to find Paul linking Psalm 19:4 to the preaching of the gospel? Because within the traditional understanding of the boundaries between natural revelation and special revelation, it is usually affirmed that Psalm 19:4a–b relates to natural revelation. For example, John Murray states that Psalm 19:1–6 relates to general or/and natural revelation, whereas Psalm 19:7–14 relates to special revelation.[16] Many say that Psalm 19:1 denotes the content of natural revelation for the first six verses: "The heavens declare the glory of God; And the firmament shows his handiwork."[17] However, here lies the problem: Paul does not apply the first part of Psalm 19:1–6 exclusively to the distinct category of natural revelation. Rather, in Romans 10:18 Paul applies Psalm 19:4 to the gospel, that is, to special revelation.[18]

---

16. Murray, *Romans*, 2:61.

17. In fact, the Belgic Confession captures the element of communication that pertains to natural revelation in Psalm 19 when it discusses that natural revelation is a book that is read. After all, as the Psalmist says that nature speaks and propels knowledge, we note that such speech is so broad that everyone has heard its voice. Hence, Reformed theologians have said correctly that natural revelation manifests the truth that all humanity has heard the voice of God.

18. There is a wide range of perplexity over this text, particularly Paul's use of Psalm 19:4. Hodge clearly states that Paul does *not* intend that Psalm 19:4 be applied specifically to the "preaching of the gospel." Rather, Hodge contends that Paul uses Psalm 19:4 to state that the "proclamation of the gospel was now free from all national and ecclesiastical restrictions" in order to go to Jew and Gentile (Hodge, *Romans*, 443–4). Calvin rejects the ancient "allegorical" interpretation in which the sun equals Christ (Ps 19:4) and the heavens equal the apostles (Ps 19:1). Rather, for Calvin, Paul invokes his teaching from Romans 1. Paul is using Psalm 19:4 not to declare that "the Gospel" has gone to the Gentiles, but that "the whole workmanship of heaven and earth spoke and proclaimed its Author by its preaching." In the fashion of Aquinas, Calvin is holding that Paul's use of Psalm 19:4 here is a reference to natural revelation alone—that God preaches through natural revelation his "divinity" to Jew and Gentile (Calvin, *Romans and Thessalonians*, 234). Murray saw the "difficulty" here. Murray wonders if Paul had a lapse of memory since he seems to be quoting Psalm 19:4 in the context of special revelation instead of natural revelation. After all, Murray indicates, we must remember that the Psalmist deals with general revelation in verses 1–6 and with special revelation in verses 7–14. For Murray, although in the strict sense Psalm 19:4 applies to natural revelation, Paul has the liberty to use it in any way he pleases. Simply put, according to Murray, Paul is using Psalm 19:4 as a pattern for the gospel going "to the uttermost parts of the earth." To put it another way, general revelation (Ps 19:4), as it testifies of God to all humanity, is now an analogy for the gospel (special revelation) going out to all humanity (Murray, *Romans*, 2:61). C. E. B. Cranfield suggests a simple solution; he holds that "probably all that

A Reassessment of Natural and Special Revelation

Has Paul lost his way? Should he be understanding the following theological prescription: that Psalm 19:1–6 only reveals the divine attributes of God's wisdom and power from natural revelation, whereas verses seven through fourteen reveal the law (righteousness) of the Lord from God's supernatural revelation in his Word? Can he really quote Psalm 19:4 to verify that the gospel has gone forth to all humanity by virtue of the testimony of the creation? Although study is yet needed on this, allow me to suggest two biblical assumptions that underlie Paul's thinking: (1) the creation declares the supernatural deeds/acts of the Lord; and (2) within the fabric of natural revelation lies the essential nature of supernatural revelation.

First, regarding creation declaring God's supernatural deeds (assumption 1), we note that in various passages in the Old Testament the heavens are described as witnessing and testifying to the acts of God. For example, in passages in Deuteronomy, God seems to be holding court, and the witnesses are the "heavens and the earth" (4:26; 30:19; 31:28; 32:1). Simply, the witness is the created order (also true for prophetic literature: Isa 1:2; Amos 4:13; Mic 6:1, 2). Isaiah (1:2) may capture best this point: the Lord testifies to the heavens that he has "nourished and raised his children" (they are objects of his acts of redemption) and that those same children are sinful and corrupt, and, therefore, objects of God's anger (judgment). The Lord makes his appeal to the heavens because they have witnessed God's blessing and judgment with respect to God's activity; on the terrain of the creation God has performed his deeds. The heavens and the earth have seen how God has actually pruned his children—whether he has brought them through the Red Sea on dry ground, or whether he has hosted them in a land that flows with milk and honey. In this context God does not partition or divide himself as if there are certain attributes only revealed by

---

he [Paul] wants to assert is that the message has been publicly proclaimed in the world at large—the significant thing is that it has been quite widely preached to the Gentiles." Like Murray, Cranfield maintains that Psalm 19:4 is being used by Paul as an analogy of expanding the preaching of the gospel (Cranfield, *Romans*, 2:537). Barth avoids the reference of Psalm 19:4 altogether. In light of his dialectical view of transcendence and cosmos this is not surprising. Barth avoids the traditional view of natural revelation with respect to Psalm 19:4, and, thus, he places the verse in the context of the preaching of the Word of Christ within the church. As the church goes into the world, it proclaims the *kerygma* (Barth, *Romans*, 389). N. T. Wright holds that Paul's quote of Psalm 19:4 is directing us back to the "created order" as stated in Romans 1:18–20, but Wright admits that Paul is not clear concerning how the reference to Psalm 19:4 is related to the gospel. Wright realizes that Paul's use of the Psalmist is a reference to the proclamation of the gospel, but he does not know how (Wright, *Romans*, 2:37).

natural revelation and certain attributes only revealed by special revelation. God's revelatory activity is one; it is supernatural as well as comprehensive. Moreover, such revelatory activity is always the product of the God of the Bible—the triune God—the Father, Son, and Holy Spirit. The heavens witness his activity—even the activity of special revelation—upon the terrain of natural revelation; the acts of God done in the creation. To put it another way, the heavens serve to declare the glorious supernatural deeds of God by simply witnessing his activity upon the landscape of creation (cf. Ps 97:6).[19]

In order to further illustrate that within the fabric of natural revelation lies the essential nature of supernatural revelation (assumption 2), I want to direct our attention to Romans 8:12–31, and then on the basis of some observations about that text, I want to make a connection with Romans 10:18 and Psalm 19:4.

ROMANS 8

In Romans 8, Paul opens by speaking of the believer in union with the effectual work of Christ; there is no condemnation for those in Jesus (v. 1). On the plane of redemptive history, a transformation has occurred in the believer by virtue of the coming of Christ and the sending of the Holy Spirit. The believer is now under the "law of the Spirit of life in Christ" who has released the believer from the law of sin and death (vv. 2, 5b). The believer's life in the Spirit is now in distinct contrast to the life of one walking according to the flesh (vv. 3, 5a, 7–8).

With this context before us, Paul tells us that the believer has received the Spirit of adoption (vv. 12–17), which brings the believer into intimate communion and fellowship with his heavenly Father (v. 15). Through the work of Christ and the entrance of the Spirit, the believer has moved into the eschatological presence of the Father as his adopted child—and such a child is not an object of his wrath (cf. Rom 1:18). The believer is assured of this adoption by virtue of the Holy Spirit's bearing witness to the believer's spirit (v. 16). Moreover, as the adopted child of God, the child of the Spirit is being conformed to the eschatological state of being a joint-heir with Christ (v. 17). Meanwhile, as the children of God continue their pilgrimage

---

19. The material in this paragraph is stimulated by a sermon delivered by Rev Charles G. Dennison (1945–1999) on Psalm 19 that was preached on November 27, 1994, at Grace Orthodox Presbyterian Church in Sewickley, PA.

A Reassessment of Natural and Special Revelation

here on earth, they assume the *pattern* of Christ in this world. Like Christ, the child of God lives the pattern of suffering to glorification (v. 17).

Paul is so overcome by the final glorified state of believers (i.e., their future reception as joint-heirs with Christ) that he declares the present state of suffering in this world cannot be compared with the glorious state of heavenly inheritance (v. 18). As Paul makes his argument, verse eighteen serves as the *hinge pin* for what follows. For not only do we suffer in this world as an anticipation of our glorified state, but also the creation shares in our suffering condition as the creation itself waits for the glorification of the sons of God (v. 19; cf. Ps 102:25–28; Isa 51:6). As we keep in mind that the creation is in a state of futility and bondage because God has subjected it to such a state by virtue of Adam's fall into sin (vv. 20–21),[20] Paul directs our attention to the fact that, as in the birth of a child, the creation is going through the pains of labor—groaning and crying out for the release of her child and the ceasing of pain (v. 22). Likewise, the believer, who already has received the firstfruits of the Spirit, groans like a mother in labor for the final adoption of his glorified body (v. 23; cf. v. 26). For Paul the parallel is clear: the believer lives the life of suffering waiting for his release, and the creation exists in a state of suffering waiting for its release.[21] Paul seems to infer here that the creation is a joint-sufferer with the children of God as those children wait for the day to be joint-heirs with the glorified Christ.

Viewing the pattern more directly—we must not miss the fact that *Christ sets the pattern*! Christ's redemptive work begins in suffering here on earth and moves to glorification in heaven. Likewise, following the pattern of Christ, the believer experiences suffering here on earth and glorification in heaven. *We must not stop there*: following the pattern of Christ and the believer, the pattern for the creation involves suffering in its present state while it waits for the glorification of the "sons of God." Clearly, since the fall, God has subjected the creation itself to the visible pattern of Christ—moving from suffering to exaltation. God wrote this pattern of suffering to exaltation upon the very fabric of natural revelation; the creation

---

20. Going back to the fall seems to be agreed upon by Murray, *Romans*, 1:303; Wright, *Romans*, 1:151; Cranfield, *Romans*, 1:413; and Calvin, *Romans*, 173.

21. Wright draws the analogy between Israel and their bondage, not Christ (Wright, *Romans*, 1:151). Cranfield goes so far as to say that Christ is not in view at all in verses 18–23 since Paul does not mention him (Cranfield, *Romans*, 1:416–7). On the other hand, Hodge thinks "glorious liberty" in verse 21 (see also v. 18) is a phrase that has been applied to Christ, and now is applied in a similar manner to the creation (Hodge, *Romans*, 337).

was not meant to be an end for itself. Rather, the creation's own pattern is always a witness and a testimony to that of both Christ and the believer.[22]

The creation takes this pattern because it is the fiat creation of Christ; as the product of Christ's creative word, the creation takes on the pattern that the Father has marked for his Son as Christ is delivered into the creation. *In light of this Christocentric pattern, the special revelation of the gospel's pattern of suffering to glorification is written upon the deepest framework of natural revelation.* For this reason, as Paul moves to his discussion in Romans 10 about the gospel being heard by all, he quotes Psalm 19:4 as the sure evidence that creation itself has proclaimed the *kerygma*; indeed, the gospel message of suffering to exaltation has been preached to every single person on the face of the world. Everyone has seen and heard this testimony. Indeed, the creation proclaims its message in sermonic form. As the creation groans and cries, it is declaring the pattern of the cross *for* the exaltation of Christ's church! In this way, Paul applies Psalm 19:4, which is usually restricted by theologians to the realm of natural revelation, to the universal proclamation of the gospel!

Here is the biblical picture—God's revelatory work and activity come to humanity in two forms: special revelation and natural revelation. Although there are two forms, they are inseparable. In fact, the creation (natural revelation) declares the supernatural deeds/acts of the Lord (special revelation). This observation does not mean that the creation (natural revelation) tells us that the death of Christ will be on Calvary, or that Christ's resurrection will occur in the tomb owned by Joseph of Arimathea (John 19:38). Even so, the creation witnesses that Christ died on the cross, and the creation witnesses that the resurrected Christ broke the bonds of the tomb (Matt 27:45, 50–54; 28:2–3). The creation has witnessed the entire story of redemption and testifies to that entire story by virtue of its pattern of existence—suffering waiting for the exaltation of the Christ and the church! Within the fabric of natural revelation lies the essential blueprint (pattern) of special revelation. The creation receives its freedom and release from bondage when the children of God are released from their suffering state in the creation—the creation serves redemption; the creation serves the church.[23] Creation gives way as the church, the eternal flock, enters into

---

22. Wright sees a restorationist view of creation here (Wright, *Romans*, 1:152). Barth works with his transcendence-cosmos dialectic (see Barth, *Romans*, 302–15).

23. The creation also seems to assume the position of the sacrificial system that obviously points us to Christ (see Lev 6:1–13; 9:23–24). Note that offerings must be consumed (burned up) in order to bring peace and holiness (note the eschatological

A Reassessment of Natural and Special Revelation

joint-inheritance with the glorified Christ. The restoration of the creation is not the end; rather, the joint-inheritance of the church and Christ is the end; creation serves grace. Creation serves eschatology!

ROMANS 1

We have been proceeding in reverse order: Romans 10:18 to 8:12–30, and now 1:18–25. If we pause, however, to look at these texts in sequence, we can make an important observation. In Romans 1:18—3:20, Paul sets up a strict antithesis between the righteous and the unrighteous upon the landscape of creation in revelational history. In Romans 8:12–30, Paul informs the church of her final end—the creation will surrender itself for her consummation. From Romans 1 to Romans 8, we move from creation to consummation; we move from the plane of creation history to the plane of the transcendent age to come. In Romans 10, however, Paul returns to the present task of the church in light of her mission to both Jew and Gentile, and that present task is the preaching of the gospel (10:8–21). In terms of the sequence of Paul's argument in Romans, therefore, the present task of preaching is done on the backdrop of both the antithesis of the kingdom of God and the kingdom of Satan (1:17—3:20) and the clarification of the final end for the glorious children of God. Indeed, the final flock of the Lamb enjoys the justifying and sanctifying grace of God the Father through the Son by the work of the Holy Spirit (8:12–30).

In making this journey in reverse order to the sequence of the text (Romans 10, then 8, then 1), I have aimed to achieve a more organic understanding of supernatural revelation. In my mind, if the problems surrounding the exegesis of Romans 10:18 can approach resolution, then issues in Romans 8 and Romans 1 may be reexamined in a clearer light. Indeed, Paul tells us by quoting Psalm 19:4 in Romans 10:18 that the heavens have witnessed the supernatural activity of God upon the plane of the natural creation, and, furthermore, that the creation proclaims that testimony every single day to all men. Further, in Romans 8, Paul notes that an essential characteristic of the gospel is inherently written upon the fabric of natural revelation: it is the pattern of suffering to exaltation (a component of

---

structure of the sacrifice being on the altar from night to morning [creation language from "evening and morning"]). What happens to the sacrifice will happen to the creation (2 Pet 3:10–13)—the creation is consumed by fire so that the sons of God may be brought into the consummation of God's peace.

special revelation). Keeping these fundamental truths about supernatural revelation before us, we now proceed to Romans 1.

Paul's argument in Romans 1 is redemptive-historical. In verses 17–25 Paul does not prescribe the foundations of theological prolegomena for future theologians as a defense for theism and/or a construct for natural theology. Rather, Paul places us in the midst of the redemptive-historical conflict between the seed of the woman (the kingdom of God) and the seed of the Serpent (kingdom of Satan). The contrast is grounded in eschatology, that is, the present and final revelation of the righteousness of God (v. 17) in contrast to the present and final revelation of the wrath of God against all ungodliness and unrighteousness (v. 18).[24] Paul is mapping out the *strict antithesis between faith and unbelief*; faith results in salvation, and unbelief results in wrath.[25] There is no middle ground; moreover, theism based on natural theology does not get it half right. Rather, the strict antithesis faces the reader: there are those who are redeemed by *faith* in Christ (vv. 16–17), and there are those who are condemned by their own *unbelief*, and, thus, are objects of God's fury (1:18—3:20).

The reason that unbelievers are condemned is that they are "without excuse" for their unbelief (v. 20: *anapologētous*); their rebellion is self-imposed.[26] They not only know God as image-bearer (v. 19 "sense of divinity within them"), but they also know God "through the things that are made" (v. 20). For Paul, the knowledge of God is not limited to the divine attributes of a theistic being deduced logically and exclusively from natural revelation. In fact, Paul declares that the God who is revealed and known is the God of the Bible. Human beings are the image-bearer of the Father, Son, and Holy Spirit (1:19 corresponding to Gen 1:26–28), and the creation is the product of the activity of the Father, Son, and Holy Spirit (1:20 corresponding to the passages Gen 1, John 1:2–3, and Gen 1:2, with reference to Father, Son, and Holy Spirit respectively). In addition, Paul states that the arena on which the triune God of the Bible displays himself is the creation (1:20). In light of this point, verse 20 deserves reassessment.

---

24. The same Greek verb appears in both verse 17 and verse 18: *apokalyptetai*. In both cases, the verb is in indicative present passive 3rd person singular.

25. Murray sees the passage in the context of strict antithesis as well: "'The wrath of God' stands in obvious antithesis to 'the righteousness of God' in verse 17" (Murray, *Romans*, 1:35).

26. One can say that unbelievers are literally "without an apology"—"without a defense"—against the testimony of the true God and his supernatural revelation.

A Reassessment of Natural and Special Revelation

Again, Paul speaks in this passage within the spectrum of the entire history of redemption. We are viewing Paul's analysis of the landscape of redemptive history since/from the creation of the world. He is telling us that since the creation of the world, the "invisible things of the Lord are clearly seen" upon the continuum of history.[27] Murray indicates that Paul seems to be caught in an "oxymoron" here, that is, he is saying that something invisible can also be clearly seen (visible).[28] In verse 20 Paul provides an explanation: the invisible is a reference to God's eternal power and divinity. Thus, God's eternal power and divinity (which are invisible) are clearly seen and understood by the things that are made.

To be sure, in order to fit into a certain theological construct, many theologians have held that verse 20 is a reference to God's creative act of bringing forth the creation, and that the creation reveals the "invisible attributes" of God (i.e., his eternal power and divinity), and this leaves humanity without excuse. Although it is absolutely true that the creation reveals the blueprint of God's invisible attributes, I am not convinced that such a theological construct is Paul's intention in this text.[29] Again, Paul has placed

---

27. In the NKJV we have: "For since the creation of the world His invisible *attributes* are clearly seen." The word "attributes" is *not* in the Greek text. The NIV has: "For since the creation of the world God's invisible qualities—his eternal power and divine nature—have been clearly seen." The 1901 ASV and the KJV both have: "For the invisible things of him since the creation of the world are clearly seen."

28. Murray, *Romans*, 1:38. Cranfield also places the concept of oxymoron before us (Cranfield, *Romans*, 1:115). Calvin ties the text to Hebrews 11:3 (Calvin, *Romans*, 32).

29. On the basis of Greek and Roman literature, Cranfield sees this as a reference to the "attributes" of God (Cranfield, *Romans*, 1:115; e.g., Homeric hymns, Hesiod, Cicero). Cranfield's assessment can be questioned, however. What is known, what is seen, and what is perceived are the "invisible things of God" (v. 20). Paul is not arguing from the visible to the visible; rather, he moves from the invisible to the visible—the invisible is revealed in the visible, and from the visible the invisible is known. We cannot overlook the Greek term that Paul uses here with respect to God's revelation of the "invisible" (*aoratos* adjective nominative plural). When this particular form of the Greek word for "invisible" appears in the New Testament, it has either a direct or indirect reference to Christ (Col 1:15, 16; 1 Tim 1:17; Heb 11:27). Simply put, the invisible things of God include the person, identity, and ordained work of Christ. Look at Colossians 1:15, 16; as Paul refers to the things that have been made in Romans 1, that is, as Paul looks at God's activity in creation, we do well to look at the Colossians passage as further commentary. In, by, through, and unto Christ were all things created—visible and invisible, including the *basic patterns* that are found in Christ's creative activity in the original creation (Gen 1) as they come to be found also in the gospel centered on Christ: for example, light testifies to the Light; chaos testifies to order; void testifies to fulfillment; formlessness testifies to resolution; a first day testifies to a final day of consummation (Sabbath day); and, eventually, a fallen groaning creation testifies to the deliverance of God's children.

us within the continuum of history "since/from" the creation, and, therefore, he is not aiming our attention solely upon the natural phenomena of the creation that God created. Rather, he is pointing out that God's eternal power and divinity are clearly seen and understood by the things the Lord is *doing* in created history (cf. Ps 136). In other words, God's creative power with respect to bringing the creation into being is *not* what is in view in this text; rather, what is in view is God's *activity*—God's *doing*—in the creation (cf. Pss 145:10–13; 146:5–9; 148:1–14; 150:1–2). Instead of using a form of the Greek word *ktizō* that usually refers to the creative work of God with respect to the creation, Paul uses a form of the Greek word *poieō* that usually refers to an *activity* (do, make, work).[30]

Let me illustrate by using Israel's exodus from Egypt. Again we must keep in mind that since/from the creation, the invisible things of God, that is, his eternal power and divinity, are clearly seen by virtue of the things that he is doing. In this light, we need to examine statements from the Lord in Exodus 14:4, 18 about the unbelieving nations:

> "Then I will harden Pharaoh's heart, so that he will pursue them; and I will gain honor over Pharaoh and over all his army, that the Egyptians may know that I am the Lord." And they did so. (Exod 14:4)

> Then the Egyptians shall know that I am the Lord, when I have gained honor for Myself over Pharaoh, his chariots, and his horsemen. (Exod 14:18; cf. also Josh 23:4–9)

Indeed, Christ, as the "firstborn of all creation" (v. 15) points to Christ being the "firstborn from the dead" (v. 18), that is, having the position of priority (pioneer, go before) in the creation order as the second person of the Trinity points to the fact that he also has the position of priority in the resurrection of the dead on behalf of his body of believers, the church—the invisible is made visible as his Father makes the tomb vacant! Christ, as the great "I am of God" (Exod 3:14; cf. John 6:35, 38), made his invisible person known to Moses out of a bush (the invisible in a visible natural object) that would not be consumed as Moses's faith exchanged fearing the wrath of God for refusing to fear the wrath of Pharaoh (Heb 11:27). The same Christ took Paul on a similar path to that of Moses (cf. 1 Tim 1:12–17). In my judgment, what Paul means when he says that "the invisible things of him [God] from the creation of the world are clearly seen" (Rom 1:20a), is not that the attributes of a theistic being are revealed, rather that the attributes of the *triune* God of the Bible as well as the essence of his being are revealed, and they are exhibited in *the pattern* of the gospel itself.

30. The Greek word for "made"—*poiēmasin*—noun dative plural ("of things done or made" would be the literal); its specific form is only found twice in the New Testament, both in the writings of Paul: Romans 1:20 and Ephesians 2:10—"we are the workmanship of Christ Jesus." Christ is active in the things that are made.

A Reassessment of Natural and Special Revelation

Looking at God's incredible act in light of Romans 1, we see that Pharaoh and the Egyptians were truly witnesses to God's invisible power and divinity; moreover, they clearly understood God's invisible power and divinity on the basis of the visible activity (doing) of the Lord. In fact, they "knew God" (Rom 1:21) on the basis of God's activity, and, thus, they were without excuse.[31] Furthermore, not only did Pharaoh and the Egyptians know God, they also refused to glorify him as God, or to be thankful; rather, they lifted up futile thoughts as they lived with darkened hearts (Rom 1:21). Indeed, the Egyptians provide a perfect example of "changing the glory of the incorruptible God into an image made like corruptible man" (Rom 1:23). Truly, they exchanged "the truth of God for the lie, and worshiped and served the creature rather than the Creator" (Rom 1:25; cf. Pss 115:1–8; 134:15–18)!

We must not stop there; we must press on from the *antithetical* structure of Romans 1 to the *consummation* of creation in Romans 8. After all, the exodus is a prototype of the consummation of God's activity upon the landscape of creation history. In the exodus, the creation witnesses its own preview of its *eager expectation* of the glorification of the sons of God (in this case, the Israelites' final release from bondage; cf. Rom 8:19). In fact, the creation subjects itself to God's sovereign activity in the exodus in the hope of being delivered from its own bondage through the glorious freedom experienced by the children of God (the exodus itself; cf. Rom 8:21).

We must press on even further to the *present* nature of *preaching the gospel* (Rom 10:18). The exodus is also a preview of the Lord preaching the gospel through the testimony of the creation (Rom 10:18)! Was not God's special revelation organically connected with the natural revelation in this event? To put it another way, in the exodus, are we not witnessing the supernatural revelation of God in its two overlapping forms—natural and special? For we are told that the "Angel of God" (Jesus Christ) and "the pillar of cloud" (Holy Spirit) moved behind the camp of Israel and stood between them and the Egyptians, giving the Israelites protection during the night (Exod 14:19–20). In fact, in the morning, as the Egyptians pursued the Israelites through the Red Sea, the pillar of fire and cloud (Holy Spirit) played havoc upon the Egyptian chariot wheels—so much so that the Egyptians say, "Let us flee from the face of Israel, for the Lord fights for them against the Egyptians" (Exod 14:25). Indeed, the creation witnesses

---

31. Cranfield is on the right track when he writes, "The result of God's self-manifestation in His creation is not a natural knowledge of God on men's part independent of God's self-revelation in His Word, a valid though limited knowledge, but simply the excuselessness of men in their ignorance" (Cranfield, *Romans*, 1:116).

and now testifies (preaches) that it has seen the gospel upon the landscape of creation history (cf. Josh 2:9–12; 5:1; 9:1–2, 8–9). The creation testifies that the children of God have gone from bondage to freedom, from slavery to resurrection by virtue of the joint operation of the Father, the Son (Angel of God), and the Holy Spirit (pillar and cloud).

IMPLICATIONS FOR APOLOGETICS

Without a doubt, this paradigm in Romans presents us with a strong tool in the apologetic arena of ideas. For example, we can look back at the debate at the beginning of the nineteenth century, when William Paley's (1743–1805) work *Natural Theology* was a popular academic science textbook throughout Britain. Like others in England, a young Charles Darwin was educated in the field of natural science and human anatomy by using Paley's textbook. When Darwin began to challenge the conclusions of Paley's natural theism, he, like many others, thought that the appropriate step was merely to remove God from the picture of naturalism. Moreover, since many naturalists had already rejected the Christian themes of redemption in Christ, they thought that all that remained for them was to reject the God of nature—a God of natural theology! In light of such thinking, we can see more clearly the genius of Paul's full-orbed understanding of Christian theistic revelation. Paul does not simplistically add supernatural revelation to a natural theology constructed by abstract reason; he does not even add supernatural revelation to natural revelation. Rather, as Paul shows us, the biblical theistic position is that natural revelation can never be truly comprehended without special revelation; natural revelation is always organically linked or united to special revelation in the entire spectrum of God's supernatural revelation.

Paul's great sermon on Mars Hill provides further illustration. As recorded in Acts 17:16–31, Paul does not attempt to reconcile natural revelation and supernatural revelation as two separate and distinct revelations. Rather, he proclaims that the same God who created all things (Acts 17:24), and even gave the Athenians life, is not only the true invisible God who cannot be served or made into finite imagery, but also the same God who will judge all humanity according to his righteousness by virtue of the fact that he has raised Christ from the dead (Acts 17:30–31). We cannot separate the fact that all humanity has life, movement, and being because of God's natural creative activity (natural revelation) from the fact that God

A Reassessment of Natural and Special Revelation

has given life, movement, and being to his Son at his resurrection (supernatural revelation).

Furthermore, this resurrection (supernatural revelation) has occurred upon the plane of the natural order (natural revelation); to reject the resurrection is to reject the true understanding of the natural (just like the Athenians); moreover, to reject the true understanding of the natural is to reject the resurrection (just like Darwin and the other naturalists). In the realm of apologetics, then, we demand that all human beings must repent because the natural and the supernatural are inseparable! The Christian apologist must be emphatic—to reject the God of the resurrection is to reject the God who made all things, including the natural world. If one rejects the God of Christianity, then one must reject the natural world as it appears to humanity since that world is linked organically to the gospel. We can conclude that a true view of natural revelation is dependent upon a true view of special revelation, which is found in the gospel of Jesus Christ.

PART 3

Book Reviews

9

A Review of Greg Bahnsen's *Van Til's Apologetic*

For those who are students and critics of the Reformed apologetic method of Van Til, the late Greg L. Bahnsen's work has become a welcome addition. As a proponent of Van Til's apologetic method, Bahnsen maps out in systematic fashion the corpus of Van Til's project. The work is encyclopedic in scope because Bahnsen arranged his treatise like a topical anthology. In fact, as each topic is presented, Bahnsen provides sections from Van Til's own writings as the essential content of each subject that is discussed. At times, one may think that the volume is merely a republication of excerpts from Van Til's works. Although this may seem like a weakness, in my judgment, it is a strength. As Bahnsen brackets and interweaves each section with his own introduction, explanation, and commentary (in the main text as well as in footnotes), the reader has the benefit of Bahnsen's insights as well as Van Til's own thoughts. The reader can evaluate and engage Bahnsen's interpretation with Van Til's original text before him.

In service to his reader, Bahnsen arranged Van Til's thoughts in a logical sequential manner: introduction to apologetics, task of apologetics, epistemological side of apologetics, apologetic side of epistemology, psychological complexities of unbelief, presuppositional apologetic, comparisons and criticisms of apologetic methods, and how to defend the faith.

In each section, Bahnsen unfolds the complexities of Van Til's definitions and insights, for example, Christian apologetics is a defense of Christian theism,[1] the "absolute certain" proof for Christian theism,[2] defending and arguing by presupposition,[3] the rejection of epistemological neutrality,[4] revelational epistemology,[5] epistemology and antithesis,[6] brute facts as mute facts,[7] antithesis and common grace,[8] and the transcendental nature of critique.[9] As Bahnsen deals with each of these subjects (among others), he places the reader in the context of the scholarly debate with respect to Van Til's positions. Perhaps, at this point, we are confronted with Bahnsen's own scholarly prowess. In such cases, whether in footnote or in the main text, Bahnsen provides insightful commentary as he maps out the position of Van Til's opponents while providing further analysis into Van Til's own position. Bahnsen demonstrates the ability to understand and explain the interplay between Van Til and his opponents. Moreover, he is competent to place Van Til's thought on the landscape of philosophy, the broad context of intellectual thought, and the life of the church. This analysis is an invaluable asset and resource to Van Til, especially when Bahnsen engages Van Til's critics who have constantly misrepresented his position.

For example, based on the Reformed doctrine of total depravity, Van Til has been criticized that he believed that the non-Christian could not know anything at all. Bahnsen provides clear insight into Van Til's position:

> But Van Til never taught that the natural man is so consistent and successful in his rebellion against God that he actually reaches the stage of knowing nothing whatsoever, becomes a blithering idiot, and never reaches true conclusions (or believes true propositions) in any sense on any subject at all. Asked whether he means to assert that unbelievers do not actually discover any truth by the methods they employ, Van Til replied firmly and categorically: "We mean nothing so absurd as that." Indeed, if the unbeliever were to be utterly ignorant on everything, he would no longer be responsible

1. Bahnsen, *Van Til's Apologetic*, 34–38.
2. Ibid., 78–82, 112–4.
3. Ibid., 88–143.
4. Ibid., 144–54.
5. Ibid., 165–94, 203–19.
6. Ibid., 261–317.
7. Ibid., 376–9.
8. Ibid., 414–41.
9. Ibid., 495–529.

before God for his sin and rebellion. Because he is made as God's image, confronted with God's inescapable revelation, and restrained by the common grace of the Holy Spirit, the unbeliever cannot fail to know God and, by extension, to understand something of himself and God's world. Van Til thus taught: "There is a sense in which he knows something about everything, about God as well as about the world. . . . Many non-Christians have been great scientists. Often non-Christians have a better knowledge of the things of this world than Christians have. . . . From a relative point of view he knows something about all things."[10]

From this quote, we have a clear sense of Bahnsen's project; he interweaves careful commentary as well as fair scholarship. In this case, it should be clear that Van Til never held that the unbeliever can know nothing at all. In fact, if such were the case, then the unbeliever would not be held responsible before his Creator. Herein, Bahnsen shows that Van Til's critics have failed to examine his corpus responsibly.

On the other hand, Bahnsen is aware that Van Til's continental philosophy (idealism) and its terminology are difficult to comprehend. Laity, pastors, and theologians (critic or comrade) have all complained that his terminology is complicated. Perhaps, even more problematic, trained philosophers, even those trained in idealistic philosophy, find themselves struggling with Van Til's terminology. Specifically, these philosophers struggle with how Van Til changed the meaning of idealistic terminology in order to make it fit God's revealed religion as found from Genesis to Revelation. Bahnsen seems especially sensitive to these criticisms about Van Til's terminology; he attempts to break down the philosophical language while maintaining the integrity of Van Til's thought. As he encourages both friend and critic to read Van Til carefully, Bahnsen's volume provides a lucid interpretation of his language. For example, at the heart of Van Til's apologetic method is "transcendental analysis." Such a method of analysis arises out of the tradition of Kant's idealistic philosophy. Bahnsen writes: "Kant proposed to engage in 'transcendental' analysis, which asks what the preconditions are for the intelligibility of human experience."[11] Bahnsen spends thirty-three pages of meticulous explanation to clarify Van Til's own variation of transcendental analysis in counter-relationship to Kant.[12] Simply put, Kant's transcendental analysis was limited to human experience,

10. Ibid., 415.
11. Ibid., 499.
12. Ibid., 496–529.

whereas Van Til pushed all transcendental analysis and its relationship to human experience to the necessity of Christian theism. In other words, all experience and knowledge is dependent upon the God of the Scriptures.

Although Bahnsen's work may be the finest and fairest encapsulation of Van Til's apologetic system to appear in print, it has a flaw; it fails to grasp the control that biblical progressive revelation had upon Van Til's apologetic. This failure becomes apparent in Bahnsen's discussion of Van Til's view of "logical and conceptual reasoning."[13] In this section, Bahnsen provides a quotation that correctly exposes the inner core of Van Til's view of reason: "Van Til clearly declared: 'The Christian finds, further, that logic agrees with the [biblical] story. Human logic agrees with the story, because it derives its meaning from the story.'"[14] As Bahnsen continues to exposit upon Van Til's view of logic, he never penetrates the impact and genius of the quote that he has just provided the reader. Oblivious to that quote, he returns to a discussion about the "laws of logic" in the context of the relationship between the universal and the particular in the realm of experience, thought, language, and mathematics.[15]

Ironically, as a Van Tilian, Bahnsen fails to apply Van Til's transcendental analysis upon Van Til. In other words, he fails to grasp the transcendental starting point of Van Til's view of logic and how Van Til applied his starting point to the philosophical issues dealing with the "laws of logic." In more than one place in his writings, Van Til was clear that "logic" and "facts" only have meaning in the context of the "story."[16] For Van Til, the "story" is the "Christian story"—meaning the story of redemption unfolding progressively upon the pages of Scripture. Specifically, logic and facts have no meaning outside the redemptive-historical revelation of Christ. Like so many comrades of Van Til's apologetic, Bahnsen shows no evidence of penetrating this Archimedean as well as biblical hermeneutical point in Van Til's system that was impressed upon him by his most influential professor and teacher, Vos. In my judgment, as long as Van Til's students fail to wrestle with Vos's influence upon this great Reformed apologist, they will never comprehend fully the depth and uniqueness of the person of Christ in Van Til's entire apologetic system.

13. Ibid., 235.
14. Ibid., 237.
15. Ibid.
16. For example, Van Til wrote: "Aquinas sought to show the unbeliever that the Christian story is in accord with fact. Calvin sought to show that 'logic' and 'fact' have meaning only in terms of the 'story'" (Van Til, "Calvin," 5).

10

A Review of John Muether's *Cornelius Van Til*

John R. Muether's *Cornelius Van Til: Reformed Apologist and Churchman* is a triumph as an ecclesiastical biography! Muether's well-written and easy to read volume is not for the casual reader of biographies; rather, his achievement comes with a challenge as each page demands reflection and candid engagement. Our OPC historian masterfully coordinates the narrative to entice the reader into being an engaging spectator of Van Til's life journey. If you have a passion for the Reformed faith, then you will share in the concerns, anxieties, disappointments, frustrations, delights, joys, and triumphs of this churchman, apologist, seminary professor, husband, father, grandfather, confident uncle, and respectful sibling. You will be gripped by a penetrating look into his difficult decisions: Farmer or academician? Christian Reformed or Orthodox Presbyterian? Calvin Theological Seminary or Westminster Theological Seminary (a few occasions)? You will be captivated by the nature of his respect for, and critique of, fellow Reformed comrades (e.g., Hodge, Warfield, Kuyper, Bavinck, Jellema, Daane, the De Boers, Masselink, Clark, Carnell, Dooyeweerd, Schaeffer, Gerstner, and Clowney), evangelicals (e.g., Buswell, Henry, Graham, and Lewis), and the modernists (e.g., Barth, Brunner, and Marty). While using primary and secondary sources effectively, Muether's exhaustive labors into letters of correspondence and personal interviews pull the reader into the inner dynamics of his subject.

Usually the work of a good historian and biographer is timely. Muether's effort is prompt for the life of the OPC. He correctly appraises Van Til's contribution to the identity of the first fifty years of the OPC and the first generation of Westminster Theological Seminary. In my estimation, the highpoint of Muether's urgent challenge and thesis comes from the words of Van Til himself: "By 1979 Van Til regretfully described the student population at the seminary as 'a generation that knows not Van Til.'"[1] In the same paragraph, Muether carries the same idea into the OPC, pointing out that Van Til also feared "that the OPC was losing its militant edge."[2] The author's assessment of Van Til's concern for the OPC is crucial. Herein, Muether's aim comes to the forefront—he informs us from the beginning that the volume is about an apologist and a churchman.[3] He is not writing another volume on Van Til's apologetic method and system, although he demonstrates a firm grasp of both. Rather, Muether pleads that the OPC must self-consciously reflect upon the Lord's work in Van Til. After all, the faces among OPC church officers and members have changed significantly over the last fifteen years. Do most in the OPC know Van Til and the identity that the OPC took over the course of his generation—that is, no compromise with the Christ of Scripture as articulated in the orthodox creeds and the Reformed confessions? While the world, modernism, and evangelicals have despised such a commitment to biblical revelational theology, by God's grace, this is the identity that Van Til carved for the OPC. Sadly, like Machen before him, the twilight of Van Til's life was an experience of continued marginalization and disenfranchisement, even within the churchman's OPC. Nevertheless, Muether's closing section on "the ecumenical Van Til"[4] may be his most brilliant and most penetrating section to the soul of the reader. Muether captures what ecumenicity truly looked like through the eyes of a biblically conscious and militant Van Til and how it needs to be defined currently if the OPC is going to be truly an ecumenical denomination within Protestantism. Does such an ecumenical spirit exist in the OPC today?

1. Muether, *Van Til*, 224.
2. Ibid.
3. Ibid., 15–20.
4. Ibid., 237–40.

A Review of John Muether's *Cornelius Van Til*

Before moving to specifics, I must stress that I found each section instructional and a delight to read. In light of personal interests, I found chapters 4 and 5 particularly enlightening. "Reformed or Evangelical?" (chapter 4) contains an excellent section on "debating the theology of Gordon Clark."[5] "The New Machen against the New Modernism" (chapter 5) expounds Van Til's assessment of Barth's theology and the personal pain that accompanied his appraisal. Also, in terms of some general observations, Muether grasps correctly Van Til's view of the antithesis, of the Creator-creature distinction, as well as Van Til's view of the relationship between antithesis and common grace. Furthermore, Muether has correctly understood that the history of redemption, conditioned by God's covenant, grounds Van Til's view of antithesis. On this exact point, he has correctly assessed the influence of Vos upon Van Til's apologetic—often missed by others. From here Muether notes well that a wrong assessment of the depth and breadth of Van Til's antithesis leaves the door open for evangelicalism, or modernism, or secularism.

Are there some gaps in the work? Like any work, there are, but those gaps do not damage its fine quality. For example, although I understood Muether's point, I found his section on "Van Til and Hodge" in the last chapter[6] to be a trivial inclusion. Also, I found his discussion on "debating common grace"[7] lacking a clear synopsis of Van Til's unique and intriguing position on common grace.

Permit me to conclude by issuing a challenge to Mr. Muether and the OPC. First, I wish to encourage Mr. Muether to write a study volume, essentially a synopsis of each chapter and questions that relate to the main substance of each chapter. Mr. Muether, your masterful volume needs to be studied in the Sunday schools of our churches. Second, every officer in the OPC needs to read this volume; it is essential reading for understanding the identity of the OPC and its humble tradition. Third, Candidates and Credentials Committees in the OPC need to consider it as required reading for any candidate for licensure and/or ordination. Last, it is imperative to reflect upon what it means to be a churchman. In some circles, the term has received popular use, yet it seems to have a vague meaning.

Mr. Muether, thank you for a splendid study; it is truly a gift to Christ's church from our church historian!

5. Ibid., 100–113.
6. Ibid., 232–4.
7. Ibid., 152–3.

11

A Review of Timothy Keller's *The Reason for God*

John R. Muether's fine biography entitled *Cornelius Van Til: Reformed Apologist and Churchman* suggests that Van Til was marginalized by Westminster Theological Seminary and the OPC by the end of his life. Concerning Westminster Theological Seminary, in 1979 Van Til speculated whether its academic environment understood his apologetic.[1] Van Til's assessment in 1979 may have been skewed, but if he were alive today, his assumption may have been confirmed as he listened to Timothy Keller's approach to apologetics on March 11, 2008 in the very hall that bears Van Til's name.[2] Specifically, if one truly understands Van Til, then one would know that Timothy Keller's *The Reason for God: Belief in an Age of Skepticism* exists outside the bounds of Van Til's own method. Countless pages of ink flowed from Van Til's pen in opposition to the apologetic that Keller presents. Although Keller's presentation at Westminster Theological Seminary did not indicate fidelity to Van Til's apologetic method, hopefully a consistent attitude of commitment to Van Til will be advanced in the OPC when reviewing Keller's volume.

Keller's volume is divided into two parts: 1) "the leap of doubt"; and 2) "the reasons for faith." In light of his ministry in the Manhattan borough of New York City, Keller addresses the "seven biggest objections about

1. Muether, *Van Til*, 224.
2. See Keller, "WTS."

A Review of Timothy Keller's *The Reason for God*

Christianity" he has confronted over the years of his ministry (part one), and then he examines "the reasons underlying Christian beliefs" (part two). The apologetic aspect of the volume addresses the urban skeptic who Keller describes as "sophisticated but ignorant," meaning that the individual is highly educated in their field of specialization (vocation) and, yet, has many misconceptions of the Christian religion.[3] The underlying thesis of the entire volume is that the requirements for proof that skeptics apply to the Christian faith should be applied consistently to their own belief system. In this exercise, skeptics should discover that their doubts are not as solid as they seem to be.[4]

In part one, the reader is presented with some typical objections to Christianity: the claim of one true religion, a good God allowing suffering, Christianity as an enemy to freedom, the church as a source of injustice, a loving God sending people to hell, science proves Christianity false, and the Bible cannot be viewed literally. To each objection, Keller employs an argument that attempts to remain consistent to his thesis, but it needs to be noted that his argument employs an inductive method, that is, the evidence for Christianity is more rational and probable than any argument to the contrary. In the second part, Keller presents the essential biblical narrative of the Christian story. Herein, God is presented as a playwright whose "drama" provides many "strong clues" ("divine fingerprints") in the universe as evidence for the Christian religion. The analogy of "dance" is also employed to depict the interrelationship between God and all he has created.[5] Although Keller tells us more than once that "there cannot be [an] irrefutable proof for the existence of God,"[6] in the second part he argues that God's play "has greater power to explain what we see and experience than does any other competing account."[7] In fact, for Keller, "the gospel . . . is not just a moving fictional story about someone else [Jesus]. It is a true story about *us*."[8]

With this overview before us, I now turn to assess the volume's two sections, making no apology for my commitment to Van Til and his importance for the OPC. My appraisal proceeds in two directions: 1) Keller's

---

3. Ibid., 12:50.
4. Keller, *Reason*, xviii.
5. Ibid., 213–26.
6. Ibid., 127.
7. Ibid., 213.
8. Ibid., 200.

apologetic method in relationship to Van Til's method; and 2) Keller's depiction of the Christian story.

First, Keller has stated that he is interested in how consistent his work is with Van Tilian apologetics.[9] In terms of the holistic method of Van Tilian apologetics, no resemblance exists. No matter what percentage one gives to the strength of an evidential argument for God's existence, Van Til would not give credibility to any probability argument. This criticism dominated Van Til's analysis of any apologetic method that applied the inductive method to apologetics, a method that he found embodied in Bishop Joseph Butler (1692–1752) and those whom he called the "less-than-consistent Calvinists" (Old Princeton). Ironically, Keller jumps on the current bandwagon of criticizing Enlightenment Cartesian foundationalism (rationalism),[10] and yet he employs the late Renaissance and early Enlightenment use of the inductive method (empiricism) as embodied in Francis Bacon's (1561–1626) *New Organon* (1620) to encounter modern skepticism. Again, Van Til would claim this is a flaw in Keller's approach. Keller is attempting to meet the skeptic on his own ground. (In fact, in René Descartes's [1596–1650] *Meditations* [1641], he attempted to meet the revival of Pyrrhonian skepticism on the skeptic's ground as he constructed his foundational rationalism. Keller seems to be telling us that he prefers meeting the skeptics on their own turf with a method that incorporates Enlightenment inductivism [empiricism] rather than Enlightenment deductivism [rationalism]).[11] If one attempts to meet the skeptic on his own ground, Van Til says that the Christian apologist has already given away the merchandise since the apologist is allowing the skeptic to define the epistemological ground of the discussion (the probability of truth). Perhaps it would be helpful to think about the issue this way: As you stand in the presence of God, do you think God would affirm that there cannot be any irrefutable proof of his existence? In fact, on the basis of the Word of God and God's providential sovereign activity in history, can we not hear the Lord's response: the triune God of the Bible irrefutably exists! According

9. Keller, "WTS," 20:8.

10. Keller, *Reason*, 118, 268n6.

11. A digest of the fine works of Richard H. Popkin (1923–2005) on skepticism during the Enlightenment can be very instructive concerning the problems that both deductive and inductive reasoning faced encountering the skeptics. See Popkin's *The History of Scepticism from Erasmus to Spinoza*. Also incredibly challenging to anyone putting confidence in deductive and inductive arguments for God's existence is Alan Charles Kors's volume, *Atheism in France, 1650–1729*.

to Scripture, God's existence is indubitable, and all of humanity is without excuse because the irrefutable proof of his existence is clearly seen in his activity (Rom 1:18–25). Paul does *not* teach in Romans 1 that humanity is without excuse because God provides more rational and probable evidences than the argument to the contrary. Van Til echoes Paul's sentiment, but Keller does not. In fact, the modern skeptic's questions, which Keller wishes to give so much sympathy, fairness, and credence, are nonsense before the presence of God.[12]

The directive of Keller's argumentation relies heavily upon the cultural milieu. His argument on each subject follows a basic pattern. The skeptical question is raised in its cultural context, and then a statement or argument of response from a prominent cultural figure is placed before the reader (e.g., Stephen L. Carter, Dostoevsky, G. K. Chesterton, David L. Chappell, Robert Bellah, Ian Barbour, Jan Vansina, Alvin Plantinga, and foremost, C. S. Lewis and N. T. Wright). The response is used to turn the question of the skeptic on its head so that Keller can proceed to demonstrate that it is more reasonable to believe the Christian position. For this reason, one will strain to find any example of Keller confronting the skeptic with the absolute authority of the triune God and his Word. One may wish to counter my observation by arguing that the initial part of the volume presupposes the content of biblical revelation, but I found it to be an afterthought at best. Specifically, the apologetic directive found clearly in WCF 1.4 and 1.5, which was employed so masterfully by Van Til, is clearly missing in Keller. WCF 1.4 tells us that the Holy Scripture is to be believed because it is the Word of God (God is truth). The absolute authoritative claim that Scripture makes about itself *precedes* the evidence that it is the Word of God (WCF 1.5). Van Til applied the same principle to any discussion about God's existence. Van Til grounds his epistemology in a philosophy of history: this means that he begins with the self-attesting and self-authenticating activity of the triune God in history as declared in Holy Scripture. The evidences for God's existence are constitutive of this covenantal/redemptive-historical

---

12. At this point, I need to be fair to Keller. Of course, in his pastoral role he needs to be gracious and loving to the questions of the modern skeptic; he needs to listen well and make every attempt to respond to their concerns. His book clearly indicates that this is his honorable passion. My point is this: although the gospel demands that we be pastorally gracious to the skeptic's questions, the believer must also realize that the skeptic's questions come from a heart of unbelief. Thus, those questions against God are unfair because they are against the authority and the fulfilled eschatological work of our Godhead. One may wish to consult the instructive article by Warfield, "Doubt."

paradigm as the Trinity discloses himself in his revelation. In the scope of biblical, historical revelation, God, history, facts, and God's interpretation of those facts are inseparable. Keller never uses this biblical paradigm in order to respond to the modern skeptic. Rather, Keller exchanges the irrefutable proof that God provides in revelational history for a probability argument of God's existence in the relative cultural context of his own era. From God's perspective, however, the argument is over; redemptive and covenantal history is fulfilled. On the authority of God's work in Christ, all men everywhere stand presently before God and need to repent and believe (Acts 17:30–31). God's providential history is not a "play" in which human beings are the spectators trying to comprehend rationally, understand, and put together the "clues" that God has left for us.[13] Rather, from God's perspective, the play, if you wish, portrays facts that must be believed without reservation since today is the day of salvation (2 Cor 6:2).

Furthermore, one should not be surprised about the popularity of Keller's volume. Cultural relevance enamors Christians. For the most part, however, the same popular questions of skepticism arise in every age since the skeptics of each era think that they are reinventing the wheel. In reality, they are not thinkers; they just drift through history espousing the "same old, same old," yet updated, versions of their popular notions—repeating the whimsical, pompous criticisms of academicians; supposed intelligent inquiries from friends and blogs; amoral discussions in locker rooms, dorm rooms, chat rooms, bars and the workplace; the recurring themes in music, film, and stage; and the continual therapies of psychological anxiety and alienation. The products of culture always demand a cultural response. Keller capitulates to that culture. In contrast, the genius of Van Til's apologetic is to engage the culture by beginning with the God of the Bible who is the same yesterday, today, and tomorrow—demanding that the culture conform its existence to the eternal and constant truth of the gospel.

So, what about the story of the gospel, which is Keller's focus in the second part of the volume? Does he present the story found in the Bible as summarized in the historic Reformed confessions? Interestingly, Keller defends the content of the historic ecumenical creeds from the early church, but the Reformed confessions are mysteriously missing. This omission is important. Van Til maintained that the starting point for the defense of the Christian faith is the self-attesting Christ of Scripture and that the best summary of the message of Scripture is found in the ecumenical creeds

---

13. Keller, *Reason*, 127.

as well as the Reformed confessions. In other words, the true defense of the Christian faith is the defense of the Reformed faith! Van Til's position has not been popular within evangelical and Reformed circles. Obviously, his position did not find sentiment in Keller's volume. So, what view of Christianity is Keller defending? I found it difficult to come to a precise response to that question, but it was apparent that certain eclectic nuances emerged, for example, there is a Reformed element (salvation by grace), an evangelical element (experiential and relational emphasis on community without any depth of covenant consciousness or a doctrine of the church), and a liberal element (social restoration).

From a historic Reformed perspective, the reader should be surprised to learn that Martin Luther King Jr. (1929–1968) had a "deeper and truer" view of Christianity with respect to justice,[14] that the existential philosopher Søren Kierkegaard (1813–1855) provides the launching point for the truth about sin, and in perhaps the strangest chapter, that Dietrich Bonhoeffer's (1906–1945) life is "the marvelous example of human forgiveness to understand the divine."[15] After all, according to Keller, "no one embodied the costliness of forgiveness any better than Dietrich Bonhoeffer."[16] In terms of Christ's death on the cross, Keller comments, "As Bonhoeffer says, everyone who forgives someone bears the other's sins. On the Cross we see God doing visibly and cosmically what every human being must do to forgive someone, though on an infinitely greater scale."[17] Personally, I find Keller's endorsement of Bonhoeffer's notion of human forgiveness as a bearer of another's sin perplexing. How can such a position be reconciled with the Bible's teaching that Christ's sacrificial atonement is a once and for all expiatory and propitiatory event on behalf of sinners (Rom 6:10; Heb 10:8–18)? Christians forgive each other not as bearers of sin but because Christ forgave us. Even so, Keller's puzzling language about the cross of Christ continues: "This is a God who becomes human and offers his own lifeblood in order to honor moral justice and merciful love so that someday

---

14. As I point out in my classroom discussion of King's famous "Letter from a Birmingham Jail," his key paragraph in presenting his view of justice is an eclectic synthesis of Aquinas, Martin Buber's (1878–1965) "I-thou" concept, and Paul Tillich's (1886–1965) view of sin. These three men are not pillars of Reformed orthodoxy, and, thus, a serious employment of the transcendental critique is needed of King's view of justice before it is affirmed as a "deeper and truer" view.

15. Keller, *Reason*, 191.

16. Ibid., 190.

17. Ibid., 192.

he can destroy all evil without destroying us."[18] Although one will find the terminology of the satisfaction view of atonement scattered throughout Keller's presentation, it would seem that Keller is advocating more directly the moral theory of the atonement. Hence, the reader should not be surprised that the justice achieved by Christ on the cross is a restoration of the social order of human activity.[19] Ironically, I am *skeptical* whether the reader will find an exposition of the penal substitutionary work of Christ's atonement as taught in the Reformed confessions in Keller's presentation of the "true" story of the cross. In my estimation, Keller's exposition appears dangerously close to Horace Bushnell's (1802–1876) moral theory of the atonement, which was assessed and critiqued correctly by Charles Hodge.[20]

Since a biblical and confessional view of the atonement is in question in Keller's presentation, what can be said about the grand narrative of the biblical story? Herein, Keller adopts the popular neo-Calvinist scheme: "creation, fall, redemption, and consumption."[21] This "story line" has its roots in nineteenth-century Dutch neo-Calvinism, which eventually evolved into a paradigm that teaches the "absolute harmony of humanity with nature."[22] Moreover, Keller endorses the neo-Calvinist's canon when he writes: "The purpose of Jesus' coming is to put the whole world right, to renew and restore the creation, not to escape it."[23] Herein, justice and *shalom* finally embrace. Keller continues: "The work of the Spirit of God is not only to save souls but also to care and cultivate the face of the earth, the material world."[24] Keller's approval of the neo-Calvinist horizontal scheme of the biblical story is quite distant from Calvin's pastoral gem regarding the believer's pilgrimage in this creation: "If heaven is our homeland, what else is the earth but a place of exile?"[25] Furthermore, with respect to the WCF, a serious revisionist view of the biblical narrative is put in place by the scheme and content of creation, fall, redemption, and consummation.

18. Ibid.

19. Ibid., 196–7.

20. I recommend the reading of Keller, Bushnell, and Hodge alongside of each other. See Bushnell, *Vicarious Sacrifice*, 1:449–552; and Hodge, *Systematic Theology*, 2:566–73. Hodge refers to Bushnell's *Vicarious Sacrifice: Grounded in Principles of Universal Obligation*, published in 1866.

21. Keller, *Reason*, 214.

22. Ibid., 222.

23. Ibid., 223.

24. Ibid.

25. Calvin, *Institutes*, 3.9.4.

A Review of Timothy Keller's *The Reason for God*

Although one can *infer* this pattern as a subordinate scheme in the WCF, that blueprint is *not* the self-conscious model of the authors of the Confession. Rather, the paradigm of the WCF is the "fourfold state of man." The ninth chapter reveals the broad outline of the Confession: state of innocency (9.2), state of sin (9.3), state of grace (9.4), and state of glory (9.5). For the authors of the WCF, the focus of God's activity in the creation is *anthropology* (God in covenant with man from the covenant of works to the covenant of grace in Christ). But during the nineteenth century a paradigm shift occurred, mainly in continental Reformed thought. This shift emphasized God's activity in the *creation*. Herein, man is called as a servant and instrument in God's teleological plan to restore and secure the *creation*. This post-Enlightenment paradigm shift from anthropology to creation reached its high point in the famous quip by Bavinck, "grace restores nature." For many, Bavinck's phrase has come to define the canon of neo-Calvinist dogma for the twentieth century and beyond as the content of that quip has evolved.[26] Perhaps a simple way to state the difference between the two paradigms is this: the WCF understands that the believer's (i.e., Christ's bride's) end is the inheritance of God himself, through Christ, in the glorious transcendence of heaven (see the Westminster Shorter Catechism Q&A 1), whereas neo-Calvinism understands the end as a restored creation in which believers "labor" in "deeds of justice and service" with the "expectation of a perfect world."[27] I would suggest that the neo-Calvinist needs to reread Romans 8:18–25. Paul teaches in Romans 8:18–25 that creation serves redemption, nature serves glory, the universe serves eschatology—specifically, creation serves the "sons of God" (the church: see also Matt 6:24–34; 2 Cor 4:16—5:8; Eph 1:15–23; Phil 3:20–21; Heb 3:14; Rev 21:22—22:5). In my judgment, the neo-Calvinist's scheme is guilty of deconstructing the vertical realm of eschatology taught clearly in Holy Scripture and our Reformed standards. More importantly, however, it is deconstructing the entire biblical narrative and replacing it with a post-Enlightenment gospel of cultural and social relevance.

Well, in light of this analysis, is there something positive to glean from Keller's book? Yes. Although the holistic character of Keller's apologetic method is antithetical to Van Til's method, he does provide certain

---

26. An introductory survey of the neo-Calvinist movement appears in W. Dennison, "Dutch Neo-Calvinism and the Roots for Transformation." A succinct counter to the neo-Calvinist horizontal view of eschatology is found in Vos's superb sermon, "Heavenly-Mindedness (Hebrews 11:9–10)."

27. Keller, *Reason*, 225.

particular (common grace) perceptions into the skeptic that can be used by a perceptive Van Tilian reasoning from the "impossibility of the contrary."[28] Members of the OPC seriously need to adopt a discerning spirit with respect to Keller's volume. We must remain steadfast to the directive that Van Til placed before us. We must not turn the question of God's existence over to Keller's method of "critical rationality."[29] "Critical rationality" assumes that "belief in God offers a better empirical fit, it explains and accounts for what we see better than the alternative account of things. No view of God can be proven, but that does not mean that we cannot sift and weigh the grounds for various religious beliefs and find that some or even one is the most reasonable."[30] Keller's position does not provide *the* reason for God; rather, his empirical method puts its trust in human rationality to bow before the most rational and probable argument for a certain religion. In contrast, one would be better served by bowing before the method of God's infallible self-witness of his own activity in covenant and redemptive history. After all, the Bible is God's own infallible commentary on his own activity. In his Word, his testimony is self-authenticating. No unbeliever stands presently or in the future before the God of biblical history with justified skepticism. Furthermore, it is imperative for the OPC to remain faithful to our confessional standards as the true summary of the gospel of Jesus Christ. We must not cave to a revisionist view of biblical history in order to be socially and culturally relevant in our era. Such a revisionist position ends up altering the core of the gospel from Genesis to Revelation.

---

28. To look into Van Til's notion, see Van Til, "My Credo," 5; and Bahnsen, *Van Til's Apologetic*, 4–6, 113, 485–7.

29. Keller, *Reason*, 120–1.

30. Ibid., 121.

Bibliography

Ammerman, Robert R. "A Short History of Analytic Philosophy." In *Classics of Analytic Philosophy*, edited by Robert R. Ammerman, 1–12. New York: McGraw-Hill, 1965.

Aristotle. "Metaphysica." In *The Basic Works of Aristotle*, edited by Richard McKeon and translated by W. D. Ross, 681–926. New York: Random House, 1941.

Augustine. *The City of God Against the Pagans*. Vol. 4. Translated by Philip Levine. Cambridge, MA: Harvard University Press, 1966.

Babelotzky, Gerd. *Platonische Bilder und Gedankengänge in Calvins Lehre vom Menschen*. Wiesbaden: Steiner, 1977.

Balke, Willem. *Calvin and the Anabaptist Radicals*. Translated by William Heynen. Grand Rapids: Eerdmans, 1981.

Baltzell, E. Digby. *Puritan Boston and Quaker Philadelphia: Two Protestant Ethics and the Spirit of Class Authority and Leadership*. New York: Free Press, 1979.

Barth, Karl. *The Epistle to the Romans*. 6th ed. Translated by Edwyn C. Hoskyns. London: Oxford University Press, 1972.

Bavinck, Herman. "Common Grace." Translated by Raymond C. Van Leeuwen. *CTJ* 24, no. 1 (April 1989) 38–65.

———. *Our Reasonable Faith*. Translated by Henry Zylstra. Grand Rapids: Baker, 1977.

———. *Reformed Dogmatics*. Edited by John Bolt. Translated by John Vriend. 4 vols. Grand Rapids: Baker, 2008.

Beale, Gregory K. "Already and Not Yet Eschatology and the Temple." Lecture. Park Woods Presbyterian Church. Overland Park, KS. March 8–10, 2002.

———. *The Book of Revelation: A Commentary on the Greek Text*. Grand Rapids: Eerdmans, 1999.

———. "Eden, the Temple, and the Church's Mission in the New Creation." *JETS* 48, no. 1 (2005) 5–32.

———. "Garden Temple." *Kerux: The Journal of Northwest Theological Seminary* 18, no. 2 (September 2003) 3–50.

———. *The Temple and the Church's Mission*. Downers Grove, IL: InterVarsity, 2005.

Benne, Robert. *Quality with Soul: How Six Premier Colleges and Universities Keep Faith with Their Religious Traditions*. Grand Rapids: Eerdmans, 2001.

Berkhof, Louis. *Systematic Theology*. 4th ed. Grand Rapids: Eerdmans, 1972.

Berkouwer, G. C. *General Revelation*. Grand Rapids: Eerdmans, 1955.

———. *Man: Image of God*. Translated by Dirk Jellema. Grand Rapids: Eerdmans, 1962.

Bibliography

Bos, A. P. *The Soul and its Instrumental Body: A Reinterpretation of Aristotle's Philosophy of Living Nature*. Leiden: Brill, 2003.

Bostock, David. *Plato's Phaedo*. Oxford: Clarendon, 1986.

Bratt, James D. *Dutch Calvinism in Modern America: A History of a Conservative Subculture*. Grand Rapids: Eerdmans, 1984.

———. "Puritan Schools in a Quaker Age." *Perspectives* 10, no. 7 (August/September 1995) 12-15.

———. "What Can the Reformed Tradition Contribute to Christian Education?" In *Models for Christian Higher Education: Strategies for Success in the Twenty-First Century*, edited by Richard T. Hughes and William B. Adrian, 125-40. Grand Rapids: Eerdmans, 1997.

Bratt, James D. and Ronald A. Wells. "Piety and Progress: A History of Calvin College." In *Models for Christian Higher Education: Strategies for Success in the Twenty-First Century*, edited by Richard T. Hughes and William B. Adrian, 141-62. Grand Rapids: Eerdmans, 1997.

Burnet, John. "Introduction." In *Plato's Phaedo*, edited by John Burnet, ix-lix. Oxford: Clarendon, 1911.

Burtchaell, James Tunstead. *The Dying of the Light: The Discouragement of Colleges & Universities from their Christian Churches*. Grand Rapids: Eerdmans, 1998.

Bushnell, Horace. *The Vicarious Sacrifice: Grounded in Principles Interpreted by Human Analogies*. Eugene, OR: Wipf and Stock, n.d.

Cahn, Steven M., ed. *Classics of Western Philosophy*. 3rd ed. Indianapolis: Hackett, 1990.

Calvin, John. *The Epistles of Paul the Apostle to the Romans and to the Thessalonians*. Edited by David W. Torrance and Thomas F. Torrance. Translated by Ross MacKenzie. Grand Rapids: Eerdmans, 1960.

———. *Institutes of the Christian Religion*. Edited by John T. McNeill. Translated by Ford Lewis Battles. Philadelphia: Westminster John Knox, 1967.

———. *Tracts and Treatises in Defense of the Reformed Faith: Psychopannychia*. Translated by Henry Beveridge. Vol. 3. Grand Rapids: Eerdmans, 1958.

———. *Treatises Against the Anabaptists and Against the Libertines*. Edited and translated by Benjamin Wirt Farley. Grand Rapids: Baker, 1982.

Clark, Kelly James. *Return to Reason: A Critique of Enlightenment Evidentialism and a Defense of Reason and Belief in God*. Grand Rapids: Eerdmans, 1990.

Cooper, Laurence D. "Beyond the Tripartite Soul: The Dynamic Psychology of the *Republic*." *The Review of Politics* 63, no. 2 (Spring 2001) 341-72.

Cranfield, C. E. B. *A Critical and Exegetical Commentary on the Epistle to the Romans*. 2 vols. Edinburgh: T&T Clark, 1979.

Cullmann, Oscar. "Unsterblichkeit der Steele und Auferstehung der Toten." *TZ* 12, no. 2 (1956) 126-56.

Daane, James. "Common Grace versus Individualism." *Reformed Journal* 1, no. 2 (April 1951) 11-12.

———. "A Theology of Grace—II." *Reformed Journal* 5, no. 4 (April 1955) 9-11.

———. *A Theology of Grace: An Inquiry into and Evaluation of Dr. C. Van Til's Doctrine of Common Grace*. Grand Rapids: Eerdmans, 1954.

De Boer, Cecil. "Editorial: The New Apologetic." *The Calvin Forum* 19, no. 1-2 (August/September 1953) 3-6.

De Boer, Jesse. "Professor Van Til's Apologetics: A Linguistic Bramble Patch: Part I." *The Calvin Forum* 19, no. 1-2 (August/September 1953) 7-12.

Bibliography

———. "Professor Van Til's Apologetics: God and Human Knowledge: Part III." *The Calvin Forum* 19, no. 4 (November 1953) 51–57.

Dennison, Charles G. Untitled sermon on Psalm 19. Grace Orthodox Presbyterian Church. Sewickley, PA. November 27, 1994.

Dennison, James T. Jr. *Reformed Confessions of the 16th and 17th Centuries in English Translation: Volume I, 1523–1552*. Grand Rapids: Reformation Heritage, 2008.

Dennison, William D. "Biblical Theology and the Issue of Application." In *Reformed Spirituality: Communing with Our Glorious God*, edited by Joseph A. Pipa Jr. and J. Andrew Wortman, 119–51. Taylors, SC: Southern Presbyterian, 2003.

———. "Dutch Neo-Calvinism and the Roots for Transformation." *JETS* 42, no. 2 (June 1999) 271–91.

———. *Paul's Two-Age Construction and Apologetics*. Eugene, OR: Wipf and Stock, 2000.

Diekema, Anthony. *Academic Freedom & Christian Scholarship*. Grand Rapids: Eerdmans, 2000.

Dubs, Homer H. "The Socratic Problem." *The Philosophical Review* 36, no. 4 (July 1927) 287–306.

Edwards, Jonathan. *The "Miscellanies" (Entry Nos. 501–832)*. Vol. 18 of *The Works of Jonathan Edwards*. Edited by Ava Chamberlain. New Haven: Yale University Press, 2000.

Fine, Gail. *On Ideas: Aristotle's Criticism of Plato's Theory of Forms*. Oxford: Clarendon, 1995.

Frame, John M. *Apologetics to the Glory of God: An Introduction*. Phillipsburg, NJ: P&R, 1994.

———. *The Doctrine of the Knowledge of God*. Phillipsburg, NJ: P&R, 1987.

———. "God and Biblical Language: Transcendence and Immanence." In *God's Inerrant Word: An International Symposium on the Truthworthiness of Scripture*, edited by John Warwick Montgomery, 159–77. Minneapolis: Bethany, 1974.

———. "Letter from John Frame." *Journey*, March/April 1988.

———. *Perspectives on the Word of God: An Introduction to Christian Ethics*. Phillipsburg, NJ: P&R, 1990.

———. *Van Til: An Analysis of His Thought*. Phillipsburg, NJ: P&R, 1995.

———. "Van Til: His Simplicity and Profundity." *NH*, October 1985.

———. *Van Til: The Theologian*. Phillipsburg, NJ: Pilgrim, 1976.

Friedman, Michael. "The Re-evaluation of Logical Positivism." *Journal of Philosophy* 88, no. 10 (1991) 505–51.

Gaffin, Richard B. Jr. "Epistemological Reflections on 1 Corinthians 2:6–16." In *Revelation and Reason: New Essays in Reformed Apologetics*, edited by K. Scott Oliphint and Lane G. Tipton, 13–40. Phillipsburg, NJ: P&R, 2007.

Genderen, J. van and W. H. Velema. *Concise Reformed Dogmatics*. Translated by Gerrit Bilkes and Ed M. van der Maas. Phillipsburg, NJ: P&R, 2008.

Greidanus, Sidney. *Sola Scriptura: Problems and Principles in Preaching Historical Texts*. Toronto: Wedge, 1970.

Hackforth, R. "Commentary." In *Plato's* Phaedo, translated by R. Hackforth, 42. Indianapolis: Bobbs-Merrill, 1955.

Haynes, Stephen R., ed. *Professing in the Postmodern Academy: Faculty and the Future of Church-Related Colleges*. Waco, TX: Baylor University Press, 2002.

Hodge, Charles. *A Commentary on the Epistle to the Romans*. Philadelphia: Grigg & Elliot, 1835.

Bibliography

———. *Systematic Theology.* 3 vols. New York: Charles Scribner's Sons, 1899.

Hoitenga, Dewey J. Jr. *Faith and Reason from Plato to Plantinga: An Introduction to Reformed Epistemology.* Albany: SUNY Press, 1991.

Homer. *Homeri Ilias.* Edited by Thomas W. Allen. Vol. 3. Oxford: Oxford University Press, 1931.

Hughes, Philip E. *Paul's Second Epistle to the Corinthians.* NICNT. Grand Rapids: Eerdmans, 1982.

Hughes, Richard T. and William B. Adrian, eds. *Models for Christian Higher Education: Strategies for Success in the Twenty-First Century.* Grand Rapids: Eerdmans, 1997.

Hunter, James Davison. *To Change the World: The Irony, Tragedy, & Possibility of Christianity in the Late Modern World.* Oxford: Oxford University Press, 2010.

Johnston, Robert K. *Rethinking Common Grace: Toward a Theology of Co-relation.* Ithaca, NY: Snow Lion, 2002.

Kahn, Charles H. *Plato and the Socratic Dialogue: The Philosophical Use of a Literary Form.* Cambridge: Cambridge University Press, 1996.

Keller, Timothy. *The Reason for God: Belief in an Age of Skepticism.* New York: Dutton, 2008.

———. "Tim Keller at WTS." Westminster Theological Seminary video. April 18, 2008. http://www.wts.edu/flash/media_popup/media_player.php?id=117&paramType=video.

Kline, Meredith G. *Kingdom Prologue: Genesis Foundations for a Covenantal Worldview.* Overland Park, KS: Two Age, 2000.

Kors, Alan Charles. *Atheism in France, 1650–1729: The Orthodox Sources of Disbelief.* Vol. 1. Princeton: Princeton University Press, 1990.

Kuyper, Abraham. "Common Grace." In *Abraham Kuyper: A Centennial Reader,* edited by James D. Bratt and translated by John Vriend, 165–201. Grand Rapids: Eerdmans, 1998.

———. "Common Grace in Science." In *Abraham Kuyper: A Centennial Reader,* edited by James D. Bratt and translated by John Vriend, 442–60. Grand Rapids: Eerdmans, 1998.

Lane, Belden C. "Dragons of the Ordinary: The Discomfort of Common Grace." *The Christian Century,* August 21–28, 1991.

Leithart, Peter J. "The New Classical Schooling." *The Intercollegiate Review* 43, no. 1 (Spring 2008) 3–12.

Machen, J. Gresham. "History and Faith." *Princeton Theological Review* 13 (July 1915) 337–51.

Marsden, George M. *The Outrageous Idea of Christian Scholarship.* New York: Oxford University Press, 1997.

———. *Reforming Fundamentalism: Fuller Seminary and the New Evangelicalism.* Grand Rapids: Eerdmans, 1987.

———. *The Soul of the American University: From Protestant Establishment to Established Nonbelief.* New York: Oxford University Press, 1994.

Marsden, George M. and Bradley J. Longfield, eds. *The Secularization of the Academy.* New York: Oxford University Press, 1992.

Masselink, William. *General Revelation and Common Grace: A Defense of the Historic Reformed Faith Over Against the Theology and Philosophy of the So-called "Reconstructionist Movement."* Grand Rapids: Eerdmans, 1953.

Bibliography

Montasani, John. "Marsilio Ficino and the Plato-Aristotle Controversy." In *Marsilio Ficino: His Theology, His Philosophy, His Legacy*, edited by Michael J. B. Allen et al., 179–202. Leiden: Brill, 2002.

Mouw, Richard J. *He Shines in All That's Fair: Culture and Common Grace*. Grand Rapids: Eerdmans, 2001.

Muether, John R. *Cornelius Van Til: Reformed Apologist and Churchman*. Phillipsburg, NJ: P&R, 2008.

Murray, John. "Common Grace." In *Collected Writings of John Murray*, vol. 2, 93–119. Edinburgh: Banner of Truth Trust, 1977.

———. *The Epistle to the Romans*. 2 vols. Combined edition. Grand Rapids: Eerdmans, 1982.

Notaro, Thom. *Van Til and the Use of Evidence*. Phillipsburg, NJ: P&R, 1980.

Oliphint, K. Scott. *Covenantal Apologetics: Principles and Practice in Defense of Our Faith*. Wheaton, IL: Crossway, 2013.

Patzer, Andreas. *Der Historische Sokrates*. Darmstadt: Wissenschaftliche Buckgeshellschaft, 1987.

Plantinga, Alvin. "Advice to Christian Philosophers." *Faith and Philosophy* 1, no. 3 (1984) 253–71.

———. "Reason and Belief in God." In *Faith and Rationality: Reason and Belief in God*, edited by Alvin Plantinga and Nicholas Wolterstorff, 16–93. Notre Dame: University of Notre Dame Press, 2009.

———. "The Reformed Objection to Natural Theology." In *Rationality in the Calvinian Tradition*, edited by Hendrik Hart et al., 363–83. Lanham, MD: University Press of America, 1983.

———. *Warrant and Proper Function*. New York: Oxford University Press, 1993.

Plato. *Gorgias*. In *Platonis Opera*, vol. 3, edited by Joannes Burnet, 447–527. Oxford: Clarendon, 1903.

———. *Phaedo*. In *Platonis Opera*, vol. 1, edited by Joannes Burnet, 57–118. Oxford: Clarendon, 1900.

———. *Phaedrus*. In *Platonis Opera*, vol. 2, edited by Joannes Burnet, 227–79. Oxford: Clarendon, 1901.

———. *Republic*. In *Platonis Opera*, vol. 4, edited by Joannes Burnet, 327–621. Oxford: Clarendon, 1902.

Popkin, Richard H. *The History of Scepticism from Erasmus to Spinoza*. Berkeley: University of California Press, 1979.

Prior, William J. "The Socratic Problem." In *A Companion to Plato*, edited by Hugh H. Benson, 25–35. Malden, MA: Blackwell, 2006.

Quintilian. "From *Institutes of Oratory*." In *The Rhetorical Tradition: Readings from Classical Times to the Present*, 2nd ed., edited by Patricia Bizzell and Bruce Herzberg, 364–428. Boston: Bedford/St. Martin's, 2001.

Quistorp, Heinrich. *Calvin's Doctrine of the Last Things*. Translated by Harold Knight. Richmond: Westminster John Knox, 1955.

Raines, John C. "Tools and Common Grace." *Cross Currents* 40, no. 3 (Fall 1990) 314–27.

Rogers, Arthur Kenyon. *The Socratic Problem*. New Haven: Yale University Press, 1933.

Ross, W. D. "The Socratic Problem." *Proceedings of the Classical Association* 30 (1933) 7–24.

Sayers, Dorothy L. "Image of God." In *The Mind of the Maker*, 19–31. Westport, CT: Greenwood, 1941.

Bibliography

Sproul, R.C. *Defending Your Faith: An Introduction to Apologetics.* Wheaton, IL: Crossway, 2003.
Stroud, Barry. "Logical Positivism." In *A Companion to Epistemology*, edited by Jonathan Dancy and Ernest Sosa, 262–65. Cambridge: Basil Blackwell, 1992.
Swindoll, Charles. *Moses: God's Man for a Crisis.* Fullerton, CA: Insight for Living, 1976.
Tewksbury, Donald G. *The Founding of American Colleges and Universities Before the Civil War.* New York: Archon, 1965.
Thesleff, Holger. *Studies in Platonic Chronology.* Helsinki: Societas Scientiarum Fennica, 1982.
Turretin, Francis. *Institutes of Elenctic Theology.* Edited by James T. Dennison Jr. and translated by George Musgrave Giger. 3 vols. Phillipsburg, NJ: P&R, 1997.
Vander Stelt, John C. *Philosophy and Scripture: A Study in Old Princeton and Westminster Theology.* Marlton, NJ: Mack, 1978.
Van Til, Cornelius. "Antitheses in Education." In *Fundamentals in Christian Education: Theory and Practice*, edited by Cornelius Jaarsma, 437–59. Grand Rapids: Eerdmans, 1953.
———. Apologetics syllabus. n.p.: n.p., n.d.
———. "Calvin as a Controversialist." In *Soli Deo Gloria: Essays in Reformed Theology: Festschrift for John H. Gerstner*, edited by R. C. Sproul, 1–10. Nutley, NJ: P&R, 1976.
———. "A Calvin University." *The Banner*, November 9, 1939.
———. *Christian Apologetics.* 2nd ed. Edited by William Edgar. Phillipsburg, NJ: P&R, 2003.
———. *Christian-Theistic Evidences* syllabus. n.p.: P&R, 1976.
———. *A Christian Theory of Knowledge.* n.p.: P&R, 1969.
———. *Common Grace and the Gospel.* Phillipsburg, NJ: P&R, 1972.
———. *The Defense of the Faith.* 3rd ed. Philadelphia: P&R, 1967.
———. *The Dilemma of Education.* 2nd ed. n.p.: P&R, 1956.
———. "The Education of Man—A Divinely Ordained Need." In *Fundamentals in Christian Education: Theory and Practice*, edited by Cornelius Jaarsma, 39–59. Grand Rapids: Eerdmans, 1953.
———. *Essays on Christian Education.* Phillipsburg, NJ: P&R, 1979.
———. "God and the Absolute." In *Christianity and Idealism*, 7–35. Philadelphia: P&R, 1955.
———. "God: The Purpose of a Christian School is that Mankind Might Do Everything to God's Glory." In *The Purpose of a Christian School: A General Introduction for Parents, Teachers, Administrators, and College Students*, edited by David B. Cummings, 115–30. Phillipsburg, NJ: P&R, 1979.
———. *The Great Debate Today.* Nutley, NJ: P&R, 1971.
———. *The Intellectual Challenge of the Gospel.* London: Tyndale, 1950.
———. *Introduction to Systematic Theology* syllabus. Philadelphia: n.p., 1971.
———. *An Introduction to Systematic Theology: Prolegomena and the Doctrines of Revelation, Scripture, and God.* 2nd ed. Edited by William Edgar. Phillipsburg, NJ: P&R, 2007.
———. "My Credo." In *Jerusalem and Athens: Critical Discussions on the Theology and Apologetics of Cornelius Van Til*, edited by E. R. Geehan, 3–21. Nutley, NJ: P&R, 1971.
———. "Plato." In *Proceedings of the Calvinistic Philosophy Club*, edited by Jacob T. Hoogstra, n.p. Englewood, NJ: n.p., 1939.

Bibliography

———. *A Survey of Christian Epistemology*. Philadelphia: den Dulk Foundation, 1969.

Vogel, Cornelia J. de. "The Present State of the Socratic Problem." *Phronesis* 1, no. 1 (November 1955) 26–35.

Vos, Geerhardus. *Biblical Theology: Old and New Testaments*. Edinburgh: Banner of Truth, 1992.

———. "Christian Faith and the Truthfulness of Bible History." *The Princeton Theological Review* 4, no. 3 (July 1906) 289–305.

———. "Heavenly-Mindedness (Hebrews 11:9–10)." In *Grace and Glory: Sermons Preached in the Chapel of Princeton Theological Seminary*, 103–23. Edinburgh: Banner of Truth, 1994.

Wallach, John R. "Plato's Socratic Problem, and Ours." *History of Political Thought* 18, no. 3 (1997) 377–98.

Warfield, Benjamin B. "Doubt." In *Selected Shorter Writings of Benjamin B. Warfield*, vol. 2, edited by John E. Meeter, 655–9. Nutley, NJ: P&R, 1973.

———. "The Old Testament and Immortality." In *Selected Shorter Writings of Benjamin B. Warfield*, vol. 1, edited by John E. Meeter, 339–47. Nutley, NJ: P&R, 1970.

Weissman, David. "Logical Positivism." *Journal of Philosophy* 88 (1991) 505–51.

Wengert, Timothy J. Review of *Philip Melanchthon's Rhetorical Construal of Biblical Authority: Oratio Sacra*, by John R. Schneider. *The Sixteenth Century Journal* 25, no. 1 (Spring 1994) 202–3.

Williams, George Huntston. *The Radical Reformation*. 3rd ed. Vol. 15 of *16th Century Essays & Studies*. Kirksville, MO: Truman State University Press, 2000.

Wilson, Douglas. "Introduction to Antithesis in Education." In *Repairing the Ruins: The Classical and Christian Challenge to Modern Education*, edited by Douglas Wilson, 13–25. Moscow, ID: Canon, 1996.

Wolterstorff, Nicholas. "Can Belief In God Be Rational If It Has No Foundations?" In *Faith and Rationality: Reason and Belief in God*, edited by Alvin Plantinga and Nicholas Wolterstorff, 135–86. Notre Dame: Notre Dame Press, 1983.

———. "Thomas Reid on Rationality." In *Rationality in the Calvinian Tradition*, edited by Hendrik Hart et al., 43–69. Lanham, MD: University Press of America, 1983.

Wright, N. T. *Paul for Everyone: Romans, Part Two (Chapters 9–16)*. London: SPCK, 2004.

———. *Surprised by Hope: Rethinking Heaven, the Resurrection, and the Mission of the Church*. New York: HarperOne, 2008.

Yancey, Philip. "Chords That Bind." *Christianity Today*, September 1, 1997.

Yandell, Keith E. "Modernism, Post-Modernism, and the Minimalist Canons of Common Grace." *Christian Scholar's Review* 27, no. 1 (Fall 1997) 15–26.

Other Works by William D. Dennison

BOOKS

A Christian Approach to Interdisciplinary Studies: In Search of a Method and Starting Point. Eugene, OR: Wipf and Stock, 2007.
Karl Marx. Great Thinkers. Phillipsburg, NJ: P&R, forthcoming.
Paul's Two-Age Construction and Apologetics. Eugene, OR: Wipf and Stock, 2000.
The Young Bultmann: Context for His Understanding of God, 1884-1925. American University Studies Series 7, Theology and Religion. New York: Peter Lang, 2008.

ESSAYS AND ARTICLES

"Abraham: The Prophet (Gen. 20:1–18)." *Kerux: The Journal of Northwest Theological Seminary* 13, no. 2 (September 1998) 25–32.
"Bethel: House of God (Gen. 28:10–22)." *Kerux: The Journal of Northwest Theological Seminary* 2, no. 3 (December 1987) 23–30.
"Biblical Theology and the Issue of Application." In *Reformed Spirituality: Communing with Our Glorious God*, edited by Joseph A. Pipa Jr. and J. Andrew Wortman, 119–51. Taylors, SC: Southern Presbyterian, 2003.
"Christian Education: Is it a Mess? (Part I)." *The Outlook*, June 2003.
"Christian Education: Is it a Mess? (Part II)." *The Outlook*, July/August 2003.
"Christian Education: Is it a Mess? (Part III)." *The Outlook*, September 2003.
"Christ, Our Starting Point." *NH*, December 1991.
"Comparing J. Gresham Machen and Rudolf Bultmann: Reflections upon the Marburg Experience, 1905–06." *JHMTH* 16, no. 2 (2009) 217–35.
"Creation and Re-creation: Reflection on Salvation." *Journey*, January/March 1991.
"Darwin on Christian Theism." *NH*, July 2009.
"Dutch Neo-Calvinism and the Roots for Transformation." *JETS* 42, no. 2 (June 1999) 271–91.
"The First Wedding: A Copy of the Last Wedding." *The Outlook*, June 2005.
"For a Better World? Response to David C. Ward." *JIS* 26, no. 1 (2014) 57–72.

Other Works by William D. Dennison

"From the Department of Apologetics." *His Story is . . . Our Story* 5, no. 1 (March 2004) 3–4.

"Indicative and Imperative: The Basic Structure of Pauline Ethics." *CTJ* 14, no. 1 (April 1979) 55–78.

"Introduction" to Charles G. Dennison's "Evangelism and the Church." *Ordained Servant* 18 (2009) 42–51.

"In Search of a Starting Point and a Method for Interdisciplinary Studies in the Context of Christian Theism." *Pro Rege* 35, no. 1 (September 2006) 10–23.

"J. Gresham Machen's Letters Home from Marburg, 1905–06." Edited by William D. Dennison. *JHMTH* 16, no. 2 (2009) 241–75.

"Joseph: Justified by Faith." *The Outlook*, December 2004.

"Luther and Calvin on Interpretation." *The Outlook*, October 1996.

"Mary: The Image of the Christian Life." *The Outlook*, December 2003.

"Miracles as 'Signs': Their Significance for Apologetics." *Biblical Theological Bulletin* 6, no. 2–3 (June/October 1976) 190–202.

"Parenting the Baptized." *NH*, June 2008.

"The Passion Narratives of Mark and Luke: Christ's Loneliness and the Christ of Compassion." *Kerux: The Journal of Northwest Theological Seminary* 19, no. 2 (September 2004) 32–44.

"Reason, History, and Revelation: Biblical Theology and the Enlightenment." *Kerux: The Journal of Northwest Theological Seminary* 18, no. 1 (May 2003) 3–25.

"The Redemptive-Historical Hermeneutic and Preaching." *Kerux: The Journal of Northwest Theological Seminary* 21, no. 1 (May 2006) 11–39.

"Resurrection Living (Col. 3:1–4)." *Kerux: The Journal of Northwest Theological Seminary* 9, no. 1 (May 1994) 24–31.

"Rudolf Bultmann: Pastor?" *CTJ* 34, no. 1 (April 1999) 179–87.

"Rudolf Bultmann's Review of J. Gresham Machen's, *The Origin of Paul's Religion*." Edited by William D. Dennison. Translated by Richard B. Gaffin Jr. *JHMTH* 16, no. 2 (2009) 236–40.

"So, What is Faith? Hebrews 11:1, 17–19; Gen. 18:14; 22:1–14." *Kerux: The Journal of Northwest Theological Seminary* 24, no. 1 (May 2009) 28–33.

"Van Til: Raising a Question." *Journey*, September/October 1987.

"Your Life is the Worship of Jesus Christ (Jn. 1:1–18)." *Kerux: The Journal of Northwest Theological Seminary* 1, no. 2 (September 1986) 37–43.

REVIEWS

Biblical Hermeneutics: Five Ways, edited by Stanley E. Porter and Beth M. Stovell. *NH*, July 2013.

Interpreting the Bible: A Popular Introduction to Biblical Hermeneutics, by Terence J. Keegan. *CTJ* 24, no. 1 (April 1989) 139–40.

Natural Law and the Two Kingdoms: A Study in the Development of Reformed Social Thought, by David VanDrunen. *WTJ* 75, no. 2 (Fall 2013) 349–70.

New Testament Theology, by Leon Morris. *CTJ* 27, no. 1 (April 1992) 102–6.

The Pattern of Sound Doctrine: Systematic Theology at the Westminster Seminaries: Essays in Honor of Robert B. Strimple, edited by David VanDrunen. *CTJ* 40, no. 2 (November 2005) 380–3.

Other Works by William D. Dennison

Surprised by Hope: Rethinking Heaven, the Resurrection, and the Mission of the Church, by N. T. Wright. *NH*, April 2009.

Subject Index

A

abstract, xiv, xxiii, xxv, xxvi, 18, 31, 40n8, 43, 47, 49, 77, 90–94, 97, 97n29, 99, 129, 138, 150
adoption, 119, 142, 143, 145n23, 149, 169
aesthetic, 58, 120
Anabaptist, 74n46
analogical (knowledge/thinking), 40, 87, 87n9, 88, 90
analytic philosophy, 9–35
anthropology, 64, 169
antithesis, xxiii, 6, 7, 11, 17, 18, 39, 47, 53, 54, 55, 61n10, 62, 63, 66, 67, 69, 70n38, 73, 74n46, 75, 76n53, 77, 78, 79, 86, 86n6, 87n7, 92, 92n20, 95n27, 97n29, 100n35, 101, 107, 145, 146, 146n25, 149, 156, 161, 169
apologetics, xxiii–xxvii, 3–8, 105–17, 118–31
archaeology, xiii, xv
Archimedean point, 4, 21, 24, 27, 35, 73, 77, 158
argument, xxvi–xxvii, 3–8, 24, 25, 41, 68, 105–6, 163–66
Aristotelian, 40n8, 52, 81, 82, 93, 136
arithmetic, 82
Arminian, 37, 38n2, 89, 89n16, 93, 107
astronomy, 82
atheism, 83, 100
atonement, 167–68
Augustinian, xi-xii
autonomy, xi, 29, 46, 83, 97, 100, 100n35, 106, 126, 127

B

Baptist, 55
Belgic Confession, 136n11, 140n17
biblical theology, xi, xii, xxi, xxiv, 31, 32, 33, 48, 109
biology, 71–72, 100
Buddhism, 112

C

Calvin College, 9, 11, 79n57, 85
Calvinism, xi–xii, xxiv, 39, 57–60, 89, 89n16, 93, 107, 164
Calvin Theological Seminary, 11, 159
canon, xiv, 58n5, 105, 106, 116
capitalism, 112
Cartesian, 164
Catholicism, 16, 17, 25, 37, 38n2, 89, 89n16, 93, 107
chain of being, 66n20, 67, 69, 72
Christ (Jesus),
  as apologist, 126–28
  as second/last Adam, 106–7, 126–28, 130
  as self-attesting, xix, xxiv, 3–8, 33, 35, 61, 79, 84, 98, 101, 106, 127, 130, 166
  union with, xxiii–xxvii, 7–8, 18, 61–62, 105–17, 119, 121, 128–30, 131, 142–45

Subject Index

Christian Reformed Church (CRC), 11, 12, 16, 18, 19, 33, 38n4, 43, 85
Civil War, 57–59
comprehensive knowledge, 88, 120
consummation, 50, 76, 119, 121, 145, 145n23, 147n29, 149, 168
continental philosophy, 157
cosmonomic law, 29
covenant, xi, xiv, xxiv, 22, 23, 48, 49, 51, 55, 79n57, 81, 82, 83, 93, 94n26, 100, 101, 106, 108, 111, 112, 115, 122, 124, 131, 134, 135, 136, 161, 165, 166, 167, 169, 170
Covenant College, xx
creation, xxv–xxvi, 13, 28, 29, 30, 35, 41, 44, 45, 46, 50, 65n19, 78, 79n57, 83, 89n16, 90, 92n20, 93n23, 94, 98, 108, 113, 115, 119, 120, 121, 122, 124, 132–51, 168, 169
Creator/creature distinction, 13, 21, 98, 99, 161
criticism (historical/higher/literary), xi–xii, xiii–xviii, 32, 58n5, 63, 98n32

D

Darwinian, 83
deconstruction, 83
deism, 135
dialectic, 4, 31, 82, 96, 97, 98, 101, 141n18, 144n22

E

ecclesiastical, xvii, xxvii, 10, 56, 57, 57n2, 58n5, 59, 61, 78, 79, 140n18, 159
ecumenical, xvi, 60, 61, 79, 84, 160, 166
education, xxvi, 10, 56, 57, 58, 59, 77, 80, 81–101
empirical, 22, 23, 24, 25, 26, 27, 34, 37, 41, 42, 43, 60, 64, 66, 68, 72, 77, 89, 91, 92n20, 93, 98, 107, 124, 126, 127, 164, 170
Enlightenment, xi, xii, 5, 7, 58n5, 84, 98n32, 164, 169
Episcopal, 55

epistemology, xxvii, 9–35, 36–54, 62, 67, 70, 77, 79n57, 94, 94n26, 95, 98, 106, 127, 138, 155, 156, 164, 165
eschatology, xxiii–xxvii, 18, 33, 48, 54, 56, 77, 80, 86, 105–17, 118–31, 132–51, 165n12, 169, 169n26
ethics, xvii, 27n46, 28, 50, 53, 54, 77, 95, 96, 97, 97n29, 99, 100, 100n36, 101, 101n37, 106
evangelical, 16, 17, 55, 58n5, 74n46, 112, 159, 160, 161, 167
evidence, xxiii, 17, 23, 28, 28n49, 105, 106, 112, 133, 163–65
evolution, xiii, 46, 100
existentialism, 60, 77, 100, 167
experience, xv, xxiii, 3–8, 15, 21, 23, 29, 32, 34, 37, 41, 42, 54, 60, 90n16, 91, 96, 97n31, 105–17, 126, 129, 131, 157–58, 167

F

facts, 12–14, 18, 24n34, 28, 28n49, 30, 30n55, 32, 33, 34, 36–54, 60, 61, 61n10, 83–94, 95, 98, 101, 150–51, 156, 158, 158n16, 166
faith, xii, xiv–xvi, xxii, xxiii, xxvii, 6, 7, 12n5, 41, 42, 54, 56, 57, 59, 67, 68, 79, 85, 100n36, 105–17, 119, 129, 136, 139, 146, 148n29, 155, 159, 162, 163, 166, 167
federal head, 49, 50, 51, 106, 107, 123
form (Platonic), 40, 46, 63–72, 73, 91–94
foundationalism, 24, 164

G

Geneva College, 36
Geometry, 82
God,
 analytical knowledge of, 14, 15, 27
 attributes of, 94, 141–42, 146–48
 as author of Scripture, xiii–xviii
 as Father, 108, 111, 114, 117, 127, 128, 133, 136, 142, 144, 145, 146, 148n29, 150

Subject Index

as Holy Spirit, 8, 39, 42, 43, 65n19, 101, 108, 109, 110, 111, 116, 117, 119, 128, 129, 130, 131, 136, 142, 145, 146, 149, 150, 157
as incomprehensible, 14, 41–42
as Son, 7, 99, 101, 106, 109, 111, 114, 117, 120, 121, 127, 133, 136, 142, 145, 146, 150, 151
as sovereign, xi, 7, 37, 41, 47, 48, 52, 78n55, 86n6, 91, 93, 100n36, 101, 105, 124, 149, 164
gospel, 3–4, 7, 32, 36, 79, 95n27, 97n31, 99, 101, 105–17, 128, 129, 133, 139, 140, 140n18, 141, 141n18, 144, 145, 147n29, 148, 149, 150, 151, 163, 165n12, 166, 169, 170
grammar, 82, 84, 96, 98, 101
Greek (culture/thought), 42, 44, 68n27, 76n53, 82, 84, 87, 88, 89, 90, 91, 93, 95n27, 96, 97, 97n31, 100, 101, 139, 147n29

H

Harvard, 57–58
Heart, xviii, xxiii, 4, 39–40, 45, 46, 52, 54, 88, 101, 105–17, 118, 149, 165n12
Heaven, xxiii–xxvii, 64, 92n20, 105–17, 119–22, 125, 128, 129, 137n14, 140, 140n18, 141–42, 143, 145, 168–69
Hegelian, 9
Heidelberg Catechism, 75n48, 76, 76n52, 123n5
hermeneutics, xiii–xviii, 78, 97n31, 158,
Hinduism, 112
humanism, 5–6, 83

I

idealism, xii, 7, 9–35, 60, 77, 92, 157
image of God, 5, 39, 47, 50, 53, 64, 65, 65n19, 73, 75, 86, 122, 146, 156–57
immortality, 55–80,
Islam, 34n69, 112

J

Judaism, 34n69, 112

K

Kantian, 15, 40, 40n8, 87n8, 99, 100, 157–58
kingdom of God, xi, xvi, 16, 33, 48, 78, 86, 100, 106, 119, 137, 145, 146
kingdom of Satan, 16, 19n19, 33, 48, 86, 114, 145, 146
knowledge (understanding/interpretation), xxiv–xxvi, 9–35, 36–54, 132–51

L

liberal arts, 81–83, 98
linguistic analysis, 23, 25, 26
logic, 9, 15, 17n17, 22, 23, 24, 25, 27, 29, 30, 31, 34, 44, 52, 61n10, 69, 82, 84, 94, 96, 106, 107, 124, 146, 155, 158, 158n16
Lutheran, 55, 60n8

M

Marxism, 83, 112
materialism, 60, 77
mathematics, 18, 24, 37, 47, 52, 54, 84, 158
Mennonite, 55
metaphysics, 17n17, 22, 23, 29n51, 41, 45–47, 50, 53, 54, 77, 106
Methodist, 55
modernity, xi–xii, 5, 40n8, 43, 58, 59, 83, 86, 87, 92, 95, 98n32, 100, 138, 159, 160, 161
multiculturalism, 83
music, 39, 82, 166
mythology, 82, 91, 96

N

naturalism, 60, 77, 150
natural law, 28n49, 84
natural theology, 89, 93, 125, 146, 150
Nazarene, 55
neo-Calvinism, 168–69

185

Subject Index

neutrality, xv, xvi, xxiii–xxiv, 17, 18, 29, 37, 46, 47n23, 54, 85, 86, 89, 107, 126, 156
nihilism, 100
noetic, xxvi, 18, 34, 61

O

Old Princeton, 12n5, 30, 31, 35, 37, 38, 60n8, 89n16, 98n32, 164
one and many (problem), 90–91
ontology, 23, 24, 25, 28, 29, 126, 127, 136
organic, xi, xiv, xxv, 97, 112, 136, 136n11, 145, 149, 151
Orthodox Presbyterian Church (OPC), xviii, xxii, 11, 81, 82, 83, 84n2, 159, 160, 161, 162, 163, 170

P

pantheism, 9, 12, 13, 14, 18, 136
patristic, xiv, xvi
perspectivalism, 19–27, 31
phenomenalism, 40
philosophy of education, 58, 85, 95,
philosophy of history, 10, 10n3, 12, 21, 27, 28, 29, 31, 32, 33, 34, 35, 47, 86, 94, 94n26, 98n33, 132, 134, 137, 165
philosophy of life, 12, 19, 28, 32, 130, 130n6
philosophy of nature, 30
philosophy of revelation, 132–51
plan (of God), xxiii, xxv, xxvi, 9, 28, 33, 46, 86n6, 87n9, 88n12, 91, 91n19, 93, 94, 97, 98, 98n33, 99, 100, 101, 105, 106, 133, 134, 135, 137, 138, 169
Platonism, 40, 66n22, 74n46, 75, 76n53, 78, 81, 84n3, 87n8, 92, 93, 99, 100
point of contact, 28, 29, 38n2, 45–47
political philosophy, 6, 100
positivism, 23, 24, 25, 33, 100
postmodernity, 58, 59, 83, 95
poststructuralism, 60
pragmatism, xii

pre-redemptive revelation, xxv, 48, 48n27, 49–50, 53, 54, 119, 124, 125, 128
Presbyterian, 55, 57–58
presupposition, xi, xii, xv, xvi, xxi, xxiv, 3–8, 10, 15, 17, 20, 26, 29n52, 30, 31, 32, 35, 45, 58, 62, 85, 88, 94n26, 113, 120, 124, 134, 137, 155, 156, 165
Protestantism, 74n46, 160
providence, xiv, xvi, 7, 28, 28n49, 49, 51, 86, 91, 91n19, 94, 100, 115, 137n12
psychology, 50, 53, 54, 100, 106, 155, 166

Q

quadrivium, 82, 96

R

rationalism, 41, 60, 77, 164
realism, 34, 41, 42, 60, 77, 91, 92, 95n27
reason, xxiii, xxvi, 4, 6, 15, 16n16, 23, 29, 30, 41, 42, 43, 44, 47n23, 54, 60, 61n9, 67, 68, 69, 89, 93–94, 96, 107, 108, 111, 113, 126, 129, 131, 150, 158, 164n11
redemption, xvii, xxiii–xxvii, 30, 32, 33, 43, 48, 51, 65n19, 76, 77, 97n31, 98, 99, 99n34, 101, 105–17, 118–31, 132–51, 158, 161, 165, 166, 168, 169, 170
Reformed theology, xi, xii, xv, xvi, 11, 17n17, 25, 27, 43, 60, 60n8, 64n15
regeneration, 39, 40, 60, 119
reincarnation, 67, 68, 70, 71, 72
Renaissance, 58n5, 83, 94, 164
resurrection, 74, 75n48, 76, 99, 101, 106, 108, 110, 117, 119, 128, 144, 148n29, 150, 151
revelation, xi–xii, xiii–xviii, xxi–xxvii, 132–51
rhetoric, 82, 84, 94–101
Roman (culture/thought), 82, 84, 96, 97, 101, 107, 111, 112, 113, 114, 115, 147n29

Subject Index

romanticism, 60, 77

S

sanctification, 108, 116, 119, 145
scholasticism, 35, 41, 42, 43, 44, 93
science, 17, 23, 24, 28n49, 39, 41, 43, 45, 56, 58, 83–91, 100, 138, 150, 157, 163
socialism, 112
sociology, 100
sophists, 82n1, 95
soteriology, 118–19
soul, 55–80
speech act (theory), 25,
starting point, xix, xxiv, 3–8, 23, 29n52, 33, 34, 40, 43, 89, 93, 94, 99, 101, 116, 126, 130, 131, 158, 166
story (biblical), 30, 32, 33, 34, 35, 61n10, 98, 144, 158, 158n16, 163, 164, 166, 168
structuralism, 60, 77
systematic (dogmatic) theology, xvi, 10, 22, 31, 41, 54, 58n5

T

tabernacle, 119–24, 126, 128
temple, 119–30

total depravity, 16n16, 36–54, 60, 60n8, 64, 65n17, 65n19, 89n16, 156
transcendental (analysis/critique), xxvi–xxvii, 3–8, 59, 74n46, 78n55, 79, 131, 156, 157–58, 167n14
Trinity
  as ontological, xi, 21, 25, 28, 29, 29n51, 32, 33, 35, 40, 52, 101, 127
  as economic, 29, 30, 32, 33, 35
Trinity Evangelical Divinity School, 27n46
trivium, 82, 82n1, 94–101

U

United States of America, 57–58

W

Westminster Confession of Faith (WCF), 47n24, 58n5, 74–75, 107, 136, 165, 168–69
Westminster Shorter Catechism, 79n57, 169
Westminster Theological Seminary, 11, 34, 37, 159, 160, 162
worldview (world-and-life view/*weltanschauung*), xi, xxiii, xxiv, xxvi, 5, 19, 27–28, 58, 62, 69, 78, 84, 94, 95, 98n33, 100, 105

Names Index

A

Alexander, Archibald, 89
Aquinas, Thomas, 30, 34, 35, 61n10, 89n16, 135, 136, 136n11, 140n18, 158n16, 167n14
Aristotle, 63, 63n11, 66n22, 74n46, 87, 91, 92, 93, 94, 108, 135
Augustine, xi, 5, 75n51, 91n19
Austin, John L., 26

B

Bacon, Francis, 164
Bahnsen, Greg L., 94n26, 155–58
Baltzell, E. Digby, 57, 58n4
Barbour, Ian, 165
Barth, Karl, 34, 141n18, 144n22, 159, 161
Bavinck, Herman, 12n5, 35, 38, 39, 41, 42n15, 43, 54, 60n8, 75, 76, 76n53, 94, 134n6, 135n8, 159, 169
Beale, Gregory K., 119, 122
Bellah, Robert, 165
Berkhof, Louis, 12n5, 29n51
Boethius, 82n1
Bonhoeffer, Dietrich, 167
Bos, Abraham P., 63n11, 66n22
Buber, Martin, 167n14
Bushnell, Horace, 168, 168n20
Buswell, J. Oliver, 159
Butler, Joseph, 89n16, 164
Bratt, James, 57, 58n4, 59n6, 60n8
de Brès, Guido, 136n11

C

Calvin, John, xi, 29, 30, 34, 61n9, 61n10, 64, 64n17, 65, 65n19, 65n20, 66n21, 70n38, 73, 73n46, 74, 76, 76n53, 79n56, 94, 140n18, 147n28, 158n16, 168
Carnap, Rudolf, 24
Carnell, Edward J., 159
Carter, Stephen L., 165
Cebes, 68, 69, 70
Chappell, David L., 165
Chesterton, G. K., 165
Cicero, 52, 147n29
Clark, Gorden H., 84n2, 159
Clement of Alexandria, xiv
Comte, Auguste, 100
Cranfield, C. E. B., 140n18, 143n21, 147n28, 147n29, 149n31

D

Daane, James, 11, 11n5, 43, 159
Danhof, Henry, 38
De Boer, Cecil, 9, 10, 11, 12, 13, 14, 15, 18, 19, 20, 21, 27, 28, 30, 33, 159
De Boer, Jesse, 16, 17, 18, 19, 20, 21, 27, 28, 30, 33, 159
Dennison, Charles G., 142n19
Descartes, René, 164
Diekema, Anthony, 79n57
Dionysius, 97
Dooyeweerd, Herman, 12n5, 37, 38, 40n8, 44, 45, 159
Dostoevsky, Fyodor, 165

Names Index

E

Edwards, Jonathan, 135n9, 137n12, 137n14, 138n15

F

Foucault, Michel, 80
Frame, John M., 10, 19–27, 28, 30, 31, 31n61, 32, 34, 35, 35n75, 94n26
Freud, Sigmund, 100

G

Gabler, Johann Philipp, xi
Gerstner, John, 159
Graham, Billy, 159

H

Hackforth, R., 67
Hegel, G. W. F., 10, 14
Henry, Carl, 159
Hepp, Valentine, 12n5, 38, 39, 42, 43, 54
Heraclitus, 70n35, 90
Hesiod, 147n29
Hippias of Elis, 82n1
Hodge, A. A., 38n2, 89n16
Hodge, Charles, 12n5, 38n2, 76n53, 89n16, 140n18, 143n21, 159, 168
Hoeksema, Herman, 11, 38, 43, 44, 48
Hyppolytus, xiv

I

Irenaeus, xiv
Isocrates, 82n1, 95

J

Jellema, William, 159

K

Kant, Immanuel, xi, 10, 14, 15, 19n19, 40, 40n8, 41, 87, 97, 157
Keller, Timothy, 162–70
Kierkegaard, Søren, 167
King, Martin Luther, Jr, 167, 167n14

Kline, Meredith G., 119
Kuyper, Abraham, 12n5, 35, 38, 39, 40, 40n8, 42, 43, 45, 54, 60n8, 159

L

Lewis, C. S., 159, 165
Locke, John, 108
Lucretius, 52

M

Machen, J. Gresham, 12n5, 98n32, 98n33, 160
Machiavelli, 6
Marsden, George, 59n6
Marty, Martin, 159
Marx, Karl, 100
Masselink, William, 12n5, 43, 159
Mill, John Stuart, 6, 7
Muether, John R., 159–61, 162
Murray, John, 140, 141n18, 146n25, 147

N

Nietzsche, Friedrich, 100

O

O'Brien, Dennis, 25

P

Paley, William, 150
Parmenides, 87
Plantinga, Alvin, 33, 34n69, 165
Plato, 14, 34, 40, 46, 62, 63, 63n11, 63n12, 64, 64n13, 65, 65n18, 65n19, 65n20, 66, 66n21, 66n22, 67, 67n23, 68, 68n27, 68n29, 69, 70, 70n38, 71, 72, 73, 74n46, 75, 75n50, 75n51, 76, 78, 87, 91, 91n20, 92, 93, 95, 95n27, 97
Popkin, Richard H., 164n11
Poullain, Vallérandus, 73

Q

Quistorp, Heinrich, 74n46

Names Index

S

Sayers, Dorothy L., 89n16
Schaeffer, Francis, 159
Schilder, Klaas, 11n5
Simmias, 70, 71
Socrates, 63, 64n12, 64n13, 67, 67n23, 68, 68n27, 69, 70, 70n35, 71, 108
Sproul, R. C., 133,
Steen, Peter, 36, 37
Swindoll, Charles, 97n31

T

Tillich, Paul, 167n14
Turretin, Francis, 75n49

V

Vansina, Jan, 165
Van Til, Cornelius,
  on antithesis, 45–47, 61–63
  on common grace, 47–54
  on education, 85–86
  on epistemology, 27–35, 156–57
  life of, 159–61
  on metaphysics, 45–47, 90–94
  on revelation, 49–50, 134–38
  on transcendental argument, 3–8
  and Vos, 27–35
Vollenhoven, D. H. Th., 12n5, 37, 38, 44, 45
Vos, Geerhardus, xi, xii, xxiv, xxv, 30, 31, 32, 33, 34, 35, 48, 49, 94, 98n33, 130, 137, 158, 161, 169n26

W

Warfield, Benjamin B., 12n5, 38n2, 75n50, 89n16, 159
Weber, Max, 100
Weissman, David, 24,
Williams, George Huntston, 74n46
Wilson, Douglas, 84n4, 100n35
Wittgenstein, Ludwig, 26, 27
Wolterstorff, Nicholas, 33, 34n69
Wright, N. T., 66n22, 141n18, 143n21, 144n22, 165

Scripture Index

GENESIS

1	138, 146, 147n29,
1:1	136
1:1–5	138
1:2	136, 146
1:3–5	113, 132
1:26–27	122
1:26–28	73, 146
2:7	73
2:15	119, 122, 123n5, 124, 125, 126, 129, 130
2:21–23	73
3:1–5	124
3:1–7	125
3:8	122
3:15	86
8:21	135
9:9–11	135
9:12–15	135
12:7	112
17:5	112

EXODUS

3:14	148n29
14:4	148
14:18	148
14:19–20	149
14:25	149
17:6	136
20:2	99
20:3–17	99

LEVITICUS

6:1–13	144n23
9:23–24	144n23
26:12	122

NUMBERS

3:6–8	123
3:17—4:49	123
3:38	123
18:7	123

DEUTERONOMY

4:26	141
6:4–9	101
7:6–11	101
10:12–13	123
30:16–17	123
30:19	141
31:28	141
32:1	141

JOSHUA

2:9–12	150
5:1	150
9:1–2	150
9:8–9	150
23:4–9	148
23:6–7	123

2 SAMUEL

7:6	122

Scripture Index

1 KINGS

6:20	120
9:6	123
10:3–5	101
10:4–5	80

2 KINGS

1:6	100

1 CHRONICLES

28:8–9	123

2 CHRONICLES

9:3–4	80
26:1–4	101

PSALMS

2:1–12	7
16:10	73
19:1	140, 140n18
19:1–6	140, 141
19:4	139, 140, 140n18, 141, 142, 144, 145
19:7–14	140
27:1–3	117
84:10	125
95:1	136
97:6	142
102:25–28	143
114:7–8	136
115:1–8	149
118:6	111, 117
118:9	7
134:15–18	149
136	148
145:10–13	148
146:3	7
146:5–9	148
148:1–14	148
150:1–2	148

PROVERBS

3:7	81

ECCLESIASTES

12:7	73

ISAIAH

1:2	141
7:14	126
51:3	122
51:6	143
52:7	139
53:1	139

EZEKIEL

28:13	122
31:8–9	122
40—48	120
47	122

AMOS

4:13	141

MICAH

6:1	141
6:2	141

MATTHEW

1:23	126
4:1–11	126
4:17	119
6:24–34	169
10:28	73
12:34–35	4
15:18–19	4
16:18	100
16:21	127
16:24–25	80
26:42	127
27:45	144
27:50–54	144
28:2–3	144

MARK

1:12–13	126–27
1:15	106, 119
7:21	4

Scripture Index

LUKE

4:1–13	127
4:16–21	106
4:43	106
11:43	80
12:1	109
12:9–10	109
12:11–12	109, 110
12:34	4
16:14–41	74, 76
16:15	4
16:22–23	73
16:23–24	73
20:46	80
21:12	109
21:12–15	110
21:14	109
21:14–15	109–11
23:43	73

JOHN

1	138
1:1	126
1:2–3	146
1:3	136, 137
1:3–10	133
1:14	120, 126
2:19–22	120, 126
3:16–21	138
6:35	148n29, 136
6:38	148n29
8:12	133
8:44	126
19:38	144
20:9	127

ACTS

1:8	112, 114
7:59	73
9:1–9	111
9:3	112
9:15	112, 113
9:15–16	114
17:1–4	128
17:16–31	150
17:18	128
17:24	150
17:30–31	150, 166
17:31–32	128
18:26	xvii
22:1	111
22:3–21	112
22:6	112
23:11	112
24:10	111, 115
25:8	111, 115
26:1	111, 112, 115
26:2–27	112
26:16	112
26:16–17	112
26:17	113

ROMANS

1	47n24, 140n18, 145–50
1:16–17	146
1:17	145, 146, 146n24, 146n25, 146
1:17–25	146
1:17—3:20	145
1:18	53, 142
1:18–20	141n18
1:18–21	107
1:18–25	138, 139, 145, 165
1:18—3:20	145, 146
1:19	146
1:19–20	xxv
1:20	148n29, 148n30
1:21	149
1:23	149
1:25	124, 149
3:9–20	60
5	47n24, 49
5:12–21	107
6:1–14	99, 107, 119, 128
6:10	167
8	142–44, 145, 149
8:1	142
8:2	142
8:3	142
8:5	142
8:7–8	142
8:9–11	128
8:12–17	142
8:12–30	138, 139, 145

ROMANS (continued)

8:12–31	142
8:15	142
8:16	142
8:17	142, 143
8:18	106, 143
8:18–23	143n21
8:18–25	169
8:19	143, 149
8:19–23	xxv
8:20–21	143
8:21	149
8:22	143
8:23	143
8:26	143
8:31–39	111, 117
10:8–21	145
10:10	111
10:11–13	139
10:14	139
10:15	139
10:17	139
10:18	xxv, 138, 139, 140, 142, 145, 149
11:36	101
12:1–2	76

1 CORINTHIANS

1:30–31	107
2:2	101
2:4	101
2:6–16	60
3:16–17	129
6:12–20	76
6:19	129
6:19–20	108
10:4	136
15	47n24, 49
15:20–23	107

2 CORINTHIANS

4:4	xxvi, 107
4:6	xxvi
4:11—5:8	119
4:16—5:8	169
5:1–8	73
5:6	73
5:8	73
5:17	106
6:2	106
10:5	xxvii, 16, 16n16, 108

GALATIANS

2:20	7, 99, 119
3:15–19	106
3:28–29	106
3:29	106
4:4	106, 114
6:14–15	107

EPHESIANS

1:2	114
1:3	119
1:21	106
1:15–23	169
2:1–10	107
2:2–3	106
2:6	114, 119
2:7	106
2:10	148n30
2:12–13	106
4:10	73
6:4	81

PHILIPPIANS

1:23	73
2:15	106
3:20	106, 114
3:20–21	169

COLOSSIANS

1:15	147n29
1:16	136, 137, 147n29
2:8	xxvii
3:1–2	119
3:1–4	xxiii, 107, 114, 119
3:1–17	99

1 THESSALONIANS

5:23	76

Scripture Index

1 TIMOTHY

1:12–17	148n29
1:17	147n29
3:16	128
4:1	106
6:16	73

2 TIMOTHY

3:1	106
4:1	106

TITUS

2:12	106

HEBREWS

1:1	106
1:1–3	109
1:1–4	119
3:14	169
5:8	127
6:1–2	xiv
10:8–18	167
11:1	109
11:3	147n28
11:27	147n29, 148n29
12:9	73
12:23	73

1 PETER

1:1	119
1:3	116
1:3–5	108
1:9	73
1:11–12	116
2:12	116
2:21–25	80
3:10–17	115
3:14	115, 116
3:15	108, 109, 116
3:15–16	5
3:16	116, 117
3:19	73
4:6	73

2 PETER

3:10–13	145n23

1 JOHN

2:18	106, 119

REVELATION

21:1	120
21:2	120, 128
21:3	120
21:3–7	126
21:3–8	120
21:6	121
21:6–7	120
21:9	121
21:9–13	128
21:10	120
21:12–13	121
21:14	120
21:16	120
21:18–21	120
21:19	120
21:21	120
21:22	121
21:22–23	120
21:22–27	120
21:22—22:5	169
21:23	120, 133
21:23–24	121
21—22	108, 120, 120n3, 121, 122
22:2	120, 121
22:5	120
22:13	121, 131
22:17	128

www.ingramcontent.com/pod-product-compliance
Lightning Source LLC
Chambersburg PA
CBHW052058230426
43662CB00036B/1413